A Boal Companion

Theatre of the [...] niques. Yet this does not d [...] Augusto Boal, TO's founder a [...] of ov [...]

A Boal Companion [...] plores performative and cu [...] practices that inform Boal's work by putting them alongside those from related disciplines. Contributors in this anthology put TO into dialogue with complexity theory, Merleau-Ponty, Emmanuel Levinas, race theory, feminist performance art, Deleuze and Guattari, and liberation psychology to name just a few. In this way, kinship between Boal's project and multiple fields including social psychology, ethics, biology, comedy, trauma studies, and political science is made visible.

This collection not only expands the knowledge of TO practitioners and scholars but invites into TO those readers unfamiliar with Boal's work whose primary interests lie in one of the related disciplines addressed in these chapters. The ideas generated throughout the collection will:

- expand readers' understanding of TO as a complex, interdisciplinary, multivocal body of philosophical discourses;
- provide a variety of lenses through which to practice and critique TO;
- make explicit the relationships between TO and other bodies of work.

Jan Cohen-Cruz and Mady Schutzman hosted Boal at NYU in 1987–88, brought a group of 20 cultural practitioners to Rio de Janeiro for three weeks to study with Boal in 1989, and co-edited *Playing Boal: Theatre, therapy, activism* in 1994.

Jan Cohen-Cruz wrote *Local Acts: Community-based performance in the US* (Rutgers University Press: 2005) and is the editor of *Radical Street Performance*. She is an associate professor at New York University where she teaches in the Drama and the Art and Public Policy Departments.

Mady Schutzman is author of *The Real Thing: Performance, hysteria, and advertising* (Wesleyan University Press: 1999). She teaches at California Institute of the Arts and is an advisory board member of the Los Angeles Center for Theatre of the Oppressed.

A Boal Companion

Dialogues on theatre and cultural politics

Edited by Jan Cohen-Cruz and
Mady Schutzman

Routledge
Taylor & Francis Group

NEW YORK AND LONDON

First published 2006 in the USA and Canada by Routledge
270 Madison Avenue, New York, NY 10016

Simultaneously published in the UK by Routledge
2 Park Square, Milton Park, Abingdon, Oxon OX14 4RN

Routledge is an imprint of the Taylor & Francis Group

© 2006 Jan Cohen-Cruz and Mady Schutzman; individual chapters, the contributors

Typeset in Goudy by The Running Head Limited, Cambridge
Printed and bound in Great Britain by TJ International Ltd, Padstow

Library of Congress Cataloging in Publication Data
A catalog record for this book has been requested

British Library Cataloguing in Publication Data
A catalogue record for this book is available from the British Library

ISBN10: 0–415–32293–6   ISBN13: 9–78–0–415–32293–5 (hbk)
ISBN10: 0–415–32294–4   ISBN13: 9–78–0–415–32294–2 (pbk)

Contents

Contributors

Awam Amkpa is Associate Professor of Drama at New York University's Tisch School of the Arts. He has also taught at King Alfred's University College and Mount Holyoke College. He is the author of *Theatre and Postcolonial Desires* (Routledge: 2003) and two forthcoming books: *Postcolonial Drama* and *Theatres of the Black Atlantic*. Awam has facilitated numerous community-based projects in Africa, Europe, and North America. He is also a playwright, theatre director, and director of documentaries, as well as a film scholar.

Ann Elizabeth Armstrong is an Assistant Professor at Miami University of Oxford, Ohio. She has created community-based performances in Williamsburg, VA and published an article about that experience in *Theatre Topics*. She is currently editing an anthology about feminist pedagogies of theatre and also directing an interdisciplinary project that will culminate in an original play about Freedom Summer 1964. The play will document the experiences of college students who volunteered to go down to Mississippi and engage in civil rights activism.

Gianpaolo Baiocchi is Assistant Professor of Sociology at the University of Massachusetts, Amherst. He researches and writes about cities, inequalities, politics, and social theory. His book *Militants and Citizens: The Politics of Participation in Porto Alegre* has recently been published (Stanford University Press: 2005).

Daniel Banks is Associate Teacher in the Undergraduate Drama Department at New York University, where he has created the Hip Hop Theatre Initiative. He has directed and choreographed extensively in the US and abroad and holds a PhD from the Performance Studies Department at NYU.

Brent Blair is a designated Linklater voice instructor and Senior Lecturer at the University of Southern California's School of Theatre where he founded a program in Applied Theatre Arts. He teaches Liberation Arts and Community Engagement, Theatre and Therapy, and Theatre in Education. Blair is co-founder of the Center for Theatre of the Oppressed in Los Angeles, works part time as a therapist with high-risk teens in central Los Angeles, and is completing his PhD in Depth Psychology at Pacifica Graduate Institute.

L.M. Bogad, Assistant Professor of Theatre and Dance at the University of California, Davis, is author of *Electoral Guerrilla Theatre: Radical ridicule and social movements* (Routledge: 2005). His articles appear in *TDR*, *Contemporary Theatre Review*, and numerous other journals and anthologies. He has worked as a performer, writer, and organizer across the US and the UK. His play, *Haymarket*, was the first full-length drama/tragedy about the Haymarket Square Riot. He is a veteran of the Lincoln Center Theatre Director's Lab and the Clandestine Insurgent Rebel Clown Army.

Campbell Britton is currently Theatre Arts Visiting Assistant Professor at Loyola Marymount University. She has created seminars in South American Theatre and Theatres of the Avant-Garde and also teaches theatre history and acting techniques. Recipient of a 2001 Fulbright Fellowship to Brazil and a University of California at Los Angeles Distinguished Teaching award, she has lectured abroad on a wide range of international theatre traditions. Her PhD dissertation, "Prismatic dialogues: Antunes Filho, Nelson Rodrigues, and Brazilian cultural identity," is due for completion this year.

Jan Cohen-Cruz, an Associate Professor of Drama and director of the New York University Tisch School of the Arts' Office of Community Connections, wrote *Local Acts: Community-based performance in the US* (Rutgers University Press: 2005), edited *Radical Street Performance* (Routledge: 1998), and, with Mady Schutzman, coedited *Playing Boal: Theatre, therapy, activism* (Routledge: 1994). Past projects include coconception with Sabrina Peck, of a play with community gardeners and students. Current projects include an arts-based exploration of the impact of war on youth and the development of a training program in community-based performance.

Lori S. Katz, PhD, is a clinical psychologist and the Director of the Long Beach Sexual Trauma Center. She has testified before the US Congress and worked with the Department of Defense as an expert on the treatment of victims of sexual assault. She is the author of *Holographic Reprocessing: A cognitive-experiential psychotherapy for the treatment of trauma* (Routledge: 2005). She is a national and international speaker and educator on treating trauma.

Suzanne Lacy is a conceptual/performance artist and writer. Her complex performances address significant social issues and engage local populations in a place-specific manner. A founding member of the Feminist Studio Workshop at Los Angeles' Woman's Building, Lacy pioneered the exploration of art as a force in the community and in media. She edited *Mapping the Terrain: New genre public art* (Bay Press: 1995) and is Chair of Fine Arts at Otis College of Art and Design in Los Angeles.

Warren Linds is Assistant Professor in the Department of Applied Human Sciences, Concordia University, Montreal, Canada. He is a popular theatre facilitator and community educator applying Theatre of the Oppressed in antiracist education programs. His doctoral dissertation (2001) was on the facilitation of Theatre of the Oppressed in a North American context. His articles have been published in a wide range of drama/theatre and research journals. Warren was a coeditor of *Unfolding Bodymind: Exploring possibility through education* (Holistic Education Press: 2001).

Helene S. Lorenz is a core faculty member and former academic Dean at Pacifica Graduate Institute in Santa Barbara, where she teaches cultural studies and depth psychology, and makes use of Boal's theatre techniques in her classroom. She is the author of *Living at the Edge of Chaos: Complex systems in culture and psyche* (Daimon: 1997) and numerous articles on the intersection between internalized colonialism and psychological life. She also works with the Center for Theatre of the Oppressed in Los Angeles.

Randy Martin, Professor of Art and Public Policy and Associate Dean of Faculty at Tisch School of the Arts, has written on performance and politics as the author of *Performance as Political Act: The embodied self* (Bergin and Garvey: 1990); *Socialist Ensembles: Theater and state in Cuba and Nicaragua* (University of Minnesota Press: 1994): *Critical Moves: Dance studies in theater and politics* (Duke University Press: 1998); *On Your Marx: Relinking socialism and the left* (University of Minnesota Press: 2001); and *Financialization of Daily Life* (Temple University Press: 2002).

Deborah Mutnick is a Professor of English at the Brooklyn campus of Long Island University. Her book *Writing in an Alien World: Basic writing and the struggle for equality in higher education* received the W. Ross Winterowd Award for the most outstanding book published that year on composition theory. In addition to basic writing, she has written about Bakhtinian dialogics, narrative theory, and the intersection between geography and composition studies.

Shari Popen lives in Tucson and teaches educational philosophy, postcolonial studies, and democratic theory in the College of Education and the Department of Political Science at the University of Arizona. Her work focuses on rethinking relations of disciplinary power in our current pedagogical and social landscapes.

Marc D. Rich, PhD, is an Assistant Professor of Communication/Performance Studies at California State University, Long Beach. Since 1993, he has jokered workshops in community and educational settings throughout the United States. Marc's essays appear in *Text and Performance Quarterly, Journal of Contemporary Ethnography, American Communication Journal, Race, Ethnicity and Education,* and *Death Studies.* His article on the efficacy of Boal's techniques is featured in *Communication Activism.* His current project (with Lori S. Katz) uses Rainbow of Desire techniques with survivors of sexual assault .

Julie Salverson is a playwright, workshop animator, and scholar. Chapters from her dissertation, 'Performing Testimony: Ethics, pedagogy, and theatre beyond injury', have been published in book anthologies and in journals including *Theatre, Theatre Topics,* and *Canadian Theatre Review.* She is Associate Professor at Queens University in Kingston, Ontario and is writing the libretto for a clown opera about the atomic bomb.

Mady Schutzman is Assistant Dean of the School of Critical Studies and faculty of the Master of Fine Arts Writing Program at California Institute of the Arts. She coedited *Playing Boal: Theatre, therapy, activism* (Routledge: 1994), with Jan Cohen-Cruz and authored *The Real Thing: Performance, hysteria, and advertising* (Wesleyan University Press: 1999). In Los Angeles, Mady produces writing workshops for disadvantaged youth, serves on the advisory board of the Center for Theatre of the Oppressed, and works as a dramaturg. She is currently researching/writing on divination, humor, and ventriloquism.

Acknowledgments

A number of people contributed to our thinking about this collection. They include Paul Heritage, Jill Dolan, Toni Sant, and, of course, our editor, Talia Rodgers. Others were helpful in a range of ways: Diane Parker and Minh Ha Duong for making the details, duties, and deadlines of publishing as pleasant as such things can be; Dante Eaton for his meticulous transcription of the round-table discussion; Kevin Kuhlke, chair of the Drama Department at New York University, for lightening Jan's academic load as our deadline approached; the School of Critical Studies and the Faculty Development Fund at California Institute of the Arts for administrative support and for funding several of Mady's cross-country trips, allowing the editors to actually work on this book in person.

Jan would like to acknowledge Mady's incisive and original idea that led to this volume: foregrounding Boal as not only a major innovator of theatre practice but also a truly significant theoretician. To that end, her vision of focusing on ideas and systems that engage around similar concerns as does Boal but in a range of interdisciplinary contexts is, to my mind, a brilliant way of looking at theatre "out-of-the-box." I am grateful that she brought me into this challenging and fascinating project.

Intro... Cohen-Cruz

I

Theatre of ... as a body of theatrical techniques. And
yet this doe... an theatre director Augusto Boal, its
founder and ... es, potent as they may be in revolu-
tionizing parti... ships, point to a much greater "body"—a
complex, intero... of philosophical knowledge that encompasses,
among other thi... aulo Freire and Bertolt Brecht, carnival and circus, the
Brazilian theatrica... rde of the mid-twentieth century, the influences of political theorists such as Hegel and of aesthetic theorists such as Aristotle. Boal's work has spread to
seven continents and is practiced by innumerable Jokers, or facilitators.[1] In this way, TO's
modularity allows people around the globe who share the TO vocabulary and repertoire an
opportunity to meet and dialogue across vast differences. But as with all such translations of
theory into practice, of thought into action—especially those like TO that are named and
marketed as reproducible systems—there are tendencies to delimit the underlying generative power of the work itself. We tend to take a how-to approach, forgetting that the "how"
needs to be as mutable as the ideas that inform it; we tend to replicate what "worked" in one
context into another, forgetting that TO is predicated on a vigilant receptivity to difference
across time, circumstance, geography, culture, race, ethnicity, sexual orientation, and
gender; we tend to restrict our critical dialogue to an analysis of what is explicit, forgetting
the more invisible, implicit, foundational keystones of which the visible is a mere sign.

As students of Boal's work, we are fortunate that he is a writer and scholar as well as a
practitioner of his techniques. His teachings are complex expositions as much as they are
embodied theatre games and exercises. His wisdom comes to us through the written word
with all its incumbent abstraction as much as it does through the body with all its incumbent visceralities. Simply put, Augusto Boal is a theorist as much as he is a practitioner, and
his work is, in fact, a demonstration of the false divide between theory and practice that has
plagued so many social movements, artistic communities, and interdisciplinary endeavors.
Strangely, however, TO is both undertheorized and insufficiently contextualized within a
broader domain of companion theories and practices.

One goal of this book is to return to and expand Boal's theoretical underpinnings. Such a
return is offered not as idle reflection but rather as a way to develop our critical resources,
refresh our interpretive capacities, and inspire our improvisational abilities as we participate
(whether as Jokers or spect-actors) in innumerable TO workshops and performances that
raise demanding and sometimes paralyzing questions that the techniques themselves do not

always answer. It will, hopefully, revive and hone our creative capacities when we face inter-ventions that curtail dialogue, empower an antagonist, thwart a protagonist, or obscure the power dynamic we seek to unearth from any scene. We are thus better equipped as practi-tioners to design techniques and approaches that speak to an ever-changing global context. Immersion into critical thought keeps our practices adaptable and honest—as radical in practice as they are in theory.

Another equally significant goal of this book is to recontextualize TO. One way to expand our understanding of how TO works is to place Boal's oeuvre in critical dialogue with exemplary thinkers and practitioners of other expertise who have brought rigorous attention to similar subjects in different ways. In so doing, Boal enthusiasts, as well as those readers simply interested in the basic tenets of Boal's work, are provided with different defi-nitions, interpretations, applications, and points of reference for familiar Boalian tropes. For instance, metaxis in Boal's lexicon (whereby we live in "reality" and our images of "reality," simultaneously) suggests aspects of complexity theory and research in biological cognition; principles of witnessing in TO echo ethical concerns in the work of philosopher Emmanuel Levinas; cross-identity interventions in Forum Theatre can be seen anew and critically prob-lematized through race theory and an analysis of minstrelsy; Boal's Invisible Theatre takes on new dimensions when likened to the work of Chris Burden, Vito Acconci, and a family of 1970s feminist performance artists including Adrian Piper and Linda Montano; the actual and imagined of Boal's "aesthetic space" interact all the more dramatically when in dialogue with Deleuze and Guattari's "smooth" and "striated space"; the potential of Rainbow of Desire techniques to heal the social landscape is invigorated by liberation psychology. Boal himself may not be aware of these diverse resonances and intersections of TO-based con-cepts in the fields of cultural studies, political science, ethics, humor studies, systems theory, theories of space, performance art, race theory, trauma theory, and feminism.

Why do this? In part, because we so easily can. Because the breadth of TO is, in fact, that resonant, its principles that plastic. Because TO is, at its core, already a synthesis of what has become divided, packaged, and consumed, mostly in the academy, as separate and discrete bodies of disciplinary knowledge. In a way, what we have done in making these cross-disciplinary links is merely to tease out the threads that are, in fact, already always operable in TO's intention and methodology. Bringing them to the surface allows TO access to more rigorous application and critique. Conversely, this collection invites into TO those readers whose primary interests lie in one of the related disciplines addressed in these chapters. In making explicit the relationship between TO and other bodies of work, we imagine enhanc-ing the potency of them all. The bearing of TO in multiple realms of knowledge is testament to the relevance and agility of the doctrines upon which it is founded. And herein lies its promise.

II

For readers not acquainted with Boal, what follows is a brief summary of key developments in his work. Theatre of the Oppressed, the name of Boal's system, is an homage to educator Paolo Freire (1988) who in *Pedagogy of the Oppressed* foregrounds the movement of seem-ingly powerless people from being acted upon, and thus objects, to initiating action, and thus becoming subjects of their own lives. Freire referred to this process as *conscientização* (consciencization) whereby poor and exploited people learn to conduct their own analysis of their social, political, and economic reality, "to enter the historical process as responsible

Subjects" (Freire 1988: 20) and to take action against their oppressors. For Freire, central to this transformation is replacing the prevalent banking method of education (filling students' heads with what experts deem important) with a dialogic approach to learning in which students and teachers are interactive partners. Boal translated this idea into a theatrical context with his concept of the spect-actor, who replaces the spectator sitting passively in the dark watching the finished production. As Freire broke the hierarchical divide between teacher and student, Boal did so between performer and audience member.

Concrete circumstances provoked Boal to explore an array of theatrical strategies of liberation. Boal was a theatre director at the Arena Stage in São Paulo (1956–71) when military coups in 1964 and 1968 caused him to bring his theatre activity more directly in line with his progressive politics. After performing an agit-prop play preaching revolution to peasants, Boal and his company were invited to take up rifles and join in an attack on the land owners. Ashamed that he had told other people to do something that he had no intention of participating in himself, Boal went on to create Forum Theatre, which begins with the performance of a short play, or anti-model, that embodies a social problem. It features a protagonist working hard to solve a problem but who nevertheless does not succeed. Spect-actors who identify with that oppression are invited to replace the protagonist and act out their own possible solutions to the particulars the play presents, thus rehearsing action for revolution in everyday life.

Boal was jailed in Brazil for his political activities and once released was warned that further activities would lead to a worse fate. He and his wife Cecilia moved to Argentina, her homeland, where they were based from 1971 to 1976. Invited to participate in a national literacy campaign in Peru in 1973, Boal designed Image Theatre, a physical form of aesthetic communication not reliant on verbal mastery. Participants silently sculpt each other into tableaux that express ideas and experiences that are then dynamized to further explore their ramifications. Returning to Argentina where political theatre had become dangerous under an increasingly repressive regime, Boal designed Invisible Theatre. Staged in public spaces and masquerading as everyday life, these theatrical scenarios addressing urgent current social issues were constructed to engender public dialogue among people who did not know that they were witnessing preplanned enactments.

From 1976 to 1986, Boal was in exile in Europe where he responded to different circumstances with a new (and revised) set of exercises. At first he was frustrated that the seemingly less terrible subjects of alienation and loneliness came up in workshops rather than the life-threatening material oppressions he had encountered in Latin America. But he was stunned to find out that despite their higher standard of living, Scandinavians committed suicide with much greater frequency than Latin Americans. Realizing the depth of pain caused by internal oppressions and their connection to external oppressions, Boal developed a body of therapeutic theatre work interchangeably called Cop-in-the-Head or Rainbow of Desire.

In 1986, Boal returned to Brazil where political change was soon to result in democratic elections. In 1992, he was elected to the city council in Rio de Janeiro. He and his company (turned staff) took Forum Theatre a step further by working with communities of educators, health practitioners, civil servants, and other professional citizenries throughout Rio with the express purpose of identifying where new laws might provide successful interventions into social oppressions. They made a dossier of problems for which spect-actors could not find solutions under current law and brought them to the city council as evidence of the need for new legislation. During Boal's term of office, upward of a dozen city laws were passed on the basis of information gathered at these "Legislative Theatre" sessions.[2]

III

This book is structured around various performative and cultural tropes that inform not only Boal's work but those of other disciplines as well. In a sense, each chapter is a dialogue between TO and another system, body of thought, or methodology. Taken as a whole, the book could be imagined as the most enthusiastic of guides, introducing TO aficionados to both recognizable companions as well as to those never imagined as such, into realms beyond and yet not so far from TO at all. Meanwhile, those unfamiliar with TO, but interested in the tropes and ideological principles themselves no matter from what field they hail, will be introduced to Boal, whose aesthetic system is an inspiring and functional montage of them all.

We open our investigation with Campbell Britton's chapter entitled "Politics and Performance(s) of Identity: 25 years of Brazilian theatre (1954–79)." While Boal (2001) himself has traced his own creative development in Brazil in his autobiography, *Hamlet and the Baker's Son: My life in theatre and politics*, Britton locates TO in relation to other Brazilian activist theatres, radical movements, political regimes, and media culture. In analyzing Boal's work in this 25-year period in relation to his Brazilian contemporaries, such as José Celso and Antunes Filho, TO can be reconsidered as one of several responses not only to military dictatorship but to the question of Brazilian cultural identity and the advocacy for positivism coming from an ultramodern, rationalist democracy. Boal's work is realigned with its influences in bossa nova, cinema novo, circus, and soccer in this jam-packed exposition of TO in the context of Brazilian cultural history.

We have grouped the remainder of the chapters into three sections. Each of the five chapters in the first section, *Sites*, foregrounds one of the realms into which Boal consciously situated his project: namely, political theatre, pedagogy, activism, therapy, and legislation.[3] Each chapter explores cultural models, theories, and methodologies currently being engaged in each context respectively and situates TO in relation to them. It is instructive to both consider these fields per se and to *re*-consider Boal's approaches *vis-à-vis* the wide-ranging research presented by the authors in this section. We find the experimentation and adaptation suggested in these chapters essential for the health of TO precisely by virtue of rendering these familiar sites a bit strange.

Sites opens with a chapter on Political Theatre. In "Staging the Political: Boal and the horizons of theatrical commitment," Randy Martin responds to critics who, declaring political theatre obsolete, see direct opposition to government actions as ineffectual and live performance as without consequence. Martin considers various ways in which the political efficacy of theatre is constituted, using Boal's extensive experiments as a touchstone. These include the relationship between theatre and the state, the role of live performance in a mediated age, and what Martin theorizes as the four sites of intervention for political theatre today—community, the popular, the national, and the postcolonial. Martin argues the importance of theatre and oppositional politics, and the innovations that Boal has brought to bear on their intersection.

In "Critical interventions: the meaning of praxis," Deborah Mutnick expands beyond Freire to an overview of critical pedagogy's origins, aims, problems in relation to Boal's work, and value for artists and activists as well as educators. Mutnick challenges arguments by liberal educators for whom radical pedagogy's association with third world literacy campaigns have called into question its viability in the US. She also critiques scholars such as Peter McLaren—on the radical end of the political spectrum—who conflate critical inquiry with polemics. Mutnick examines the notion of praxis in the context of the US invasion of Iraq, asking how one practices liberatory pedagogy in such a time.

L.M. Bogad explores performance aesthetics and tactics in social movement activism, focusing on demonstrations in public space, in his chapter, "Tactical carnival: social movements, demonstrations, and dialogical performance." Through social movement theory, he explains the importance of the public demonstration and locates TO within activist practice. He describes competing paradigms that have developed at demonstrations. Some organizations attempt to *occupy* a public space and impose call-and-response chants and lockstep marching; others attempt to *open* a space for the creative contributions of swarming individuals and affinity groups. Bogad theorizes the notion of "tactical carnival" as the most fruitful kind of participatory demonstration.

In "Social healing and liberatory politics: a round-table discussion," Mady Schutzman brings together four colleagues who engage TO in diverse settings and with diverse populations to discuss TO's therapeutic impact, its relation to other therapeutic methodologies, and its potential as social healing. Helene S. Lorenz reminds us of the shifting contexts through which TO has served as a healing art, bringing particular attention to TO in relation to liberation psychology and trauma theory. Brent Blair invites us to investigate TO's strengths and weaknesses through the lens of Carl Jung's depth psychology, putting into question some of the most assumed tenets of TO by suggesting that unconscious images become viable sites for staging TO scenes. Marc D. Rich turns our attention to ethnographic models of contact as a way to reconsider the role of the Joker. Recognizing TO as a collective form for redressing the malaise of contemporary postmodern alienation, Rich likens the Joker to a shaman and spect-actors to participants in an embodied ritual. Finally, Lori S. Katz introduces readers to the therapeutic practice of Holographic Reprocessing which helps clients recognize emotional patterns and repeated interrelational dynamics in their lives. The exploration of these imagistic projections suggests possibilities for how protagonists in TO scenes might recognize the appearance of the "same" antagonist in seemingly unrelated conflicts.

The last chapter in this section is "Performing democracy in the streets: Participatory Budgeting and Legislative Theatre in Brazil." Brazilian sociologist Gianpaolo Baiocchi first describes Participatory Budgeting as an innovative form of participatory democracy and policy-making practiced in several Brazilian cities with Workers' Party administrations. Through a year-long process of learning and discussion, participants decide on budget priorities regarding specific civic projects. Baiocchi connects Participatory Budgeting to Boal's Legislative Theatre, as both revolve around critical discussion as a pedagogical process and value the voice, experience, and knowledge of a wide range of otherwise disempowered participants as they promote dialogical problem-solving. Baiocchi explores their shared root in Paulo Freire's participatory pedagogy, their differences, and their potential to be used in tandem.

In the second section, *Tropes*, we focus on particular strategies within TO that while seminal to Boal's project are not unique to it. The authors focus on the incarnation of these practices in other conceptual and pragmatic forms, thus reframing our understanding of these practices in TO. At the same time, TO reframes these same strategies as they manifest elsewhere. Through this lively dialogue, vastly different lexicons regarding parallel dynamics continually expand, alter, and renew each other. Though this section might have incorporated chapters on any number of approaches, the ones included address the art/life continuum, storytelling, metaxis, aesthetic space, jokering, and witnessing.

Focusing on the blurring of art and life in "Activism in feminist performance art," artist Suzanne Lacy looks at parallels between her own work within a US feminist and avant-garde tradition and that of Boal's as concerns art so close to everyday life as to facilitate direct repercussions between them. She asks how Boal's Invisible Theatre and later Legislative Theatre converge and collide, theoretically and practically, with feminist performance practices in the US. Lacy grounds her inquiry in case studies from her own innovative work. She describes a 1970s collaboration with Evalina Newman, who lived in an urban housing project for older people, and a three-year project with police and teenagers in Oakland, California in the 1990s.

Storytelling is the subject of "Redefining the private: from personal storytelling to political act." Jan Cohen-Cruz looks at the roles of the teller, the listener, those who identify with the story, and various supporting social institutions, all of whom intervene (in different ways) in the injustices that the storyteller articulates. She begins with Seyla Benhabib's insight that "defining what had previously been considered private, nonpublic, and non-political issues as matters of public concern, as issues of justice, as sites of power" is the beginning of fighting oppression (1992: 100). Cohen-Cruz relates this idea to the practice of sharing personal stories to uncover political inequities, contrasting Boal's methods with those of two US performance makers, John O'Neal and Suzanne Lacy.

Warren Linds leads us from theatre into biology and phenomenology as he unpacks the notion of metaxis in his chapter, "Metaxis: dancing (in) the in-between." Metaxis is the state of living in two worlds simultaneously—the actual and the imagined. Emphasizing the significance of this potent, embodied, and yet ambivalent space, Linds introduces readers to metaxic space in our natural world. Through the work of Merleau-Ponty, Francisco Varela, Fritjof Capra, and others, Boal's metaxis is likened to the workings of anthills, fish swimming among reeds, the butterfly effect, feedback loops, and systemic reciprocity. Linds so champions the notion of groundlessness—that is, negotiating our way through a world that is not fixed or predictable—he tempts us to embrace concepts that might otherwise intimidate us.

Taking up a similar sphere as Linds, Shari Popen explores Boal's "aesthetic space" and its cross-disciplinary resonances in her piece entitled "Aesthetic spaces/imaginative geographies." First reviewing the properties of aesthetic space as transitive, telemicroscopic ("the stage brings things closer"), and self-reflexive, Popen discovers correlations in the work of scholars who are reformulating spatial logic: notably Foucault, Lefebvre, Deleuze and Guattari, and de Certeau. Popen teases out the similarities and disjunctions between them, providing us with critical tools through which to critique spatial networks of power and harness the plasticity of space toward liberatory ends. By contextualizing aesthetic space within discourses heretofore unlinked with Boal's theatrical practice, TO is infused with a new dimension.

As more and more people have become Jokers negotiating issues in various communities, the role of the Joker itself has come under scrutiny in recent years. In her chapter, "Joker runs wild," Schutzman reconsiders the role of the Joker first in light of Boal's own Joker System and then through jokers and joking in various cultural forms, such as tricksters, jokers in card and tarot decks, vaudeville performers, and clowns. Highlighting the ways in which paradox, imprecision, and fluidity have been harnessed by these jokers for purposes of resistance, Schutzman, sharing Linds' and Popen's fascination with ambiguity, asks how the notion of being everywhere and nowhere might refresh the role of the TO Joker as a leader. What tricks might the Joker learn from some other, very potent kinds of wild cards?

Critical to all social change and social healing is the role of witness and witnessing, and yet this active site through which protagonists' experiences of oppression are reconciled within a broader collectivity has remained relatively uninvestigated within TO discourse. Building upon Cohen-Cruz's exploration of witness as critical listener and Schutzman's invocation of the clown, Julie Salverson underscores this integral element in her chapter, "Witnessing subjects: a fool's help," in which she drafts a spectrum of possible modes of witnessing, advancing in the end, the outlook of the "fool." Informed by the insights of Emmanuel Levinas, Salverson walks readers through an exquisitely dangerous terrain of responsibility and courage, obligation and risk-taking, in how to radically and ethically engage the other who survives (and tells the story of) violence.

Ideologies, the final section of the book, contains chapters that investigate ideas of art and resistance contiguous with TO's agenda but that merit more serious attention in the TO world. These include postcolonial, feminist, and race theory which Boal does not specifically discuss as such, but that frequently emerge as operative but not fully addressed stakes in TO workshops. We hope that the rich ideas generated in each of these liberatory bodies of thought will expand readers' understanding of TO both as a body of philosophical discourse and as a revolutionary practice.

Awam Amkpa's "Reenvisioning theatre, activism, and citizenship in neocolonial contexts" situates TO in relationship to postcolonialism. Amkpa explains how changes incurred through African liberation movements ushered in hopes that anticolonial agitation and quests for social, political, and cultural equality were attainable ideals. The subsequent installations of neocolonial realities, however, dimmed such hopes in countries such as Nigeria. Amkpa examines how Theatre for Development (TFD) plays a pivotal role in enabling the disenfranchised to redefine themselves as cultural and political actors against marginalizing schemes of their neocolonial conditions. This he compares and contrasts with TO, describing how in the context of postcolonial conditions, both TO and TFD enable groups to imbue themselves with agency.

Correspondences between TO philosophy and the array of contemporary feminisms is unmistakable. In "Negotiating feminist identities and Theatre of the Oppressed," Ann Elizabeth Armstrong outlines both the effectively exploited contributions of feminist thought to TO practice as well as some overlooked political insights. Armstrong elucidates the contemporary debates between modern and postmodern identity, vigilant in her attention to third world feminisms while recommending those aspects of resistance within global culture that necessitate plurality, mutability, and strategies of deconstruction. Building on theories of Sandoval, Moya, and Moraga, and complementing Lacy's feminist emphasis on relationship, Armstrong bridges feminist theories of embodiment, love, and truth in ways that illuminate and question select TO practices.

In "Unperforming 'race': strategies for reimagining identity," Daniel Banks takes the reader through the making and unmaking of the notion of race. Set against the ongoing legacy of minstrelsy, Banks argues against race as a meaningful category and brings to our attention strategies to unperform and dismantle it. Race theorists and performance theorists enter into dialogue toward a problematizing of fixed notions of identity as they play out in Boal's practices. In demanding that we see race once again as the social construct it is, readers must reconcile this fictive category with the very real experience of contemporary race relations.

So what does this book foreground through its cumulative effect? What illuminating accident occurred in the unpredictable convergence of these chapters under one cover? While the echoes from chapter to chapter are manifold and far too many to articulate here, a few instructive themes surfaced that may serve as touchstones for continued critique.

One of these is the potency of in-between (or open space) and ambiguity (or paradox) as strategies of resistance. Humor, postmodern identities, nondualistic states of being, clown, fool, and carnivalesque and decentralized structures veined many of the readings, suggesting through their very reoccurrence playful, unpredictable, improvisatory, shape-shifting, and yet empowering means to challenge fixed, centralized, hierarchical, and often oppressive circumstances and/or readings.

A second recurring theme was the ethical and co-relational dimensions of dealing with stories of oppression or trauma. Whether framed as listening, love, therapy, justice, witnessing, unperforming, or participatory democracy, over and again authors recommend notions of critical empathy, engaged containment, and respectful difference. New and provocative formulations of what it means to be ethically responsible—without subscribing to any one way—pervade numerous chapters and ask readers to renegotiate their own beliefs and behaviors in relation to others, and to acknowledge how others have been unjustifiably scripted to the advantage of the privileged.

Given the current political climate in which civil liberties are being summarily erased by governmental policy and the embedded media, and notions of identity realigned by global culture, the authors in this anthology have collectively outlined TO's potential as a creative form of resistance through one of its own fundamental lessons: dialogue. The very boundaries of Boal's theatrical forms are deliberately put into question and made subject to what they border. And in so doing they meet not only with resonance and affirmation but, more importantly, with challenging dissimilarity. It seems fitting. Do we not practice art, particularly art for social change, in order to challenge categorical thinking, to dislodge a priori principles, to push the limits of what is known to cast reality back into the highly interpretive and risky business that it always is? We don't practice art or revolutionary politics to be safe—the very notion is oxymoronic. Cumulatively, the chapters in this book suggest that TO will flourish by locating it beyond its immediate horizons and turning our attention to Boal's known and unknown companions.

Notes

1   For practices and impact of TO facilitators other than Boal (available in English language anthologies), see Schutzman and Cohen-Cruz (1994) and Babbage (1995).
2   Editor's note: Legislative Theatre is the theatrical genre Boal created when he served on the city council in Rio de Janeiro. The experiment drew on situations in which spect-actorial interventions in Forum Theatre were insufficient. Boal brought a dossier of such problems to the city council as evidence of the need for new legislation. During Boal's term of office, upward of a dozen city laws were passed on the basis of information gathered in this way. See Boal 1998.
3   Boal's books bear witness to these realms. See Boal references in bibliography.

Bibliography

Babbage, F. (ed.) (1995) *Working Without Boal: Digressions and developments in the Theatre of the Oppressed*. London and New York: Routledge.
Benhabib, S. (1992) *Situating the Self: Gender, community and post-modernism in contemporary ethics*. New York: Routledge.
Boal, A. (1979) *Theatre of the Oppressed*, trans. C.A. and M.-O.L. McBride. New York: Urizen Books.
—— (1992) *Games for Actors and Non-Actors*, trans. A. Jackson. London and New York: Routledge.

—— (1995) *The Rainbow of Desire: The Boal method of theatre and therapy*, trans. A. Jackson. London and New York: Routledge.

—— (1998) *Legislative Theatre: Using performance to make politics*, trans. A. Jackson. London and New York: Routledge.

—— (2001) *Hamlet and the Baker's Son: My life in theatre and politics*, trans. A. Jackson and C. Blaker. London and New York: Routledge.

Freire, P. (1988) *Pedagogy of the Oppressed*, trans. M.B. Ramos. New York: Continuum.

Schutzman, M. and Cohen-Cruz, J. (eds) (1994) *Playing Boal: Theatre, therapy, activism*. London and New York: Routledge.

Politics and performance(s) of identity

25 years of Brazilian theatre (1954–79)

Campbell Britton

> I'm an actor . . .
> It's dull to arrive/at objectives in a flash.
> I want to live/in this walking metamorphosis.[1]

The fundamental theories in Augusto Boal's Theatre of the Oppressed (TO) grew from a turbulent era of social revolution, no less in Brazil than in other parts of the globe. A youth culture was asserting itself, artistic expression acquired a political voice, and the Cold War duality concerning "the Communist Menace" hung pregnant in the air. Boal's theatrically formative years, however, were also greatly inflected by Brazil's domestic search for cultural identity and reformation of artistic models.

Defining Brazilian identity has consistently defied even poets and scholars, such that Brazilian modernist Mario de Andrade (1893–1945) was prompted to write a 1928 "rhapsodic" novel on his nation entitled *Macunaíma, O Herói Sem Nenhum Caráter* (*Macunaíma, The Hero Without Any Character At All*).[2] And yet, in the 1950s, an official program for Brazilian self-definition was exactly what was undertaken by a freshly democratized government. Its goal was centered in a futuristic (and technocratic) vision, a positivism borrowed from those who had inscribed the motto "*Ordem e Progresso*" (Order and Progress) on the Brazilian flag. Some artists embraced a constructivist aesthetic that seemed to parallel the government's ultramodern rationalist model. They were eager to shed the image of Brazil as a tropical backwater. Yet many in the vanguard attempted to expose the "Brazil of the Future" as a false front for a country scarred by poverty, neocolonialism, and inequality, and for the first time in its history the Brazilian theatre became a major locus for social and cultural interrogation.

Tensions escalated within the government and the avant-garde as a military Ditadura (Dictatorship) starting in 1964 became ever more repressive, provoking a vibrant theatrical period of resistance through both engagé and metaphoric confrontation. American and European scholars of Brazilian theatre history have privileged this flurry of theatrical reaction to authoritarianism over post-dictatorship production, but its actual legacy remains under-investigated. I relocate theatrical activity during the dictatorship as transitional between two significant eras of democracy to uncover the period's value as a cultural metamorphosis. For by 1978–79 the military authoritarian rulers gradually began loosening controls, making way for the return of democratic elections in 1985 and, in spite of the harshest repressive tactics of the Ditadura (from 1968–74), it became clear that innovative artistic energy had not been stifled. Andrade's *Macunaíma* would become a reference point—

adapted for the stage by director Antunes Filho in 1978—and a passionate reinstatement of the Brazilian identity question; it provoked a new wave of theatrical experimentation that embraced Brazil as a uniquely contradictory and multivalent nation.

Democracy and Brazilian cultural identity (1954–64)

When Augusto Boal flew to New York City to pursue advanced studies at Columbia University in September 1953, he left behind a postcolonial country that had begun a nationalization process under the democratically elected (and former dictator) President Getúlio Vargas.[3] But Vargas committed suicide in 1954 under a cloud of multiple scandals, and shortly after Boal returned to Rio de Janeiro in July 1955, president-elect Juscelino Kubitschek (JK) prescribed an aggressive agenda for development of a uniquely Brazilian national profile. Kubitschek's term (1956–59) was followed by the brief and bizarre presidency of Jânio Quadros, until João Goulart assumed leadership (1961–64) and pushed JK's liberal agenda and dream of a Brazilian "economic miracle" even further. The national mood was euphoric in the late 1950s and early 1960s as democracy appeared to flourish and Brazil anticipated assuming a dynamic presence among the developed nations of the world.

São Paulo was becoming an industrial megalopolis, and the 1952 São Paulo Biennale resulted in active dialogues between international painters and sculptors and their Brazilian hosts. Lima Barreto's 1953 film *O Cangaçeiro* (*The Backlands Bandit*) won two prizes at Cannes and was distributed in 22 countries, classical composer Heitor Villa-Lobos' *Bachianas Brasileiras* (1930–45) had been acclaimed in Europe, and Brazil's national soccer team achieved its first World Cup victory in July 1958. A new Federal District called Brasília, constructed in the vast central plain of the country, would supplant Rio de Janeiro as the national capital. Inaugurated in 1960, it stunned the world with Oscar Niemeyer's looming modernist structures and Lúcio Costa's symbolic architectural plan. Brasília stood as a beacon of the governmental intent to unify the national identity and leap into the future.

While São Paulo and Brasília raced into the future, industrialization produced victims in other regions of the country—most importantly in the Northeastern *sertão* (backlands).[4] The working poor supplied the manpower for construction and industry, but had no means of escaping their impoverishment. Northeastern migrants were often forced off their lands and into *favelas* (urban slums), leaving them hopeless and open to abuse. Student groups, artists, and intellectuals, such as left-wing Catholic educator Paulo Freire (who used education in social and political issues as a means of overcoming adult illiteracy), became increasingly concerned with exposing and addressing the plight of these segments of society.[5]

Vigorous experimentation began among many young artists who could not conceive of the government's monolithic modernist vision without also creating a new social order. Initially, they were involved in a threefold process: to define a national cultural identity in both form and content; to demolish boundaries between artist and viewer; and to expose Brazil's poverty and inequality in the hope of stimulating socioeconomic reform by raising public consciousness.[6] The overarching objective of the artistic vanguard "sought to reach a segment of the population traditionally excluded from art discourse by tapping familiar frames of reference or by including members of this population in the process" (Barnitz 2001: 235).

Visions of cultural identity were primarily centered in the hegemonic capital of power and influence known as the Rio-São Paulo *eixo* (axis). In these two relatively proximate cities, located in the southeast and scarred by extensive slums of the shameful poverty that characterizes much of the rest of the nation, artists and intellectuals wrestled to reconcile the various and disparate Brazils within a self-reflexive (essentially middle-class) cultural paradigm.

While continually borrowing from foreign cultural models, the "new" Brazilian art was no longer content merely to ride in their wake; it sought itself in the experiences of the *povo* (the common people), drawing what it could from a mythologized past and multiple contemporary realities. Early seeds of this are found in popular music (Bossa Nova [New Beat]) and filmmaking (Cinema Novo). Bossa Nova, with its sensual and jazzy contrapuntal rhythms, drew its roots from the Samba of the *favelas*, which had originated in an Afro-Brazilian fusion that had drifted down from Bahia to the urban cultures.[7] Randal Johnson tells us in his analyses of Cinema Novo that the favelas and the *sertão* were "the places where Brazil's social contradictions appeared most dramatically," and integration of their cultural elements marked a drastic change in filmmaking away from a studio mentality (Johnson and Stam 1995: 33).[8] Films of what Johnson calls the "first phase" of Cinema Novo "share a certain political optimism, characteristic of the developmentalist years, but due as well to the youth of the directors, a kind of faith that merely showing these problems would be a first step toward their solution" (1995: 34). The gritty realism of Cinema Novo (often in black-and-white with a hand-held camera) would produce landmark works and its directors would come to perceive of their product "as a political praxis, a contribution to the struggle against neo-colonialism" (1995: 33).

The theatre, too, had European aesthetic ties to sever and a new agenda to exercise. The Teatro de Arena was founded in 1953 by José Renato (1926–), partly in reaction against the European and American fare doled out by São Paulo's Teatro Brasileiro de Comédia (TBC, Brazilian Play Theatre). Created in 1948, the TBC featured imported Italian directors and lavish production values that delighted the elite and bourgeoisie until internal stresses led to its demise in 1964. Renato was the first in Brazil to explore *teatro de arena* (theatre-in-the-round) as an alternative to the *palco italiano* (proscenium arch stage)—a great step in the process of demolishing distance between audience and actors—presenting legitimate theatre that resonated with popular identifications with the *mambembes* (traveling players) and the *circo* (circus) tradition. The Teatro de Arena acting group of the 1950s instantly appealed to students, increasing the theatre's audience base and fulfilling its desire to expand the theatre-going population, although its eclectic repertory of plays didn't differ much from the TBC's.[9]

The foreign directors of the TBC had not only set the precedent for ensemble acting within a unified directorial vision on the Brazilian stage but they also attempted to include a Brazilian play in each season and significantly contributed to apprenticing young Brazilian-born directors. Ruggero Jacobbi (1920–81), in particular, gave enthusiastic assistance to theatre groups like the Teatro Paulista do Estudante (TPE, Paulista Student Theatre) that merged with the Arena in 1955. The TPE's leaders, Oduvaldo Vianna Filho (Vianinha, 1936–74) and Gianfrancesco Guarnieri (1934–), trusted Renato's Arena to assist them in "Brazilianizing" both staging and playwriting, and when Boal joined the Arena in 1956 the young TPE actors warily agreed to work with him. It required a leap of faith, for there were attendant contradictions: anti-Americanism was on the rise and Boal was brimming with inspiration from John Gassner, the Actors' Studio, and American playwrights. Guarnieri reflects that although Boal "reinforced our position [on Brazilianizing the theatre]," his work with playwriting "came influenced by the American social theatre and principally by cinema. Italian cinema. A lot of cinema" (Guarnieri, cited in Peixoto 1989: 50). These influences grew less contentious as Boal proved his talent for "conducting" and "organizing" the fertile ideas of the other Arena members (Guarnieri, cited in Peixoto 1989: 57).

By 1958, however, the nation's economic dreams faltered and spiraling inflation caused the Arena severe financial problems. As Brazilian citizens experienced a rapid and uncontrolled decrease in their spending power, the Arena risked losing Boal and several other members, and Renato was considering closing down.[10] With nothing to lose, he serendipitously decided to direct actor/playwright Guarnieri's *Eles Não Usem Black-Tie* (*They Don't Wear Black-Tie*) as a symbolic "swan song" production. The social theme of the play—dissension within a poor family of factory workers about whether or not to support a strike—attracted unexpected attention from the public who kept it running for a year and enabled the Arena to retain full membership.

With *Eles Não Usem Black-Tie*, Arena made theatrical history and "also moved into new ideological territory: leftist consciousness-raising theatre" (George 1992: 42). Guarnieri credits the play with enabling the creation of the *seminário de dramaturgia* (playwriting seminar), and Boal's experience from the New York Writers' Group proved fundamental to Arena's emergence as a populist playwriting center with "quintessential Brazilian themes" (Damasceno 1996: 81). David George describes the seminar as:

> [T]he first systematic attempt in Brazil to develop play writing. It had taken over a decade for a theatre company to put [French director] Louis Jouvet's suggestion into practice—that the Brazilian stage would only flourish with Brazilian plays. Arena, almost by chance, with the fortuitous success of Guarnieri's play, undertook a nationalist project that had far-reaching consequences. Although the *seminário* itself was short-lived [it ran aground in 1961], in the long run national playwrights came into their own in part as a result of Arena's efforts.
>
> (George 1992: 46)

The seminar resulted in diverse works, including Boal's political comedy, *Revolução na América do Sul* (*Revolution in South America*) in 1960. From today's perspective, one of its most significant results was the emergence of actor Vianinha as a playwright. Not only did his 1959 *Chapetuba Futebol Clube* (*Chapetuba Soccer Club*) depict another overlooked aspect of Brazilian reality—the quotidian struggles of individual members of a second-string soccer club—it also inspired Vianinha to take theatre out of the confines of traditional theatrical space and interact with the *povo* who were the subjects of his dramaturgy.

In spite of *Chapetuba*'s success, Vianinha and others were impatient with Arena's progress as a force for social change:

> [They] argued that Arena was inbred, that is, it appealed only to leftists already in agreement with its politics and was incapable of acting as a politicizing force both because of its limited audience and because the means of production still followed the impresarial model controlled by petit bourgeois intellectuals.
>
> (Damasceno 1996: 72)

Vianinha left the Arena to align with legions of students, artists, and intellectuals in the Centro Popular de Cultura (CPC, Popular Center for Culture—a branch of the UNE, National Students' Union), taking a Theatre of Resistance into the union halls, slums, schools, and neighborhood organizations of Rio by 1962. Although not truly successful in making a theatre of the people, Vianinha was destined to leave a legacy of important plays and was the first writer to bring the landless rural workers' plight to the attention of the theatre-going public.

The aftermath of the *seminário* would also benefit an emerging playwright named Plínio Marcos (1935–99), a former clown, street vendor, and dock worker, who wrote of the marginalized—truly marginalized—in Brazilian society: the whores, pimps, homosexuals, thieves, and down-and-outs.[11] Like the late 1960s filmmakers who comprised the underground of the Cinema Novo movement (sometimes called the "aesthetic of garbage"), Marcos was marginalized by his work, and yet the public clearly saw an aspect of their cultural identity in his distasteful characters. Theatre critic Sábato Magaldi named him the most powerful revelation of the 1960s, and his works are perennially produced in theatres all over Brazil.

Dictatorship and Brazilian cultural identity (1964–78)

For the comfortably entrenched elite, the popular persuasion had apparently become entirely too leftist in its reformist notions and the power-brokers' fear of communism from within was exacerbated by events from outside the country, most notably the Cuban Revolution of 1959. And on the eve of April Fool's Day 1964:

> As so often in Brazilian history (1889, 1930, 1937, 1945), [a potential] civilian political confrontation was cut short by a military coup d'état . . . Within days, the new government had consolidated [and] had cast the populists from power.
>
> (Skidmore 1999: 155–57)

Hideous realities of tanks in the streets and governmental assaults against "the communist menace" were just beginning. For many in the leftist theatre community, commitment to nationalist identity seemed to redefine itself, switching from emphasis on diverse populism to overt contestation of government oppression and censorship. It also soon became dominated by heavily Marxist politics that some considered hegemonic: anyone who didn't conform to a strict engagé line was labeled "alienated." Augusto Boal rose to prominence within the engagé orientation, whereas the other two most outstanding theatre directors of this period—José Celso Martinez Corrêa (Zé Celso) and José Alves Antunes Filho (Antunes Filho)—would seek to define Brazil through different ideological and aesthetic lenses. Yet all three directors made essential contributions to revised perspectives of Brazilian cultural identity.

Augusto Boal and the engagé

One truly sees the seeds of change for Augusto Boal (1931–) in his association with the *Show Opinião*. He was invited to Rio to direct this revolutionary theatrical event by Vianinha who, together with Armando Costa and Paulo Pontes, envisioned a direct contestation of the military's abridgment of civil rights. The *Show Opinião* opened on December 11, 1964 and was "heralded as the first cultural response of any impact signaling a conscious effort on the part of left-wing artists to reaffirm their alliance with the *povo*" (Dunn 2001: 52–55).

Singer Nara Leão (1942–89), later dubbed "The Muse of Bossa Nova," was the impulse behind the show, hoping to expand the reach of Bossa Nova by performing songs with greater social content. In Vianinha's concept, the middle-class *carioca*[12] (Leão) would unite in musical protest with singer/songwriters Zé Keti (1921–99) from the *favelas* and João do Vale (1934–96) from the *sertão*. Boal's involvement would set a precedent for his collaborative use of popular music at the Arena (what he would refer to as *bossarenas*), as he developed "Brechtian arguments of the text, where the case for or against points brought up was presented in contrapuntal style, with music (and lyrics) that distanced, commented on, and complemented textual arguments" (Schwarz, in Damasceno 1996: 141). *Opinião*'s interweave of music and text stimulated both Boal's organizational skills and his belief in the power of music to "prepare the audience in an immediate way, imaginatively, for the reception of simplified texts" (Boal 1985: 170).

One year later, *Arena Conta Zumbi* (*Arena Tells the Tale of Zumbi*) would not only expand on *Opinião*'s format, but stand as another milestone in Brazilian theatre. It came about as a result of a transformative meeting while Boal was in Rio. Guarnieri's idea for a new scenario sparked Edú Lobo (1943–), the most prominent singer/songwriter of the day, to compose a new song about Zumbi that inspired the pair to research the tales of *Ganga Zumba*. They proposed their work as a project to Boal when he returned and Guarnieri and Boal developed a script that would suit the Arena's actors and small space. Guarnieri believes that Boal's theory of the *curinga*, or Joker, was born from the experience.

Arena Conta Zumbi was a complete integration of the Jazz-Samba style of protest song within a theatrical political narrative. Like Carlos Diegues' 1963 film *Ganga Zumba*, the show used the paradigm of the Quilombo dos Palmares[13] and the struggle of its inhabitants to survive being hunted in northeastern Brazil. The musical also employed a technique similar to that in Glauber Rocha's 1963 *cangaceiro* film, *Deus e o Diabo na Terra do Sol*, insofar as a unified narrative voice outlines the pedagogical intent of the show and clarifies a message of revolution. *Arena Conta Zumbi*'s Brechtian approach drew metaphor from what was wholly Brazilian, shouted and sang directly to its audience, and resonated with the fervent concerns of Brazilian youth in the 1960s. The polemical storytelling nature of *Zumbi* functioned as a call for audience identification with the actors in a single voice of protest. Photographs reveal that the production had a simple, clean aesthetic (a bare stage, minimal props and costuming in uniform pullovers and jeans) that emphasized shining young Brazilian faces and voices in a metaphoric appeal to resist oppressive authority.

Zé Celso and Tropicália

While some people were dissatisfied with a perceived lack of progress of the leftist engagé agenda as early as 1961, a real creative *ruptura* (rupture) took place in 1966–67 in a dramatic intersection among Cinema Novo, theatre, music, and environmental sculpture. The synchronicity of inspiration in these four sites gave birth to the short-lived but powerful Tropicalist movement, characterized by an aggressive self-critique that addressed the complex of contradictions in Brazil's sociopolitical fabric. Johnson describes the movement's basic procedure in cinema as "submitting the anachronisms (at first glance grotesque, in reality inevitable) to the white light of the ultra-modern, presenting the result as an allegory of Brazil" (Johnson and Stam 1995: 39).

Cinema Novo was particularly powerful in the hands of Glauber Rocha. According to Johnson, Rocha's *Terra em Transe* (*Land in Anguish*), features "pompous senators and progressive priests, party intellectuals and military leaders, [who] samba together in what Rocha calls the 'tragic carnival of Brazilian politics'" (1995: 36). The film's wrenching cry in the wilderness of 1966 urban political struggle violently influenced Zé Celso (1937–), who had professionalized his student theatre under Arena's auspices in 1959 but disengaged himself two years later with a fully independent Teatro Oficina (Workshop Theatre). Celso's carnivalizing 1967 production of Oswald de Andrade's 1933 (and previously unproduced) *O Rei da Vela* (*The Candle King*) staged an anarchistic and rebellious mélange of riotousness that linked the rebellious profile of the new Tropicalists with Andrade's 1928 *Manifesto Antropofagia* (*Cannibalist Manifesto*). David George explains the cannibalist aesthetic, an alternative to the engagé conception of artistic warfare against foreign cultural imperialism:

> Primarily, it refers to a metaphor for a nationalist aesthetic, a literary code that would "devour" rather than imitate foreign literary models, while incorporating uniquely Brazilian popular, primitivist, and folkloric modes. Armed with parody and sarcasm, the new cannibals would grind up rigid social, moral, and aesthetic codes and roast the colonial legacy of imitation and subservience . . . Anthropophagy does not respect the authority of foreign modes; rather, it blends them into a native cultural stew . . . [T]he colonial paradigm has meant that Brazilians have always been devoured (exploited economically and culturally) by foreigners. Brazilians must now devour them.[14]
>
> (George 1992: 76–77)

O Rei da Vela was completely antithetical to what audiences were seeing at the Arena. Celso's form of engagement with politics and identity aggressively depicted a perceived hypocrisy in the Brazilian mentality, with deliberately *kitsch* and garish visuals in set and costume design. The spectacle was obscenely designed to shock and assault the audience in Artaudian fashion. Not only did it manifest a desire to combat intellectualism and optimism with a bitter exposé of Brazil's incongruities, but it called for individual liberation from any form of social control, including that of the political left. Celso's artistic insurrection became a countercultural icon.

The imprint of both *Terra em Transe* and *O Rei da Vela* on singer Caetano Veloso (1942–) would lead him to announce, somewhat hyperbolically, "the death of populism" (Veloso 2003: 61). He composed the song "Tropicália," borrowing from the title of plastic artist Hélio Oiticica's (1937–80) environmental installation, *Tropicália Penetravel* (*Tropical Penetrable*). Both works parodically foregrounded Brazil's wealth of contradictions by juxtaposing signifiers for the society's coexistent exuberance and bitterness. Like Zé Celso, Veloso and Oiticica expanded the parameters of engagé art and Brazilian self-definition to include a dialectic that defeats any attempt at utopian reconciliation by either the political left or the right. Although Tropicália was only the short-term name of the movement, it liberated the Brazilian concept of tropicalism from its drowsy, orgiastic connotations to an assertive posture, as evidenced in the anthropophagic images and oxymoronic wordplay of compositions by Veloso and Gilberto Gil (1942–).[15]

Young artists were clearly contending with Brazil's radical socioeconomic and political changes in diverse, and often discordant, ways. The Left was seriously fragmented, each faction accusing the other of massive errors in judgment. In hindsight, it seems that even Boal's moves toward establishing a new theatrical form in Brazil under dictatorship were essentially anthropophagic, although they went unrecognized as such at the time; his application of experiences in New York, as well as his experiments with "Brazilianizing the classics," cinematic neo-realism and Brechtian models of distancing, were anthropophagic by their very nature as referencing and consuming foreign elements.

But in spite of these connections, Boal's explicit focus on class struggle kept him identified with the engagé Left, and some deemed his theatrical ideology either naïvely Manichean or, conversely, playing pessimistically to the power of the victimizers. The proponents of Tropicália in the late 1960s and 1970s moved the identity search in an ever more aggressive, self-critical, and heteroglossic direction, feeling that this route was the most accurate—not a forum for change, but a mirror of the nation's complex confusion. In his turn, Boal was chagrined by what he considered Tropicália's ambiguity and by the general disunity in the *classe teatral* (theatre community). The government cut the theatrical debate short when he was exiled in 1971 (along with Celso, Veloso, and many other noted artists, in the neighboring years).

Antunes Filho and the breath of redemocratization

An argumentative, passionate perfectionist, and as harangued by censors as Boal and Celso had been, Antunes Filho (1929–) managed, nonetheless, to avoid arrest and exile. Antunes had begun his career in 1952 as an apprentice director at the Teatro Brasileiro de Comédia, and quickly made a lasting impression in the theatrical community (although as an independently-minded leftist, he was sometimes called "bourgeois" or "alienated"). As an entirely different type of iconoclastic theatre director, Antunes' version of anthropophagy sought not to discard the imported inheritance of the TBC but to transform it from within, supported in his goals by the company's directors. Antunes returned to the TBC (not as a permanent member) after spending 1959–60 on scholarship abroad in Europe and directing numerous independent and innovative productions in Brazil with great success.

Antunes' mission was to discover the Brazilian way of being—the Brazilian means of human expression—as a key to cultural identity, concurrent with examining his own philosophical and spiritual disquietude in the face of the polemical fissures among artists. Politically and aesthetically, he aligned with no faction. Like Boal and Celso, he began his theatre research with experiments in realism. Like them, he explored the international canon of classics while also promoting under-investigated Brazilian authors. Unlike Boal and Celso however, he was hired by various entities as a professional director and did not form a permanent group until 1978.

Antunes' 1964 stage adaptation of Jorge Andrade's story *Vereda de Salvação* (*Path of Salvation*) at the TBC appeared as a torturous representation of life in the Northeastern *sertão*. With *Vereda de Salvação* he won his sixth Critics' Association Award, dividing critics and a shocked public with the way he "wrote" the *sertão* misery on the bodies of the rather staid TBC actors. Nowhere had Brazil seen actors (especially prestigious actors) groveling on the stage floor and immersing themselves so kinesthetically in their characters' internal distress. This "body thing" would become a lasting methodological trademark for Antunes, whose greatest impact on Brazilian theatre would emerge in 1978 with a reframing of the identity question in Mário de Andrade's *Macunaíma* (Antunes, cited in Heritage and Delgado 1999: 153).

The harshest days of the Ditadura, from the state of siege that occurred from 1968 through the mid-1970s, seemed to have exhausted the national spirit of Brazil and its artists, although several young theatrical groups still attempted to exercise what they saw as their artistic rights. A Comando de Caça aos Comunistas (Communist-Chasing Command) infiltrated and invaded theatres, newspaper offices, and neighborhood meetings, beating and arresting any suspected subversives. Performances were prevented by armed soldiers surrounding theatre buildings as Juvêncio Façanha, director of the Federal Police responsible for censorship, declared, "The theatre is rotten!" The government's Censura (Censorship Board) during this time "effectively mutilated 500 films, 450 plays, 200 books, more than 500 musical lyrics, and even *telenovela* [soap opera miniseries] scenes" (Pontes and Carneiro 1999: 58). Thomas Skidmore aptly summarizes the overall cultural legacy of the period:

> Culture in the military years was a reflection of Brazilian artists' confrontation with the realities of power in Brazil. More than a few myths had been destroyed. A large portion of the country's artists and intellectuals had endorsed the populist and often radically nationalist vision of the early 1960s. They realized, as the general-presidents succeeded one another, that those visions were dead for at least another generation.
>
> (Skidmore 1999: 172)

But Brazil's innovations in theatre did not die out completely, as some had feared they would. In a slow process following 1974, influential forces in Brazil helped to weaken the authoritarian abuses and censorship and, perhaps intuitively influenced by his "Brazilian-ized" *Peer Gynt* in 1971, Antunes' 1978 staging of *Macunaíma* was a breath of fresh air when the country needed identification with national myth and inspiration once again. In the incipient return to democracy, Antunes' adaptation of the "rhapsody" with a new generation of actors-in-training he called the Grupo Pau-Brasil (Brazilwood Group), signaled possibilities of spiritual renewal. In an ingenious and inventive (and optimistic) production, Antunes formulated a dialogue between Andrade's modernist concerns and those of his contemporary São Paulo.

The anti-heroic and tragi-comic Macunaíma, born to a fictitious Indian tribe, embarks on a quest where he encounters many regional inhabitants and customs of Brazil. In the end, believing that he has accomplished nothing with his life and unwilling to become a stone in the northeast, he transforms into a star in the Big Dipper where he might guide others to a more productive future. Antunes' actors fabricated environments and incarnated the pot-pourri of mythological creatures, birds, urban workers, villains, and even neoclassical statues along Macunaíma's journey using the simplest of materials such as newspaper and lengths of colored cloth on a bare stage.

Though his company later assumed the name Grupo Macunaíma from the eponymous "hero without any character at all," Antunes proved that Brazil had a preponderance of fascinating character—not a dearth, but an overwhelming abundance—and the group honored requests for world tours until 1985. In that decade he delved into adapting the works of Brazilian authors (most notably refashioning the works of now-legendary playwright, Nelson Rodrigues (1912–1980)), and he has continued to search out nuances in Brazil's complex national character, national culture, and national being with each new production.

The three theatre directors at the core of this chapter represent a trajectory of cultural metamorphosis entering into and emerging from Brazil's dictatorship period. Sudden shifts in the political climate from 1954–79 precipitated enactments of Brazilian identity, with most of the burden for this being shouldered by the artistic community. Antunes, Zé Celso, and Boal actively promoted the notion that ethics and aesthetics are inseparable in acts of self-definition. The theatre came to embrace paradox even as it resisted it, thus participating in what may yet emerge as a novel national and postmodern paradigm: Brazilians will proudly tell you today that their country is *not finished yet*. Augusto Boal's theatrical innovations during this tumultuous period not only provided a foundation for development of TO, but remain a defining part of this ever-evolving Brazilian puzzle.

Notes

1 From the 1988 song "Metamorphose Ambulante" ("Walking Metamorphosis"), music and lyrics by Raul Seixas, on CD *Raul Seixas—Millenium*, Polygram. All translations from the Portuguese are mine, except where noted in the bibliography.

2 A cultural identity quest immediately begs the question, which Brazil? A vast geography with a people—racially mixed (indigenous, African, and Caucasian), yet surreptitiously segregated—marked by multiple colonizations and scored with variations on numerous themes of governance, Brazil is also a land of profound enclaves (social, regional, and economic) coexisting in semi-isolation within its physical borders.

3 Vargas had been dictator until ousted by the military in 1945, in a (now ironic) move to reorganize for a democratic government.

4 The *sertão* takes up a considerable area in the interior of the northeastern states. It suffers frequent droughts, resulting in the population's complete dependence on its large landowners. The northeast is also the territory of many legends and historical communities, such as the escaped slave community of Palmares, the messianic religious compound of Canudos, and a gang of outlaws called *cangaceiros*.

5 Freire's teams taught classes, preparing the general population for great social changes and basic reforms that all had deemed necessary prior to the 1964 coup. The accelerated literacy and concurrent politicization of Brazil's poor, however, posed a threat to powerful reactionary forces within Brazil's rigid social structure.

6 Poverty in Brazil is so abject and so widespread that it is not even called poverty. It goes by the name *miséria* (misery).

7 The thematic mixture of joy and sorrow that characterizes Brazilian Samba carries the uniquely Brazilian cultural concept of *saudade* (an untranslatable sense of bittersweet longing). Later, of course, Bossa Nova would become Americanized and homogenized, losing all fidelity to the original movement.

8 *Black Orpheus*, while charming the world's audiences, was essentially a French film, and left most Brazilians indignant at how it played into exotic and infantilizing stereotypes. Vinícius de Moraes, whose play *Orfeu de Conceição* formed the basis for the film, was outraged not only at the treatment he received from the French producers but also by its final cut.

9 It is worth noting, however, that the tradition of presenting avant-garde works on Monday nights at Teatro de Arena's performance space was already in place: *Poesia Concreta* (*Concrete Poetry*), for example, was officially named in 1955 when four poems were projected on a screen and read by four voices.

10 Inflation rose from 16 percent in the years 1956–58 to 91 percent per annum in 1964. Former US ambassador to Brazil, Lincoln Gordon, retrospectively sums up "the fundamental weakness" in the government's process of "Brazilianizing" (i.e., nationalizing) and "modernizing" (i.e., industrializing) as being "irresponsible inflationary financing, which led inexorably to the ending of the economic boom and played a major part in the subsequent collapse of constitutional democracy" (Gordon 2001: 43). See Gordon (pp. 35–71) for his complete analysis of the economic factors leading to the 1964 coup.

11 To name only two of Marcos' most famous plays: *Dois Perdidos numa Noite Suja* (*Two Lost Souls on a Crappy Night*) and *Navalha na Carne* (*Razor in the Flesh*).

12 A *carioca* is an inhabitant or native of Rio de Janeiro.

13 The Quilombo dos Palmares was a settlement of runaway and free-born African slaves, founded around 1600 in the hills of northeastern Brazil.

14 "[W]hy Cannibalism? Because at one fragile point in the nation's history the native population had an effective means of dealing with the onslaught of colonialism. The Indians' first response was swift and direct: they ate the colonizers, shipwrecked explorers, and missionaries, and they even devoured an occasional bishop . . . The natives' tasteful notions of how to deal with would-be colonizers stimulated Andrade's palate, who turned Cannibalism into a nutritious way of dealing with cultural modes imposed from the outside and slavishly imitated by Brazilians. But still, what is Anthropophagy: an aesthetic theory, an anti-imperialist ideology, a nationalist cultural platform, a colossal joke, an avant-garde casserole, artistic thievery? A bit of each, actually" (George 1992: 76–77).

15 It is a marvelous turn of fate that Gil, who was forced into exile by the military dictatorship along with Veloso, is currently Brazil's Minister of Culture in president Luis Ignácio (Lula) da Silva's cabinet.

Bibliography

Barnitz, J. (2001) "Concrete and neoconcrete art and their offshoots in the Brazilian context," in *Twentieth-Century Art of Latin America*. Austin, TX: University of Texas Press.

Boal, A. (1985) *Theatre of the Oppressed*, trans. C.A. and M.-O.L. McBride. New York: Theatre Communications Group.

—— (2000) *Hamlet e o Filho do Padeiro: Memórias imaginadas*. Rio de Janeiro/São Paulo: Editora Record.

—— (2001) *Hamlet and the Baker's Son: My life in theatre and politics*, trans. A. Jackson and C. Blaker. London and New York: Routledge.

Costa, I.C. (1996) *A Hora do Teatro Épico no Brasil*. São Paulo: Editora Paz e Terra.

Damasceno, L.H. (1996) *Cultural Space and Theatrical Conventions in the Works of Oduvaldo Vianna Filho*. Detroit, MI: Wayne State University Press.

Dunn, C. (2001) *Brutality Garden: Tropicália and the emergence of a Brazilian counterculture*. Chapel Hill, NC, and London: University of North Carolina Press.

Eakin, M. (1998) *Brazil: The once and future country*. New York: St Martin's Press.

George, D. (1992) *The Modern Brazilian Stage*. Austin, TX: University of Texas Press.

Gordon, L. (2001) *Brazil's Second Chance: En route toward the first world*. Washington, DC: Brookings Institution Press.

Heritage, P. and Delgado, M. (eds) (1999) *Diálogos no Palco: 26 diretores falam de teatro*. Rio de Janeiro: Livraria Francisco Alves Editora.

Johnson, R. and Stam, R. (eds) (1995) *Brazilian Cinema*, expanded edition. New York: Columbia University Press.

Magaldi, S. and Vargas, M.T. (2000) *Cem Anos de Teatro em São Paulo (1875–1974)*. São Paulo: Editora SENAC.

Milaré, S. (1994) *Antunes Filho e a Dimensão Utópica*. São Paulo: Editora Perspectiva.

Peixoto, F. (1989) *Teatro em Movimento*, 3rd edition, São Paulo: Editora HUCITEC.

Pontes, J.A.V. and Carneiro, M.L. (1999) [1968] *De sonho ao pesadelo: Da revolta dos estudantes ao fim das liberdades democráticas*. São Paulo: Grupo o Estado de São Paulo.

Skidmore, T.E. (1999) *Brazil: Five centuries of change*. New York and Oxford: Oxford University Press.

Veloso, C. (2003) *Tropical Truth: A story of music and revolution in Brazil*, trans. I. De Sena. New York: Da Capo Press.

Section 1

Sites

Staging the political

Boal and the horizons of theatrical commitment

Randy Martin

Imagine an immediate experience that is also transcendent. A unique moment that translates everywhere. A ruthless critique of what is that provides concrete solutions. An utter negation of what is insupportable in our times that also offers an affirmation of what could be. Imagine an open map of possibilities that gives nothing away. A precipitate of crisis that also resolves it. A preparation for further action that is action for itself. A confirmation of values held in solidarity, and a call to iconoclastic rupture. An overwhelming presence and an utter mediation. A commitment to advance organizational capacity and a refusal to be beholden to institutions. A need to capture people's attentions and a willingness to let it go. A gathering of a public for its own sake, and a mobilization for other gatherings. A challenge to the authority of the state that rests upon it. Imagine all this in its contrarian fullness, and you are beginning to imagine what political theatre is.

Suspended between a critique of what is and a display of what is possible, political theatre is born of contending forces and demands that can readily bring it into crisis. Paradoxically, the very ambitions of political theatre may hasten its demise. Those who would undertake dramatic change in any medium might come to expect nothing less. Of late, some critics have pronounced political theatre to be in a condition of terminal crisis, jeopardized by a fundamental shift in the nature of politics that renders direct opposition to the state ineffectual and live performance inconsequential. From this perspective the crisis of theatre is acute, a function of an epochal shift that makes political theatre as such obsolete. Most starkly put: people today either don't believe in politics or don't believe in theatre—woe to those who would dare to combine the two.

In light of this impulse to dismiss political theatre altogether, the long trajectory of Augusto Boal's work is a most useful terrain to rethink the claims and consequences of crisis. Between the dictatorship of the 1960s and 1970s and the presidential election of Luis Ignacio da Silva in 2002, the Brazilian state has undergone changes as dramatic as any, and Boal has continued to renegotiate his relation to the state. So too, he has continued to find applications of theatre to politics, retaining a space for live performance in a mediated age. Rather than confining his work to one arena, he has operated across intersecting registers of community, the popular, the national, and the postcolonial—which could be considered the principal sites of intervention for political theatre today. From repression and censorship to exile, to electoral and parliamentary skullduggery, Boal is no stranger to crisis within the theatre and without. His engagement with disparate meanings of the political, and his persistence in finding meaningful applications for his work act against the impulse to have crisis bring theatre to an end. For those who have learned from Boal, there is also a responsibility to apply his own methods of interrogation to his work and ask what lies beyond the Theatre of the

Oppressed (TO). My contribution will dwell in successive sections on how Boal's work resists the dismissal of politics and of theatre, and concludes with some thoughts on what is implicit in his work that can allow us to continue it and consider where we might go next. In this regard, I will read Boal's own writings on the condition of theatre against the grain of the arguments that political theatre is in terminal crisis. I do so in the hope of leaving the station not with a sanctified Boal able to silence all doubters, but with the aim of thinking through his writing and treating his work as an arena where we can generate a more productive doubt about the reports of our own collective demise.

Political denial

For much of the twentieth century, political theatre (exemplified by Vsevolod Meyerhold and Bertolt Brecht early in the century, and later in the revolutionary collectives of Cuba and Nicaragua) could trace a clear alignment with that most robust form of political organization, the party. In Boal's case, party affiliation with the Brazilian Worker's Party (Partido dos Trabalhadores) allowed him to gain a seat on Rio de Janeiro's city council and promote the creation of a theatrical technique, what he calls Legislative Theatre, to create laws that reduce oppression. Political affiliation transforms theatre into a public arena where performers and audience can engage with political issues in such a way that theatre can actually have an impact on life and make a difference to the world. When a theatre audience is politically committed, a demand is placed on the performance to treat the possibilities on stage as a vehicle for advancing the audience's capacity to influence politics through existing political organizations. This dynamic alignment of political engagement, critical disposition, and utopian aspiration is not easy to achieve and presents both a resource and a burden for those who would aim to sustain it. Political theatre readily finds itself, through its very ambition, already compromised in its ability to bring all the elements together, onstage and off. That is not an argument against having the ambition in the first place, but against the idea that it should be evaluated on theatrical grounds alone.

Yet according to some accounts on the position of political theatre today, the very prospect of such alignments is a thing of the past. In a spirited refutation of the claim that theatre in Brazil is dead, David George seems to build his case on a kind of assassination of Boal as belonging to a past that must be severed from the present if room is to be made for emergent stages. Writing of a Brazilian theatre festival he attended in the early 1990s, George proclaims "that the stage is alive and well in Latin America's largest country, that it has overcome the trauma of twenty years of military dictatorship, the dismantling of arts funding agencies under the corrupt Collor administration, and the ideological patrol, epitomized by Augusto Boal's stifling dicta designated as 'theatre of the oppressed'" (George 2000: 128). Just how left criticism and tradition is equivalent to or operates as part of a series with defunding (i.e., taking away monies from previously funded organizations or programs) and dictatorship is neither specified nor documented. George gives the impression that all engagements with the state are equally suspect and passé. Illustrative as well is an otherwise trenchant critique of Boal's account of Legislative Theatre by Baz Kershaw which concludes that "the practices of Legislative Theatre may even be seen by some as a capitulation to the very forces of oppression that the theatre of the oppressed had originally hoped to vanquish." This surrender to the state, via participation in parliamentary institutions considered by revolutionaries to be bourgeois or liberal because of their faith in reform, "signals a kind of coming in from the cold of potential armed conflict to a settlement which basks in the warm glow of liberal democracy" (Kershaw 2001: 219).

Kershaw is himself no stranger to writing books on political theatre, and has recently written a book that casts theatre's very possibility into doubt. For Kershaw political theatre is dying, "infected fatally by new pathologies" (Kershaw 1999: 16), which issue from the performative quality of power outside the theatre. Kershaw is at pains to avoid a simple binary contrast between old and new worlds and modes of thought, but has his own capitulation in the form of a presumed "shift between paradigms: from fixity to flexibility, from cohesion to fragmentation, from hierarchy to equality, from unity to plurality, from culture to multi-cultures, and so on" (Kershaw 1999: 15). This now familiar invocation of a shift between the modern and the postmodern, by which universalizing narratives are put to rest, is itself typically underwritten by a still grander story of epochal shift. I cite Kershaw's version here because it is so synthetic a reckoning of the simultaneous crisis of theatre and politics:

> In the wake of the "collapse of communism" in Russia and Eastern Europe old notions of political theatre are falling into intellectual disrepute, and as corporate capitalism spreads across the globe the established estate of theatre is transformed into a play-ground for the newly privileged, a quick stop-over site on the tourist and heritage map, an emporium in which the culturally curious can sample the latest short-lived life styles. But while theatre mostly has become a marginal commodity in the capitalist cultural market-place, performance has emerged as central to the production of the new world disorder, a key process in virtually every socio-political domain of the mediatised globe.
> (Kershaw 1999: 5)

From this reflection on the proliferation of performative power outside the state, he concludes that uncertainty with respect to formal political authority undermines theatre that intends to oppose the status quo—"if few people really believe in the State then it is hardly worth attacking" (Kershaw 1999: 6).

Yet it is important to remember that this incredulity toward state authority has been voiced most strongly by successive governments, starting with Thatcher and Reagan, and achieving global resonance under the sign of neoliberalism. That the attack on the state (or more precisely public expectations that the state perform on behalf of social welfare broadly construed) has become a government function in no way diminishes the significance or prevalence of the state in the contemporary political imagination. On the contrary, those who would invoke the neoliberal assault on the state are only too willing to endorse and deploy the state's coercive powers, as we have seen in the case of the present war on terror. So too, I would argue, for the theatre. The advent of a self-conscious imperative to perform in culture at large does not cancel the theatre, as if in a zero sum game, but forces its return as a reference. The disavowal that live theatrical performance retains relevance is not unlike the dismissal of the ongoing importance of the state. Both force our attention on how the machinations of power actually get produced, and how we come to evaluate both the sources and effects of authority to convince and move us as a social body through specific public-making occasions. The meaning of performance as a generalized feature of contemporary political culture rests on the abilities to grasp the formal properties and specific operations of a given performance. Performativity does not subvert the relevance of formal performance any more than the theatricalization of politics eliminates political theatre. Both imply an aesthetic reference that is the basis of criticism. In the United States, at least, attendance at live performance events has continued apace, keeping up with population growth between 1992 and 2002. Theatre attendance actually increased a bit (from 57 to 60 million) between 1992 and 2002, despite the damaging effects of September 11, 2001 on arts economies (National Endowment for the Arts 2003).

To think that theatre could free itself from the state by fiat risks abdicating consideration of the policies and resources necessary to make theatre, the interconnection of state and civil society, and ultimately the expansive field of the political itself. The "promiscuity" of the political which Kershaw so keenly observes applies not simply to thematics or aesthetics, but to the way in which theatre is embedded across institutional sites that include arts funding, tax policy, urban planning, audience outreach, critical journalism, and the like. With or without party affinity, the question of the state remains pressing for any political theatre.

Disbelieving theatre

While it is important to refute the notion that people have stopped going to the theatre or that attendance is in decline, surely theatre has always been a minor cultural form compared to radio, cinema, television, or computers, at least in terms of the percentage of a given population that it can claim as its actual public at any given moment. Although half the US adult population has seen theatre of some kind in the last year, most will have watched television daily. If people return to the theatre year after year but it is not for most of them part of their daily lives, its role becomes a complex and open question. Even before mass media, theatre audiences were constituted by certain formal limits, be they, for instance, those who could (and could not) claim citizenship for entrance to the Athenian amphitheatre, or those rural multitudes residing outside the Javanese theatre-state. This demographic meaning of theatre's purportedly minor form is a conceptually weak one, for it does nothing to explain what theatre does or how it works.

Theatre has been tarred with a kind of metaphysics of presence, the idea that the live act is authentically self-generative and self-contained. Recently, Philip Auslander has brought this foundational distinction into question in a very productive manner by intertwining live and mediatized cultural expressions (Auslander 1999), exploring in particular what might be considered the contemporary double of the theatre, namely television. Electronic and digital technology are now very much in and of the theatre. In a more profound sense, however, theatre is a mediating technology, and always has been. Theatre is a means for drawing people together across time and space, and for representing this accomplishment once it has gotten them together by virtue of what is presented on stage. I have referred to this technology for gathering publics to reflect on their own capacity for assemblage, attention, and participation, made manifest in the theatre as the socialist ensemble (Martin 1994). Boal's work, it seems to me, is a most intriguing place to unpack this contradictory relation between theatre's call to presence and liveness on the one hand, and to ensemble and mediation, on the other. For he provides some clues as to how we might shift the terms of a debate in which theatre always seems to wind up in deficit.

If audience size is one basis for disbelieving in theatre, the concern that live performance is an anachronistic cultural form is another. For his part, Auslander says that "the televisual has become an intrinsic and determining element of our cultural formation" (Auslander 1999: 2). This notion of being determined by a medium no doubt opens a desire to be free of such determination, to locate the agency of a public or audience in the face of normalizing demands. Boal himself says that the television viewer is "converted into a mere recipient of orders" (Boal 1998: 81). Yet, in Boal's case, this coercive power is not reserved for the televisual. Theatre of the Oppressed "poetics," or analysis of immanent form, are most properly seen as precisely a theory of the audience, of what a public in attendance can do to "decolonize the mind." The spectators are thrust into historical agency by "taking possession of the stage" (Boal 2000: xxi). In Boal's analysis of Aristotelian poetics, art's political power flows from its capacity to correct what is aberrant in human behavior within the context of a particular authority. Theatre makes a spectacle of sacrifice and uses the threat of death to purge from view the will to resist. Aristotelian tragedy is coercive because the final catharsis aligns the viewer with the laws of state. "Aristotle formulated a very powerful purgative system, the objective of which is to eliminate all that is not commonly accepted, including the revolution, before it takes place. His system appears in disguised form on television, in the movies, in the circus, in the theatres" (Boal 1979b: 47). Notice that in this reckoning tragedy as a coercive form is not medium-specific. Rather, the qualities of interactivity now associated with new media approximate what Boal sees theatre as already making available. One could say, however, that because Boal approaches theatre not just as a particular medium but also as a poetics, possessed of a certain internal form that can exist in a range of media (a sculpture, a theatre piece, a television drama), he can avoid certain traps of technological determinism that haunt other discussions of cultural dominants. Ultimately, it is the poetic that is dominant in the particular sense of alignment of publics with the norms of state authority that operate against them.

As Amalia Gladhart has observed, "Boal's theory presupposes that the position of onlooker is inherently oppressive for the spectator. The nonintervening bystander, however, also *facilitates* oppression, allowing torture to continue unchecked, accepting spurious 'explanations' of disappearance and imprisonment" (2000: 21). By this reckoning there is no neutral place in theatre or in politics. It is not simply that the failure to act is a kind of complicity with dictatorial powers; coercion is imbricated in this kind of participation and, in theatre, "the audience must be whipped into shape" (Gladhart 2000: 226). This figure of coercion (whipping the audience) allows the political agency of theatre to be considered as part of a continuum of forces of violence beyond the stage. The theatre is not an innocent space of make believe but is part of a coercive economy through which state, capital, and popular opposition engage. According to Gladhart, the possibility of transformation resides in the spectator's recognition that the performance is not limited to the stage, and can be rewritten and performed elsewhere (Gladhart 2000: 227). Boal's understanding of how to conjoin theatrical engagement with concrete strategies of political organizing remains exemplary. Whether in the onstage battles with the censors when he was director of the Arena Stage, the work with literacy movements in Latin America, or the Legislative Theatre work, Boal has remained tied to a broader movement for social change.

The clear split between subject and object, the actor and the acted upon, the active and the passive is as fundamental to Boal's notion of oppression as to his notion of theatre. What joins the two is a conception of law as the source of power and its reversal—"sometimes oppression is actually rooted in the law . . . [T]o bring about the desired change would require a transformation or redrafting of the law: legislation" (Boal 1998: 9). It would be tempting to see this emphasis on law as a feature of Boal's assimilation to the apparatus of government (as suggested by Kershaw above). More accurately, I think, law has always been central to Boal's conception of politics and the role of theatrical agency within it. From exile in Buenos Aires in March 1973, he issued a manifesto for a "contrary Copernican Revolution," in which there would be "no more satellites" (Boal 1979a: 89), and Latin Americans would be the "center of their own artistic universe" (Boal 1979a: 93). Less than an advocacy for a Ptolemaic universe, this is an analogy of political principles with new laws of physics.

The ability to wipe the slate clean by redrafting legislation is not unlike the ability to stop scenic action to rehearse revolution. Both assume a kind of absolute and transcendental authority, a faith in the power of ultimate truth and justice. This idealized realm where justice is driven by the best available argument, can be ascribed to a person but is more properly attributed to a strongly rationalist conception of law. Law in this idealist sense assumes a domain of pure representation to which some particular case or reality is applied. Ensemble brings these realms together as a transitive movement of theory and practice.

Beyond oppression?

In simple terms, those who make the rules hold the power, and yet it is hard to imagine a society run by rules alone. Rather, we could say that law is not the source of power or the impetus for social change, but is itself an expression of conflicting energies and capacities that it seeks to regulate, channel, and appropriate. The gambit of any oppositional politics is that recognition by the law begins to delineate the limitations of its very authority. Theatre of the Oppressed is a demonstration that the law can be interrupted, reversed, challenged. The means to do this do not consist of law itself, nor even a sense of moral righteousness as useful as this last may be. Of what besides law, then, do the politics of oppression consist? Oppression as a category of critique has the benefit of aligning a whole range of injustices without assuming that people must first reach agreement as to what their problems are before they can act together to redress them. Rallying people around the notion that they are oppressed by some power external to them has the benefit of resisting premature and therefore tendentious and divisive calls to unity.

But the notion of oppression as something done to people can also miss a valuation of the generative, creative wealth of everyday life that those deemed oppressive may try to resist or appropriate. For with those called oppressed also lie the productive abilities that give us not only the stuff but the staff of life, the matter of feeling, imagery, and self-expansion that flash so brilliantly on stage when theatre is in the thrall of some larger societal project. The capacity to produce different outcomes than those a public is presented with as given, rests with the theatre itself as an occasion whereby a critical presence can gather. Whether or not someone literally yells "stop," action is both arrested and completed in performance. If Boal has literalized this capacity to judge, he has also implicated the public in the desire to return again and again to this scene where this critical encounter is fleshed out. The residues of this encounter do not only go by the names of so many laws, whether they be prohibitive or restorative. What political theatre inscribes beyond the capacity to mobilize in the face of rational authority, the giver of the word, is also the name under which people assemble, and by which principle I have referred to as ensemble. Inspired by what TO makes available, but also interested in what lies beyond it, in what light might we continue to imagine the grounds for and efficacy of political theatre? There is a good measure of the implicit in Boal's work that gestures toward a more expansive way of valuing political theatre.

A good reason to see theatre as something other than an anachronism in a world that has turned its back on face-to-face interaction is the prospect of understanding how to align different principles for social gathering, assembly, or ensemble. Decolonization is as much a process of opening up spaces for assembly to enhance the creative grounds for social life as it is a wresting free of habits and directives that foreclose imaginative self-reflection—part of the productive legacy of TO. That creative space of decolonization is neither homogeneous nor unidimensional. Reflecting upon the diverse occasions for political theatre, four intersecting registers of social ensemble present themselves. Less than naming a type of theatre, these registers are mutually inclusive and indicate the kind of work and sphere of operation evident in any given performance. These of course do not exhaust what political theatre can do or be, but indicate the point at which the means to gather a particular audience on a specific occasion can resonate with other social arenas and forces beyond performance. Our debt to political theatre would be in the ways it makes these social capacities and inter-sections legible and accessible. Theatre may gather its crowds under the sign of community, the popular, the national, the postcolonial. In each of these terms some reason for being together is both affirmed but also rendered problematic. Conventionally, theatre may promise the identification of a local audience with a more global concept, but when the per-formance ends, the audience disperses, and with that ends the theatre's ability to mobilize a public. Political theatre would disclose something about both the powers of assembly and the means of regulating those in attendance along lines of a particular identification and mobilization. It helps provide a different way of evaluating the significance of the public gathering for a performance beyond the empirical facts of the numbers in attendance.

Turning to the first of my four principles of assembly, community might seem the most locally coherent unit from which theatre could operate. In the most general terms, any theatre calls a community to order, and makes certain claims to a commons that allows for people to be together. More strongly, a community-based theatre will treat quotidian aes-thetics of public life as its own grounds for stages, the vernacular of its dialogue, and the epic sources of its proximate lyricism. One thinks of Boal's work with groups of poor children where, for example, a child's photograph of a nail on the wall which he must rent to hang his shoe shine kit on becomes part of a poetic language for the local meaning of oppression. Such art helps make palpable the imaginative leaps required for people to live for one another when the scarcities of divisive neglect prey upon opportunity. But typically, exactly what is common about locality is taken for granted—especially when community is treated as an uncomplicated good (Joseph 2002). When theatre is treated as community-based, it is equally an examination of the basis of authority, the maintenance of attention, the question of what was seen and known. Such theatre must offer a representation of a community and establish its resonance by means of the gathering or response of an audience. As a self-dissolving locality, theatre forces on community the question of its own conditions for self-constitution so that one social body can attach itself to others, as audience participants find themselves amidst other publics. By virtue of its assembly and disassembly in time and in space, theatre is a medium for the flow of one local body into others. To achieve this movement or circulation of localities, theatre can offer a challenge to community that it constantly opens to salient difference.

Theatre itself stands as something translocal even as it offers a momentary grounding for the local in performance. For while the audience is particularized in performance, the ideas on stage, the combination of scenic text, directorial organization, and the labor in and of performance, must act before whoever is gathered. That the show goes on despite any dis-parity between an imagined audience and who actually attends invokes a more general imagination of the people, of the generosity of spirit by which all are treated as if they were entitled to equal right, common bond, shared want. For Boal, TO seems to be precisely this. The popular, the second register of ensemble, then, is the incorporation of this general image of the people into communicative form and concrete social occasion. The popular aspect of the theatre is its authority to grant participation to all irrespective of origin, of location, a treatment in the midst of equal access that associates it with a democratic capacity that is distinct from naming the entity or community to which those people belong. By its commercial definition, the popular is a circular idea found in mass marketing: the popular is what the people want (i.e., buy); people want it (buy it) because it is popular. The collective idea of the popular as something people accomplish together is traded for the aggregate of individual consumer decisions. The question of what use is made of the popular (begged altogether when, say, someone buys a CD), is more difficult to avoid in theatre where people find themselves together and are more readily compelled to ask themselves what they have made of that fact. By this reckoning, the popular is not a demographic trait that can be read off a purchase, but a capacity for critical self-aggrandizement. As a reflection of the general capacity for participation, political theatre gathers people to ask what they want to do with the fragile, precious, and immediate fact of their being together.

The named-belonging, the assignment of a collective past when the present is divided and the future uncertain, characterizes all communities. But the political history of community has been forged into a hierarchy whose most powerful expression is a nation that enjoys the representation and authority of a state. The national as another register of social assembly is not simply an imagined community (as if any community could exist as such without some means to imagine how and why people would associate and identify with one another). Rather, it is a community that has been promised the power to achieve self-determination on a world stage. A revolutionary government presents the national in its most strident guise. The newly born state must fend off hostile greetings from those aligned with the deposed powers at home and the grip of colonial powers abroad, all the while seeking to demonstrate that the revolution is a more authentic expression of the national will of the people. Theatre, as it certainly was in the early Soviet Union, revolutionary Cuba, and Nicaragua, has been called upon as a medium in which to negotiate the competing demands to break with the prior reckoning of national origins while conserving and constructing some other notion of national identity. National identity would seem by design to work best when it is turned on others—foreigners, enemies of the state, immigrants—whereas the tendency of theatre is to invite those in attendance to interrogate their affiliation and identity by using the stage to reference dramas outside it. More complicated still, theatre companies that tour the world as national emissaries appeal to a foreign interest not available to them in their own countries. When global funding for theatre can mean that the demand for national identity is most lucrative for the expatriate director, theatre in the arena of the nation cannot do the inside job it might once have been asked to do. Throughout his career, Boal certainly negotiated the inside and outside of the nation. While nation states remain plenipotent on the world stage, their representation of the national as a definable interest has loosened its grip on many real persons who occupy the homeland. Theatres let loose on the world remain powerful machineries of representation. Unsurprisingly, they may speak of nations they can never come home to.

Finally, the postcolonial speaks to this global condition where communities, peoples, and nations have been freed from a fixed administrative relation to a metropolitan center, but without necessarily being repossessed of a deliberative means for their own development. As has been well told on stage and off, after colonial dependence, other kinds can follow. One thinks of the recent financial meltdown in Argentina where that country went from being a neoliberal poster child to one where loss of currency sovereignty eroded the ability to rule the nation. Freeing people from the shackles of structural adjustment programs mobilized crowds in the streets, but did not install some alternate means of controlling their destiny. As Jean Franco has shown so eloquently, the Cold War had a cultural front in Latin

America in which any number of artists and intellectuals were caught (Franco 2002). Political theatre was subjected to these anticommunist compromises, but also took on a range of voices and knowledges either marginalized or contained by the state, and not oriented around the colonial question of national sovereignty. In the theatre, the universal referred to a theme and value that transcended local culture, experience, and ability. When social development was subordinated to a colonial heritage, and the universal belonged to its own particular history in the West, the horizon of transcendence seemed fixed in advance. Besting the West became its own trap, as imitations in the colonies would always pale when measured against a standard given by colonial rule. Rather than mimesis, some other source of orientation and evaluation of self would have to be found to move the immediate beyond the moment—a delicacy always demanded of fine performance. Walter Mignolo (2000) has termed this other vein of self-knowledge "post-occidental reason," and woven an alternate archive of ways of understanding taken from the world over. In this the universal would begin to approximate a whole field of difference that brings the world together in a departure from the colonial demand for oneness of purpose. The postcolonial would represent the often queasy movement between colonial abandonment of administration over captured lands and a principle for assembling the world's peoples based on what each has to offer the other—a kind of global transitivity.

Whatever identifications or ideations might fill them, community, the popular, the national, or the postcolonial should not be taken as discrete choices sufficient for themselves in art or in politics. Gayatri Spivak (2003) has spoken of "planetarity" as an infidelity to the monogamy or mutual exclusivity of these four registers I have been describing. When political theatre takes these myriad associations as its materials, when it makes legible its dependencies, its limitations, its fabulations, and excesses, it finds itself an ensemble amidst so many others bearing heavily on still more to come. Theatre becomes a machinery for articulating the basis for the further expansion of social life—a wonderful and dizzying prospect when life as it is can seem quite enough. Whatever the conceptual vocabulary, the commitments of political theatre keep us open to the strangeness of our situation so as to expand our capacity to hold onto the immediate problem and to the distant possibility; they keep alive the desire for a fundamental transformation of our world while remaining very much of it. Political theatre is not only imagined in this contrarian fullness, but produces its imagination. A willingness to let the crisis of theatre and theory reach their disturbing heights allows us to return for more, like Boal himself, against so many reductive and dismissive readings of our work.

Bibliography

Auslander, P. (1999) *Liveness: Performance in a mediatized culture*. London: Routledge.

Boal, A. (1979a) *Téchnicas Latino-Americanas de Teatro Popular*. São Paolo: Editora Hucitec.

—— (1979b) *Theatre of the Oppressed*, trans. C.A. and M.-O.L. McBride. New York: Urizen Books.

—— (1998) *Legislative Theatre: Using performance to make politics*, trans. A. Jackson. London and New York: Routledge.

—— (2000) *Theatre of the Oppressed*, New edition (with preface), trans. C.A. and M.-O.L. McBride. London: Pluto.

Franco, J. (2002) *The Decline and Fall of the Lettered City: Latin America in the Cold War*. Cambridge, MA: Harvard University Press.

George, D.S. (2000) *Flash and Crash Days: Brazilian theater in the post-dictatorship period*. New York: Garland Publishing.

Gladhart, A. (2000) *The Leper in Blue: Coercive performance and the contemporary Latin American theater*. Chapel Hill, NC: University of North Carolina Press.

Joseph, M. (2002) *Against the Romance of Community*. Minneapolis, MN: University of Minnesota Press.

Kershaw, B. (1999) *The Radical in Performance: Between Brecht and Baudrillard*. London: Routledge.

—— (2001) Review of *Legislative Theatre*, *Theatre Research International*, 26: 2: 209–21.

Martin, R. (1994) *Socialist Ensembles: Theater and state in Cuba and Nicaragua*. Minneapolis, MN: University of Minnesota Press.

Mignolo, W. (2000) *Local Histories/Global Designs: Coloniality, subaltern knowledges, and border thinking*. Durham, NC: Duke University Press.

National Endowment for the Arts (2003) "2002 Survey of Public Participation in the Arts," Research Division Note #81. Washington, DC Online. Available: <http://arts.endow.gov/pub/Notes/81.pdf>

Spivak, G. (2003) *Death of a Discipline*. New York: Columbia University Press.

Critical interventions

The meaning of praxis

Deborah Mutnick

Against the backdrop of "Operation Iraqi Freedom" in March 2003, I started this chapter on critical pedagogy for *A Boal Companion*. As the editors prepare the volume to go to press, more than a year and a half later, the US occupation of Iraq continues and the sense of horror invoked by "Shock and Awe" has deepened, as scenes of barbarism—US torture of Iraqi prisoners and terrorist beheadings—multiply. Meanwhile, at home, the Patriot Act, detentions and deportations of South Asian- and Arab-Americans, and a presidential race shaping up to be yet another case of the lesser of two evils, constitute the domestic flip side of a new chapter of interimperialist rivalry.[1] And so we have endless war abroad and increasing repression at home. It is this scenario that informs my account of critical pedagogy's value for educators, performers, artists, and activists, and to which I will return after a review of its origins and aims.

Origins and aims of critical pedagogy[2]

To gather how critical pedagogy might guide us in the current conjuncture, it will be helpful, especially for readers whose primary interest is Theatre of the Oppressed (TO), to understand its origins, aims, and problems in relation to Boal's work. On the one hand, critical pedagogy is almost synonymous with the dialogic method of teaching associated with Boal's compatriot, Paulo Freire, in *Pedagogy of the Oppressed*. Diametrically opposed to the "banking method" of education, in which students are viewed as passive receptacles into whom knowledge is deposited, Freire's problem-posing pedagogy starts with students' knowledge of their existential reality, elicits generative themes based on socioeconomic conditions, and then decodes and recodifies them into units of reading and writing. As Freire puts it: "The investigation of what I have termed the people's 'thematic universe'—the complex of their 'generative themes'—inaugurates the dialogue of education as the practice of freedom" (1988: 86).

On the other hand, critical pedagogy can be traced to a wide range of theoretical influences from Marxist dialectics to Gramsci's terms of cultural hegemony and counter-hegemony, the Frankfurt School's critique of dominant culture and ideology, Myles Horton's grass-roots educational arm of the US civil rights movement, John Dewey's philosophy of democratic education and experiential learning, and various postmodern theories of representation, signification, and power.[3] In the 1920s and 1930s, the Italian Communist Antonio Gramsci worked under harsh conditions, including 10 years in prison, to illuminate the failures and successes of socialism and to envision its future. Best known for his collection of writings published as *The Prison Notebooks*, Gramsci's theory of "hegemony" was based on his understanding of the ideological rather than brute repressive force exerted by the state and civil society to control a population. Hegemony can be resisted by means of the counter-hegemonic practice of "organic intellectuals" who work with or rise from the ranks of working class or indigenous peoples. To that end, Gramsci himself taught militant workers in Turin, Italy, and wrote about education as a means of producing such intellectuals among the subaltern classes—an aspect of his writings that continues to inspire adult worker and other educational projects.[4]

Also in the 1920s, the critical theory of the Frankfurt School emerged from the Western Marxist thought of philosophers like Georg Lukacs, and in some respects served as a prologue to postmodern theory. Hallmarks of this particular school of critical theory include resistance to orthodox Marxism, technology, Enlightenment beliefs, and fixed systems generally. As Steve Bronner (1998) notes, critical theory first became influential in the US in the 1960s, providing intellectuals and radicals with a utopian belief in progress and a critique of alienation and the deadening impact of the culture industry and mass media. Its major figures, Max Horkheimer, Theodor Adorno, and Walter Benjamin, and subsequent generations, including Herbert Marcuse and Jürgen Habermas, exerted a strong influence over radical politics and theory at the same time as they spawned division and controversy on the Left. Indeed, the Frankfurt School's deep pessimism and reliance on cultural analysis to explain postwar socioeconomic realities seemed to some 1960s radicals to be a betrayal of revolutionary goals.[5]

Closer to Freire in his role as a literacy educator and his emphasis on practice is Myles Horton of the Highlander School. Horton's longtime involvement in the US civil rights movement and his radical mission gave him a sense of the big picture in political struggle. For Horton (Graves 1979), Freire's literacy programs in Brazil, Cuba, and the Citizenship School on the Sea Islands off the coast of Georgia, founded in 1954 to increase voter registration among blacks, were all united by a "revolutionary purpose" (1979: 3). His insistence on the inseparability of literacy education and social change underscores the danger of appropriating critical pedagogy for apolitical purposes. "Many people," Horton warns, "are trying to adopt Freire's educational system, but it cannot be reduced to a mere methodology; to make his system work you must have a radical philosophy" (1979: 5).

John Dewey was a leader of progressive education in the early twentieth century, which, according to Stanley Aronowitz and Henry Giroux, contains "a language of possibility for fruitful intervention into contemporary educational battles, because it poses the relationship of power and knowledge in a positive as well as a critical way" (1985: 7). However, while Dewey's philosophy corresponds with some goals of critical pedagogy, such as preparing students to participate in a democratic society, connecting critical thinking to experience, and viewing students as active learners, his perspective is decidedly liberal. As Aronowitz and Giroux admit, despite their effort to resurrect a homegrown educational theory of "possibility" for contemporary radical ends, Dewey "carefully avoids making a social and political analysis of what schools actually *are* . . . [H]e does not come to grips with the concrete obstacles to his objective of linking knowledge and power" (1985: 9). As we shall see, this importation of liberal ideas from the progressive education movement into critical pedagogy conflates political perspectives that are ultimately irreconcilable.

The problem with these eclectic philosophical underpinnings is that currents of critical, social, and educational theory tend to become a single stream of thought termed "critical pedagogy," which submerges important theoretical and ideological differences. A shallow understanding of critical pedagogy thus contributes to confusion about its objectives and conceals key internal contradictions. In the following discussion, I focus on three central contradictions in critical pedagogy: first, the contradiction between radical and liberal perspectives on democracy; second, the contradiction between historical-materialist and existential theories of reality; and third, the contradiction between theory and practice and the consequent problem of praxis.

Radical versus liberal perspectives

In a feminist critique of critical pedagogy, Carmen Luke (1992) identifies three recent sociological theories of education, starting with "a phenomenological approach" in the 1970s that emphasized interpersonal relations as "co-constitutive of the production of meaning" but which ignored structural and ideological constraints. In this period, liberal educators privileged student-centered pedagogies in the belief that recognizing students' subjectivities would ameliorate problems caused by class and other kinds of discrimination. This wave was followed by a second, compensatory wave of the reproduction theories of writers like Althusser and Bowles and Gintes, who focus on the structural limitations of schooling—economic inequality, class formations, and the impact of the dominant ideology—and dismiss the roles agency or classroom interventions might play in effecting school reforms.

The third wave, according to Luke, appeared as critical pedagogy in the 1980s, and sought to achieve a synthesis of the first two waves, acknowledging the presence of structural factors such as class stratification but reemphasizing a form of "critical self-determination" that would in turn produce "a democratic transformation of schooling and society" (1992: 27). Luke goes on to argue, however, that this third wave, including Aronowitz and Giroux in *Education Under Siege*, reinscribed a "liberal individualist ethos" by envisioning democracy in terms of equality and participatory democracy that have "historically situated the male individual at the center of theoretical, public discourse" (1992: 29). In other words, according to Luke, the problem with the third wave is its uncritical, sexist endorsement of notions of democracy, going back to the Greeks, which have historically excluded or marginalized women and other groups.

Although Luke is concerned primarily with feminist theory and practice in relation to critical pedagogy, which she contends is "entrenched in gender- and color-blind patriarchal liberalism" (1992: 49), her analysis of the tension between liberal and radical theoretical perspectives goes beyond issues of gender and race. The salient portion of her argument for my purposes might be summed up as a case of liberals dressed in the radical clothing of critical pedagogy theorists. Luke argues that the call of these theorists for participatory democracy and involvement in civic discourse is rooted in a public/private schism and utilizes a rhetoric of empowerment that echoes traditional liberal values centered on individual rights and freedoms rather than economic redistribution of material resources. It is in this sense that the adoption of Dewey—despite his important contributions to progressive education—as a major theoretical source for critical pedagogy blurs the difference between radical and liberal philosophies, leading to their confusion in classroom practice and reinforcing a bourgeois liberal ethos.

While the move to reclaim Dewey on the part of radical education theorists is understandable, it must be unpacked if we are to be clear about the social and material forces at the root of oppression. We can benefit from Dewey's philosophy of education; as Aronowitz and Giroux maintain, Dewey's emphasis on experience and participatory democracy remains vitally important to progressive-minded teachers today. It is equally important, however, for progressive teachers to understand Dewey's limitations as a liberal thinker as they grapple with the structural forces underlying social conditions, including the problems of schooling.

Historical materialism versus existential angst

In a difficult but insightful account of conflicting paradigms in critical theory, Charles Reitz traces the influence of the Frankfurt School, particularly Marcuse, on critical pedagogy. Reitz argues that Marcuse diverged from Hegelian-Marxist historical materialism to an "ontological hermeneutic" critique, by which Reitz means a critique of culture rooted in "the subjective but universally human condition" (2000: 56). In other words, Marcuse shifts the focus of Marx's critique of commodity fetishism as a historically specific product of capitalism to a view of alienation, depersonalization, fragmentation, and anaesthetization as universal conditions. According to the philosophy of historical materialism, socio-historical conditions determine consciousness. Although these conditions and the consciousness they produce are historically specific, they are often mistaken as timeless, universal realities. Hence, Marxist political critique and action are aimed at the material structures and conditions confronted in a particular epoch. An ontological-hermeneutic approach, on the other hand, is concerned with interpreting essential truths of the human condition, according to Reitz, thus defining the problems of alienation and domination as permanent, a priori fixtures of reality.

The Frankfurt School theorists' retreat from historical materialism, as Reitz observes, was spurred by the atrocities and contradictions of the twentieth century, events and conditions they ascribed to a combination of the era's scientific-technological achievements and militarist, genocidal politics. Appalled by the barbaric events of the century from World War I to the Vietnam War, Marcuse and his colleagues repudiated science and the realm of objectivity as the "first dimension" of mere fact, turning instead to the interpretive possibilities of the arts and humanities as deeper, multidimensional areas of human endeavor that require interpretation and yield, beyond objective facts, authentic significance and meaning. As Horkheimer puts it, "Art, since it became autonomous, has preserved the utopia that evaporated from religion" (cited in Jay, 1996: 179). This art became the antidote to the mind-numbing realities of twentieth-century technology, cultural conformism, and modern warfare.

Reitz argues that the concept of alienation proposed by Marcuse, and evident in Freire's "pedagogy of the oppressed," marks a departure from Marx's theory of alienation as a condition caused by economic exploitation and the fetishism of commodities. While Frankfurt School theorists and later postmodern thinkers like Derrida conclude that any objective grounds for science and philosophy are illusory—mere narrative fictions—Marx and Hegel embraced science and accepted the independent objectivity of social forces and structures— what they saw as the "rational kernel" in German idealism. Rather than criticize the forces of science and technology, Marx's critique was of the particular historical conditions produced by capitalism in which commodities obtain production and exchange value through a process of private accumulation of capital that diminishes human experience and social relations to brute market forces. Alienation, for Marx, results because the laborer is estranged from the labor process, which objectifies labor as a commodity, now alien and oppressive to the producer, whose labor converts him or her into a commodity as well. Commodity fetishism refers to the exploitative conditions and relations hidden by the socioeconomic process of production and exchange. Marcuse criticized alienation as a form of dehumanization and a debilitating loss of identity tied to the "objectivity of economic relations rather than their subjugation to the commodity form" (Reitz 2000: 55). In other words, instead of locating the problem of alienation in the capitalist mode of production, Marcuse and the Frankfurt School attacked objectivity itself as an instrument of domination and turned their criticism from the base—the economic sphere—to the superstructure composed of politics, culture, and ideology.

For educators who practice a version of critical pedagogy in their classrooms, the distinction between the ontological-hermeneutic paradigm and historical materialism is crucial because the former view of the human condition shifts attention away from an analysis of capitalism and a commitment to political activism to a critique of culture that has frequently served to deactivate and disillusion oppositional political movements. The critique of culture, though often illuminating, tends to obfuscate how the system of capitalist production reduces social relations to commodities and alienates workers from their labor. This mystification, in turn, impedes the radicalization of masses of people because it fosters a sense of despair and, at the same time, fails to provide a satisfactory explanation of alienation and exploitation. Insofar as the left academic agenda continues to be shaped by perspectives such as multiculturalism and identity politics, which tend to eschew a historical materialist analysis in their focus on ethnicity and gender and fracture coalitions into single issue concerns, we will remain in an idealist cultural sphere that neither explains the structural forces that give rise to oppressive conditions nor has the power to transform them. As vital as the critique of culture is to a fuller understanding of contemporary life, for which we owe a debt to the Frankfurt School, its substantive "revision of Marxism" challenged "the actual or even potential existence of a historical subject capable of implementing a rational society . . . [and thus] finally jettisoned that central premise of Marx's work, the unity of theory and *praxis*" (Jay 1996: 296).

Similarly, Freire seems to ally his pedagogy of the oppressed with Marxist theory when he declares: "if men produce social reality . . . then transforming that reality is an historical task, a task for men" (1988: 36). Yet in his writings the oppressor often remains nameless, produced not by a particular political economic system but "a way of life" inaugurated by "an act of violence [which] . . . is perpetuated from generation to generation of oppressors, who become its heirs and are shaped in its climate" (1988: 44). Despite his commitment to revolutionary struggle, Freire's existential proclivities lend themselves to cooptation and dilution of the revolutionary content of his pedagogy. As Reitz argues, Freire's language frequently echoes a Kantian critique of the reduction of human beings to objects or things. Like the Frankfurt School's critique, such a view mystifies the underlying conditions of exploitation and alienation of our particular historical epoch. To my mind, it is precisely knowledge of these conditions and their causes that can best help us mend the rupture between theory and practice that often occurs when we attempt to translate theoretical discussions of oppression into political action—or, in other words, achieve praxis.

Theory versus practice and the problem of praxis

The idea of praxis—reflection plus action—is both a linchpin of Freirean pedagogy and a difficult concept to appreciate, let alone employ. How, after all, does one go from one to the other, from reflective inquiry to social transformation? Freire defines praxis as follows: "Within the word we find two dimensions, reflection and action, in such radical interaction that if one is sacrificed—even in part—the other immediately suffers. There is no true word that is not at the same time a praxis. Thus to speak a true word is to transform the world" (1988: 75). He goes on to explain that reflection without action equals verbalism and action without reflection equals activism. While most of us would readily agree that we need both reflection and action, theory and practice, upon closer examination Freire's definition raises questions not unlike those Luke asks about the translation of the rhetoric of empowerment into action. Though we might read the statement "to speak a true word is to transform the world" as hyperbole or metaphor, it resonates with an idealism not unlike that which obliged Marx to stand Hegel on his head, insisting that material reality determines consciousness, not vice versa.

To provide a context for my discussion of praxis, let me return to my reference to the war in Iraq and quickly sketch out the scene at my university in Brooklyn, New York, in March 2003. In the midst of the military build-up, a graduate student teaching a first-year writing course in the English Department asked if we could hold a departmental discussion on how to teach about the impending war. The graduate student, a young, white, politically conscious English major steeped in academic culture, had introduced the topic of the war in her course and was troubled by the knee-jerk, prowar sentiment of many of her working-class, Black and Latino/a students. She worried that she could not be impartial about the war herself and would therefore impose her ideology on the students. When she articulated this concern in a hastily convened workshop I helped facilitate, it became clear she was not alone. How should we discuss an issue in the classroom that had enormous implications not only for the Iraqis but also—especially at our campus—for working-class students of color vulnerable to military recruitment? How could we provide students with information and stimulate critical inquiry and debate without abusing our power as teachers?

The teachers' perplexity over how to approach the issue of the war underscores the difficult political road ahead. The three-week war proper and what promises to be a long, bloody aftermath signal a turning point in history. Notwithstanding the pretexts of the Bush administration—the doctrine of preemptive strikes and allegations of a link between Saddam Hussein and Osama bin Laden, weapons of mass destruction in Iraq, and an American commitment to Iraqi liberation, its real goal of regime change in the Middle East was hardly a well-kept secret. All too briefly, the eyes of the world were riveted on the spectacle of the months-long US preparations for war. With the fear of genocide in Iraq, the dread of terrorist reprisals, and the horror of 9/11—horrifying in part, as many observed, because it was the first time the United States was a target of foreign terrorism of that scale—still reverberating, people poured onto the streets in the most massive global protest ever staged.

With this scenario in mind, imagine the graduate student facing her first-year writing students, her authority undermined by her youth and her rank. She had been on the streets, marching, shouting, one of billions of people who said no to war on February 15, while most of her students, she told us, supported the war and resisted her attempts to discuss it. How can she critically intervene in the classroom to provide an alternative to mainstream discourses and expose the lies of the Bush administration, the cooptation of the media, and the larger ramifications of the war while continuing to uphold the Freirean value of honoring students' subjective experience? What is the praxis, the "true word," in this instance? In what sense do, or might, reflection and action interact? And to what extent does a facile understanding of "praxis" in critical pedagogy undermine our objectives?

Neither the postmodern turn toward cultural issues of language, representation, and signification nor the move to recuperate liberal democratic traditions of civic literacy and public dialogue illuminate our reality very well. Although these theoretical turns may have alerted us to the complexity of identity and given us a "language of possibility" (Aronowitz and Giroux, 1985: 154), rather than translate into action, they obfuscate polarizing social classes and a brazen imperialist agenda. Two provisos for critical pedagogy at the turn of the century seem crucial: first, while some observers hailed the global February 15 protests in 2003 against the impending war as the "other superpower," i.e., worldwide public resistance capable of standing up to US hegemony, we are not in a revolutionary period or a stage of mass radicalization like the 1930s or 1960s. Second, we are witnessing an exercise of state power, unnerving even to some conservatives, in the expansion of imperial aims abroad and repression at home. These developments force us to rethink what "praxis" means today and how best to achieve it pedagogically.

Critical pedagogy in practice: achieving praxis

My thesis is that critical pedagogy enables an integration of theory and practice in intellectual and creative work—teaching, research, writing, performing, and political organizing. Another dimension of Freire's definition of praxis as the interaction between reflection and action is that knowledge impels and informs experience and vice versa. Words alone will not transform the world but they are necessary to comprehend and act upon it. To use a classroom to recruit students for political activities is inappropriate but so is the charade of supposed neutrality. To achieve praxis in the educational sphere, practitioners of critical pedagogy must enable students to study and analyze the world and the word critically, and act on their own conclusions accordingly.

To illustrate this approach, I turn first to two influential but—to my mind—ineffective tendencies in critical pedagogy and then to the scene on my campus in March 2003 to reconsider how praxis can best be implemented. At one end of the spectrum is Peter McLaren's call for a revolutionary pedagogy. McLaren warns against domesticating critical pedagogy by severing its methodology from its radical underpinnings. As he puts it, a radical pedagogy seeks to create "the type of critical agency necessary to contest and transform current global relations of exploitation and oppression" (2000: xxvi). It also hopes to save critical pedagogy from cooptation by a "bourgeois humanism that has frequently made it functionally advantageous to existing social relations, the employer class, and the international division of labor" (2000: xxvi). The problem with McLaren's perspective is its disjuncture from the objective conditions of the current historical moment. Were we in or close to a revolutionary period, these ambitious goals might seem more appropriate; for it is true that, historically, there have been times in this country and abroad when students and teachers have played key roles in building radical movements.[6] But it is idealistic to believe that academic theorists will lead or even galvanize masses of people in a conservative period such as this one.

Nevertheless, with Che Guevera and Freire as icons of his radical pedagogy, McLaren argues via their teachings that "the subjectivity of the working class must become the starting point for the development of the 'new man/woman' of revolutionary social struggle" (2000: xxvi). He concludes:

A revolutionary pedagogy informed by Guevarian- and Freirean-inspired leadership qualities would place the liberation from race, class, and gender oppression as the key goal for education for the new millennium. Education—as well as imperialist practices against other countries—so conceived would be dedicated to crafting a citizenry dedicated to social justice and to the reinvention of social life based on democratic socialist ideals.

(McLaren 2000: 196)

This revolutionary zeal represents a tendency in critical pedagogy to conflate education with political activism. The idea of a revolutionary pedagogy outside the context of a revolutionary movement is, at best, grandiose and, at worst, counterproductive to the aims of critical pedagogy. It suggests that educators can do precisely what the graduate student feared: impose their views on students or, to use McLaren's more disturbing language, "craft[ing] a citizenry." Such rhetoric, though aimed at large-scale social transformation, nevertheless implies a transmission model of education, in which the teacher molds rather than dialogues with students.

At the other end of the spectrum, in an oft-cited article in the *Harvard Educational Review*, Elizabeth Ellsworth rejects critical pedagogy's "rationalism"—its dependence on Enlightenment values, especially reason—and asserts instead a "pedagogy of the unknowable" based on postmodern assumptions that all narratives are partial and potentially oppressive, including progressive ones. She describes a special topics education course she designed and taught in 1988 at the University of Wisconsin in Madison specifically to intervene against incidents of campus racism. Initially hopeful about the potential to communicate across differences and empower students to fight against racism, she found, to her surprise, that the key terms of critical pedagogy—empowerment, student voice, and dialogue—functioned as "repressive myths that perpetuate relations of domination" (1989: 298). Her students splintered into "affinity groups" along ethnic, racial, class, and gender lines, reproducing the very social oppressions they sought to vanquish and making a sham of the idea "of building democratic dialogue between free and equal individuals" (1989: 317).

What emerges in a close reading of her account, however, is that the class was driven by what Freire calls "subjectivism" rather than sustained inquiry about either the particular incidents or underlying structures of racism. Although the interventions emerging from the class—such as antiracist street theatre and editorials for the school newspaper—seem to have been effective, it is unclear what the students actually learned about racism from them. Based on Ellsworth's account of the course, she seems a priori to have assumed agreement on the nature of the incidents—the class "would not debate whether or not racist structures and practices were operating at the university" (1989: 299)—and how best to counteract them. She thus took for granted students' knowledge and beliefs, eliding a key step in inquiry that might have helped them analyze the problem more complexly and historically instead of becoming mired in identity politics. Not unlike rightwing critics of "political correctness" who decry universities as hotbeds of radicalism where professors like McLaren shove Marxism down students' throats, Ellsworth concludes critical pedagogy, in the name of liberation, reproduces oppression and silences diversity. The emphasis on activism, in this case, rather than inquiry, eclipsed reflection and made praxis harder to achieve. In an abdication of classroom authority, Ellsworth explains she could not address the problems because she "did not understand racism better than my students did" because of her "white skin and middle-class privilege" (1989: 308).

These two ends of the spectrum of critical pedagogy—McLaren's revolutionary zeal and Ellsworth's postmodern despair—underscore the pitfalls of putting theory into practice. To outline an alternative, let me return to the context of the war in Iraq and suggest how critical pedagogy might indeed foster dialogue and empower students to think and act more incisively and compassionately. At the February 15 "Say No to War" demonstrations in the US, tens of millions of people chanted: "This is what democracy looks like!" Despite massive global protests against the war during the build-up to it, the Bush administration's plans for attacking Iraq were inexorable. Like many activists, I wanted to believe the global protest signified a resurgence of radical politics and resistance to the pre-fascist period into which we have descended. However, while the antiwar movement continues to build, the momentum slowed after the crisis of the war's dramatic beginning and a viable leftwing alternative to the two-party system is nowhere on the horizon as the "Beat Bush" campaign sweeps the nation. For the long haul, as activists, we need to educate ourselves on how best to respond to historical events and material conditions. As radical educators, we need to present information and analysis of the historical moment without forgetting Freire's admonition to practice a pedagogy in which "teachers and students . . . co-intent on reality, are both Subjects, not only in the task of unveiling that reality, and thereby coming to know it critically, but in the task of recreating that knowledge" (Freire 1988: 56).

Neither Ellsworth nor McLaren usefully answers questions raised by teachers on my campus about issues of authority and power vis-à-vis discussions of the war in the classroom. If we view the situation from Ellsworth's perspective, discussing the war pedagogically is simply another case of teachers deluding themselves, assuming they know more than their students and thus reproducing oppressive power relations in the classroom in the name of critical consciousness. From McLaren's standpoint, the war is another opportunity to shape students' subjectivity and prepare them for revolutionary activity. But, given political realities, concretely what would revolutionary activity entail? As the war drags on, marked by billions of dollars in military expenditures and the prospect of a long-term, bloody, military occupation, we have witnessed a rapid turn to electoral politics by progressives terrified of another four years of Bush. For students, this state of affairs might well seem more indicative of our collective perplexity than our political strength, the chant about democracy more wistful than militant. It is not that we should discourage political militancy but rather, as radical educators, be mindful of the contradictions of the current conjuncture—which, of course, will shift—as we engage students in mutual inquiry toward a deeper analysis of the structures of society that, in turn, might inform the path ahead for us all.

Toward a pedagogy of mutual inquiry

Although both Freire and Boal have been criticized as idealists, ungrounded in historical materialism,[7] I contend that their belief in ordinary people's ability to make history synthesizes Marxist theory with a profoundly democratic pedagogy. Their recognition of the crucial importance of participatory, dialogic forms of education and art can thus be seen as contributing to a concretization of radical theory, following Gramsci, who also stressed the centrality of education to radical politics, capable of enlisting working people to participate and play leading roles in transforming capitalism into a more equitable, humane social system. Nevertheless, just as Freire's humanistic philosophy sometimes obscures the concrete, specific material roots of most, contemporary human suffering, Boal's Image Theatre, according to Davis and O'Sullivan (2001), envisions a world "created out of one's head" rather than the other way around. Like Freire, the phenomenological basis, especially of Boal's therapeutic work, departs from a dialectical materialist view of the world and the revolutionary potential therein.

While noting this element of the work of both Freire and Boal, I believe their central achievement is their theoretical articulation of the relationship between teacher and student, actor and spectator. In this regard, despite individualist and phenomenological tendencies, they pose a humanizing radical alternative to ultra-leftist adventurism and postmodern despair. Their contribution to pedagogical and political praxis has been to recognize the necessity for, and develop methods of, engaging masses of people—the poor, the illiterate, working and peasant classes—in full social participation as a prerequisite for fundamental social change. As Freire tells us, insofar as critical pedagogy "must be forged *with*, not *for*, the oppressed," the task of the teacher is not to transmit knowledge but to make "oppression and its causes objects of reflection . . ." thus inspiring the "necessary engagement in the struggle for their liberation" (1988: 33). To achieve praxis, action must emanate from reflection, which in turn produces a new set of reflections, leading to the next action, and so on, in an ongoing dialectic. Unreflective action leads to adventurism and recklessness; passive reflection leaves the status quo intact. To return to McLaren's metaphor of "crafting," our work as educators or artists should not be to mold people but to enable them to become craftsmen and women—artists, writers, actors, teachers—themselves.[8]

Though more remains to be said about the mutual, largely positive impact Freire and Boal have had on the educational and artistic left in the US and elsewhere, it behooves me to note, given this volume's focus on Boal's work in relation to other theories and movements, key differences between the systems of education and theatre. As much as Boal's TO is linked historically and ideologically to Freirean pedagogy, it would be a mistake to consider the two synonymous. For one, TO builds on aesthetic as well as political and educational goals, in view of questions of content *and* form in relation to the experience and communication of social realities. While all content assumes a shape, and forms of reading, writing, and critical consciousness are integral to Freire's teaching method, the performative aspect of theatre underscores issues of form and presentation. The people-to-people contact in the realm of theatre, whether on a conventional stage or an invisible scene in a bar, and the relation of actor and audience—for Boal, all "spect-actors"—creates an exigency that is not viscerally present in written communication.

Second, because theatre is immediate and happens through the senses, Boal's techniques and performances must account for the relationship of the actor to the character, underscoring the difference between the two in ways that writing pedagogy does not always make as clear. In other words, while it is true that the individual who writes is never the same as the writer in the text—much less, the narrator—his or her disembodiment from writing physically separates one from the other. Because the actor who plays a character is always present, the one literally embodying the other, that separation must be articulated in the body. This feat requires aesthetic awareness of how theatre is made, specifically, how the actor assumes a role, knowledge that can be used to produce classical, naturalistic, or romantic theatre or to debunk their illusions and create what Brecht called an "alienation effect." Similarly, the process of rehearsing experience enables both the full development of an idea and of the dramatic relationships of spect-actors, a practice similar to drafting a text but, again, more transparent. Boalian theatre can thus deepen the rhetorical underpinnings of Freirean pedagogy through its emphasis on the importance of learning through the senses and its literal enactment of the relationship between actor, character, and audience. At the same time, Boal practitioners must continue to implement Freire's method of decoding generative themes so as to resist the banking system and instead promote theatre as the practice of freedom.

What fundamentally unites the two practices is dialogue—a true praxis of action and reflection that unfolds differently but engages the same principles in each realm. Pedagogy and Theatre of the Oppressed foster but do not dictate action; nor, I believe, is their practice, as outlined by Freire or Boal, politically neutral, liberal, or reformist. Freirean pedagogy and Boalian theatre are revolutionary in their commitment to struggles for social and economic justice; however, they do not aim to convert students to any particular organization or political philosophy. Their aims are broadly nonsectarian rather than narrowly political. The teacher eschews depositing knowledge of any kind into students, yet for real dialogue to occur, the teacher's authority must be "on the side of freedom, not against it" (Freire 1988: 67). This profound statement goes to the heart of our difficulty in defining our roles as politically conscious educators and artists: the dialectic it enacts is between the actualization of individual potential and a deep commitment to what Freire calls "humanization" and the world's historic struggle against exploitation, injustice, and oppression. It is this double commitment that enables us, for example, to criticize Operation Iraqi Freedom in the classroom without fear of silencing students or stifling creativity. As Freire understood in his use of generative themes with Brazilian peasants, the fundamental theme of our epoch is domination. As teachers, our role is not to use our power in the classroom to recruit and organize but to illuminate, analyze, and debate—to set in motion a process of inquiry that may lead to action but not compel it and may at times invite responses from students with which we may, as participants in the educational process ourselves, argue. This perspective avoids both the *postmodern error* of abandoning the possibility of rational discourse and the *ultra-leftist error* of conflating education and politics in a monologic, authoritarian discourse that, however well-intentioned, reproduces the oppressive conditions it sets out to transform.

Boal makes this distinction between polemics and politics even clearer. He contrasts the aim of catharsis in Greek tragedy to the aim of "dynamization" in the Legislative Theatre he developed as an elected official in Rio de Janeiro. In bringing the theatre "back to the heart of the city," he explains, Legislative Theatre sought "not to pacify its audiences, to tranquillise [sic] them, to return them to a state of equilibrium and acceptance of society as it is, but, again, contrarily, to develop their desire for change . . . to create a space in which it can be stimulated and experienced, and where future actions arising from it can be rehearsed" (Boal 1998: 20). He points out that despite the exclusions of women, slaves, and nonproperty holders in classical Greek society, everyone who participated in the direct democracy of the public square or agora could voice an opinion and vote. Representative democracy such as ours, even when its definition of citizenry is more inclusive, is less participatory as people rely on politicians to govern and become alienated from social structures over which they have little control. In his experiment in Brazil with Legislative Theatre, Boal embarked on a new form of transitive democracy based on dialogue in which, as he puts it, echoing Freire, "we are all subjects: pupils and teachers, citizens and spectators" (Boal 1998: 22).

Part of our frustration is that we face the hegemonic power of the US from the proverbial belly of the beast. I believe we need to situate our work as educators in the context of objective conditions for systemic change and be clear about the difference between activism and education. This distinction blurs in periods of radical upsurge; universities, schools, and other sectors like labor and neighborhoods can become sites of revolutionary struggle when societies are in motion. But especially when the contest for "hearts and minds" has disabled the Left to the extent we see today at home and abroad, it is important to distinguish between politics and polemics in the classroom. Our role should be to foster inquiry in students—"critical consciousness" or problem-posing in Freire's terms—not to indoctrinate or convert them. Such work can reveal the underlying structures and forces of capitalism; it can educate broadly and deeply, building a base of knowledge and exposing students to humanistic values. But it cannot substitute for a mass revolutionary movement. To imagine we are a vanguard is simply to delude our students and ourselves. On the other hand, to avoid critical education for fear of silencing or indoctrinating students does them a disservice and subscribes to mainstream ideology in precisely the ways we should all be criticizing it.

Notes

1   The presidential race, alas, ended in what observers who invoked the idea of "the lesser of two evils" would no doubt agree is the greater one.
2   See Darder *et al.* (2003) for a good overview of the origins of critical pedagogy.
3   I do not discuss postmodern theories here due to space limitations but am referring generally to theorists like Derrida and Foucault.
4   See, e.g., Borg *et al.* (2002).
5   See Jay for an anecdote about Weather Underground leader Mark Rudd's depiction of Adorno and Horkheimer as "craven sell-outs" (1996: 4).
6   See Hammond on the impact of popular education on the war in El Salvador, which he argues was "a critical factor . . . [that] developed the political consciousness of the *campesinos* who became the insurgency's base . . ." (1998: 5).
7   See Davis and O'Sullivan (2001) for a critique of Boal's poor grasp of dialectical materialism, leading to exercises like Cops-in-the-Head and a liberal individualist ethos in which protagonists' problems are addressed outside the context of the material conditions of their reality.
8   Boal tells a poignant story in this regard, about a group of maids who performed at various nontraditional theatre sites. The story ends with one of the maids in tears because, Boal reports, "she had looked at herself in the dressing room mirror and seen a woman instead of a housemaid" (2001: x).

Bibliography

Aronowitz, S. and Giroux, H. (1985) *Education Under Siege*. South Hadley, MA: Bergin and Garvy.
Boal, A. (1998) *Legislative Theatre*, trans. A. Jackson. London and New York: Routledge.
—— (2001) *Hamlet and the Baker's Son: My life in theatre and politics*, trans. A. Jackson and C. Blaker. London and New York: Routledge.
Borg, C., Buttigieg, J.A., and Mayo, P. (eds) (2002) *Gramsci and Education*. Lanham, MD: Rowman and Littlefield Publishers, Inc.
Bronner, S. (1998) "Of critical theory and its theorists: introduction," *Illuminations: The critical theory website*. Online. Available: <http://www.uta.edu/huma/illuminations/bron1.html> (accessed August 8, 2003).
Darder, A., Baltondano, M., and Torres, R.D. (eds) (2003) *The Critical Pedagogy Reader*. New York: Routledge.
Davis, D. and O'Sullivan, C. (2001) "Boal and the shifting sands: The un-political master swimmer," *New Theater Quarterly* 63: 288–97.
Ellsworth, E. (1989) "Why doesn't this feel empowering? Working through the repressive myths of critical pedagogy," *Harvard Educational Review* 59: 297–324.
Freire, P. (1988) *Pedagogy of the Oppressed*, trans. M.B. Ramos. New York: Continuum.
Gramsci, A. (1971) *Selections from the Prison Notebooks*, ed. and trans. Q. Hoare and G.N. Smith. New York: International Publishers.

Graves, Bingham. (1979) "What is liberating education? A conversation with Myles Horton," *Radical Teacher*, May, 3–5.

Hammond, J.L. (1998) *Fighting to Learn: Popular education and guerrilla war in El Salvador*. Rutgers, NJ: Rutgers University Press.

Jay, M. (1996) *The Dialectical Imagination: A history of the Frankfurt School and the Institute of Social Research, 1923–1950*, 2nd edition, Berkeley, CA: University of California Press.

Luke, C. (1992) "Feminist Politics in Radical Pedaogy," in C. Luke and J. Gore (eds) *Feminisms and Critical Pedagogy*. New York: Routledge.

McLaren, P. (2000) *Che Guevara, Paulo Freire, and the Pedagogy of Revolution*. Lanham, MD: Rowman and Littlefield Publishers, Inc.

Reitz, C. (2000) "Liberating the Critical in Critical Theory: Marcuse, Marx, and a pedagogy of the oppressed: Alienation, art, and the humanities," in S.F. Steiner, H.M. Krank *et al.* (eds) *Freirean Pedagogy, Praxis, and Possibilities: Projects for the new millennium*. New York: Falmer Press.

Tactical carnival

Social movements, demonstrations, and dialogical performance

L.M. Bogad

All Power to the Imagination!

Situationist International slogan

October 26, 2002: Washington, DC. A preemptive peace demonstration, responding to the Bush Administration's call for preemptive war on Iraq, is in progress. Hundreds of thousands have gathered for the largest antiwar demonstration here since the Vietnam War. Although the demonstration was first called by International ANSWER, a group largely run by the Workers' World Party, the massive turnout includes people of many walks of life and world-views, from all over the country and beyond. This diversity is encouraging for the potential growth of the peace movement.

International ANSWER has organized a very long series of orators, and while the rally is so huge that thousands of people cannot see the soundstage or hear the speakers, many stand quietly and listen to the amplified oratory, applauding and cheering when moved to do so, while others mill around, chat, and wait for the announcement that the march will begin.

However, at least one troupe of costumed performers called Absurd Response is not listening to the speakers. Instead, they move randomly through the throng, singing, dancing, and improvising with the crowd around them. They walk behind a banner that says "ABSURD RESPONSE TO AN ABSURD WAR." These are the Perms for Permawar, eight alluring men and women wearing fluorescent colored gowns, opera-length gloves, and two-foot high Marge Simpson-type wigs. Each wig sports a brightly colored letter, so their foreheads spell "P-E-R-M-A-W-A-R." The Perms, also known as Bombshells for their glamour and prowar orthodoxy, lead festive chants such as "We Need Oil! We Need Gas! Watch Out, World, We'll Kick Your Ass!" and "We Love BUSH! We Love DICK! All You Peaceniks Make Us SICK!"

The Bombshells are accompanied by dozens of other characters created around the theme of absurd response. A ghoulish trio, "The Spirit of '76 Gone Wrong," costumed in pallid skin, bloody rags, and militarist trappings, carry drum, flute, and flag (which reads "OIL"). Gibbering War Clowns bounce and pounce around the perimeter of the procession. A singing, stilt-walking Angel of Death in a red dress hovers above. She plays a squeezebox, and hanging from her neck are a miniature skeleton and a sign reading "Death ♥s W." A large number of Billionaires for Bush are there as well, in their top hats, tuxedos, jewelry, and formal dresses, to ironically support the war effort and cheer their boy "W" onward.

Finally, the speakers on the stage are finished. The enormous march begins, and Absurd Response joins the parade. At one point we are passed by an International ANSWER sound truck. ANSWER is as one-way in their communicative style as their name suggests. They are heavily amplified, overpowering the voices of those below them, as they shout decades-old, plug-in chants such as "Hey, Hey, Ho, Ho, George Bush Has Got to Go!", "George Bush! You Can't Hide! We Charge You with Genocide!" and "The People, United, Will Never be Defeated."

There is a palpable clash in style and worldview between Absurd Response, with its irony, satire, multivocality, and even ambiguity, and the monotonous monological chant of the sound truck. Before long, some new call-and-response chants emanate from the Absurd Response contingent, no longer merely mocking the warmongering White House but lampooning ANSWER's dogmatic, redundant, unimaginative style. These chants include: "Three Word Chant! (Four Words Are Better!)"; "March March, Chant Chant, Rhetoric Rhetoric, Rant Rant!"; "Hey, Hey, Ho, Ho—'Hey Hey Ho Ho' Has Got To Go!"; and "Bad Slogans, Repeated, Ensure That We're Defeated!" The people on the ANSWER sound truck, perhaps unwilling to break their rhythm or come up with a comeback, simply continue their own chants and drive down the road. A brief, instructive disruption has occurred.

This chapter is an exploration of performance aesthetics and tactics in social movement activism. It focuses specifically on what social movements are most known for to the greater public: demonstrations in public space. It draws on the praxis of the global justice movement, specifically in the United States and mostly in New York City. This is a localist effort meant to open the subject; I am not trying to arrive at final conclusions, nor to write from one locality in a way that generalizes about this incredibly diverse, dialogical, and decentralized movement. Finally, a look at social movement theory will help us understand the importance of the public demonstration and where Theatre of the Oppressed (TO) fits within the wider range of activist practice.

Building social movements

A social movement is a network of people engaged in sustained, contentious, collective action, using methods beyond established institutional procedures such as voting (Tarrow 1998: 3). For example, the global justice movement, also known as "globalization from below" (Brecher et al. 2002), or the antiglobalization movement by its detractors, seeks to oppose the disastrous effects of corporate globalization while building progressive, constructive, and dialogical connections between the people of the world. Performance, both public and private, is a key element in the formation, sustenance, and building of such social movements.

Hidden transcripts and the cycle of contention

Movements often form slowly, through the daily building of social networks, a growing awareness of a collective complaint, and an increasingly articulated conceptual frame for taking action. Even in periods of repression, people can build networks for potential social movements through the clandestine creation and nurturing of a "hidden transcript" (Scott 1990). Hidden transcripts are the highly articulated and stealthily nurtured worldview and grievance list of the oppressed. They are the stories, rumors, complaints, and utopian visions that a sub/counter-culture keeps alive for the historical moment when, because of shifts in political opportunities and constraints, substantial mass liberatory action becomes possible.

Alternative worldviews need an alternative space in which to be developed and shared. Nancy Fraser argues that the oppressed create "subaltern counterpublics" as an alternative to the dominant bourgeois public sphere because they need:

[V]enues in which to undertake communicative processes that were not, as it were, under the supervision of the dominant group . . . to articulate and defend their interests . . . [and] to expose modes of deliberation that mask domination by absorbing the less powerful into a false "we" that reflects the more powerful.

(Fraser 1997: 81)

Through this communicative process, counterpublics can develop a collective action frame, or a way of looking at the world that argues that mass mobilization for change is both possible and necessary (Tarrow 1998: 21). The development of sophisticated subaltern counterpublics, including the nurturing of hidden transcripts and/or collective action frames, is a necessary precursor to the launching of a powerful social movement.

An example of this is the development of the civil rights movement in the United States. Though locked out of the halls of power and civil society in the south, this movement was able to nurture resistance based in churches, civic organizations, and their own press and allied cultural workers (musicians, artists, theatre makers, *et al.*). They also built coalitions across region, race, and class, sustaining their struggle against American apartheid over the course of decades. After World War II, in which African-Americans had participated to defeat fascism, the US government was concerned with its image as the bastion of human rights within the Cold War contest with the Soviet Union. In this context, the civil rights movement escalated its anti-Jim Crow activity with massive, highly visible, nonviolent direct action as well as juridical, legislative, and cultural methods. The whole world was watching, including more sympathetic sections of the United States beyond the south.

A "cycle of contention" is just such a time when the incentives for contentious collective action are raised, and/or when the costs of such action are lowered for various reasons, such as when there is a perceived split in the elites, a weakening of the state's repressive apparatus, or a shift in the relative power of competing or allied forces, encouraging social movements to get active across an entire society (Tarrow 1998: 24–25):

[C]ontentious politics is triggered when changing political opportunities and constraints create incentives for social actors who lack resources on their own . . . When backed by dense social networks and galvanized by culturally resonant, action-oriented symbols, contentious politics leads to sustained interaction with opponents. The result is the social movement.

(Tarrow 1998: 2)

Social movements cannot preordain a top down loosening of national policy in order to better facilitate their own actions, but they certainly have the agency to "seize the time" if they perceive a chink in the establishment's order. When a historical opportunity for such collective agency presents itself, a cycle of contention may begin. To take advantage of the opportunity and to build group formation and cohesion, activists need to construct a cultural frame, or set of impassioned, shared meanings, that justify and motivate collective action (Tarrow 1998: 21). A cycle of contention gains momentum when social actors perceive that change is desirable, that the risks and costs of movement participation have lessened, and that the chance of victory has grown (Tarrow 1998: 24). Without a sense of shared grievance, purpose, and possibility, an effective social movement does not develop; indeed that sense of shared meaning, a role in history, and liberatory agency can sustain resistance even when the tide has turned and danger has increased (Wood 2003: 231–41).

Theatre of the Oppressed workshops can play a vital role during cycles of contention in helping members of a burgeoning movement define their issues and explore possible solutions. Whether participants are seasoned activists or people who have never engaged in overt political action, Image Theatre can help bring people together, in a common space, to creatively, nonverbally, and dialogically express and develop their perceptions of their world, power structures, and oppressions. Forum Theatre provides a relatively safe space, protected from the actual ramifications of reactive state repression, to experiment with possible contentious methods. This is oppositional praxis in action. Legislative Theatre, during this period, can help a movement develop a parliamentary agenda. Thus TO techniques, with their myriad variations, are particularly useful for social movements' development of hidden transcripts and collective action frames.

Boal was not the first to call for decentralized, anti-authoritarian methods for progressive movement building. In fact, various methods of "rehearsing for reality" are a common staple of organizing manuals from way back. However, these manuals generally call for activists to *discuss* overall strategy, and to role play and rehearse only the moment of action, public performance, and/or confrontation. For example, nonviolence training teaches activists, through practice, how to stay calm, centered, committed, and nonviolent in the face of harassment or abuse. Theatre of the Oppressed expands the role of rehearsal to help people at any level of political commitment not only to rehearse direct confrontation with the state but to use improvisatory performance to decide what their problems are, what they want, and what they are able to do about it.

There is also a long history of theatre at the service of social movements. But Boal's unique, historic contribution is the inventive systematizing of theatrical methods based on Freirian and anti-Aristotelian theory. Boal's Freirian influence leads his approach in a dialogical direction; a director or auteur does not dictate the movements on the stage but rather a Joker facilitates the creative collaboration of a group. Jokering is not unproblematic, of course, but TO strives toward the minimization of hierarchy. In his first book, Boal (1979) articulated the ways in which his theatre consciously resists Aristotelian catharsis. This is ideal for social movements' development of collective action frames and tactical and strategic praxis; a social movement seeks to galvanize, to agitate, to articulate dissent and dissatisfaction, and so the purgation of social complaint through catharsis is anathema.

Repertoires of contention

The "repertoire of contention" is the set of oppositional tactics that movements creatively accumulate over the course of many struggles (Tarrow 1998: 20–21). These tactics evolve over time as movements interact with their often-hostile environment. Some tactics become outdated; at other times, variations are invented. A new tactic can initially be incredibly disruptive, catching one's opponents by surprise. The first sit-down strike in the USA, by the United Auto Workers in Flint, Michigan in 1936–37, was a powerful innovation in the repertoire of contention and resulted in an important victory for the labor movement; the UAW won recognition and its first contract. Gandhi's philosophy and techniques of nonviolent resistance confounded the British Empire, and the American civil rights movement achieved similar successes with its own version of Gandhi's techniques. In the US and Europe, the New Left caught their opponents unaware with spectacular, symbolic pranks that disrupted what they saw as the oppressive activity of the state, drew media attention to their social issues, and provoked the imagination and sympathetic ire of many spectators. The Kabouters, for example, broke into many abandoned houses and vacant office buildings across the Netherlands, using whimsical humor in art and street performance to soften the shock of their illegal actions as they squatted in the buildings to protest at the desperate housing shortage of the time. They succeeded in garnering the sympathy of Dutch people of all ages and most classes, who were all affected by this shortage. Eventually, they forced the state to address the housing problem, including the legalization of a number of Kabouter squat-communes (Bogad 2005). While these examples of nonviolent creativity can expand the efficacy of social movements, tactics can eventually become so conventionalized that they lose a great deal of their effect. The state develops counter-tactics for containing and minimizing their potency, including what the Dutch Left bitterly refers to as "repressive tolerance." Some activists feel that prearranged, routinized civil disobedience arrests have lost much of their bite for this reason.

One of the major turns in the history of the repertoire of contention is the development of modular tactics, or tactics that can be transferred across boundaries of context, complaint, location, and identity. The public demonstration is an example, spreading across many national borders and tried by almost every social movement to date. Modular tactics have great utility; when an action is needed, the local groups of a movement across a country, or even internationally, can do the same type of action on the same day. The advantages are not to be underestimated. For example, if a corporation or state knows that if they push one union too far, the result may be not just one local strike, but a national strike, possibly with sympathy strikes against their subsidiary firms in other countries, they will at least think twice before escalating a conflict. Examples of recent coordinated global modular action include the demonstrations against the USA's buildup to invasion in Iraq on February 15, 2003, in which an estimated 10 million people across the world took part, and the Lysistrata Project, in which hundreds of groups in many countries performed that ancient Greek play as an anti-Iraq War statement (lysistrataproject.org). TO itself can be thought of as a potential modular form of resistance. Because books describing the practice have been translated into many languages, and as TO centers and groups have been working all over the world, TO techniques could be activated if desired on several continents at once.

Modular action also carries with it some risk of routinization; it too can become reductionist and mechanistic. However modular a form of resistance it may ostensibly be, an action still must be adapted to local needs, dangers, cultures, and legal/sociopolitical contexts. This is reflected in a hard-won bit of wisdom shared among experienced TO Jokers and theorists: TO facilitators must remember that TO techniques are meant to serve the local, specific, and ever-changing needs of spect-actors, and not the other way around. As a modular tactic in the repertoire of resistance of social movements, TO remains valid only to the extent that groups feel free to adapt and change its form.

Leslie Kauffman makes the corollary point that many activists fall in love with a particular tactic, and start to confuse that increasingly redundant and sometimes inappropriately used tactic, with strategy (Kauffman 2004). Strategies are comprehensive, complex plans for a long-term campaign, projecting power onto space and time; tactics are immediate actions. Tactics can be the building-block elements of a strategy; on the other hand, they may be the only items in the repertoire of a player that lack strategic power. New tactics need to be constantly innovated to feed a movement's evolving strategy; the opponents of social movements, alas, are not blocks of wood. States and corporations exercise agency, too! The tactical interaction between social movements and their opponents is a dance of competing innovation. As one tactic is used, the police (for example) will develop a tactic that disrupts or neutralizes that tactic. Another tactic will have to be innovated to respond to that response, and so on. A movement that is organized so as to maximize the creation and circulation of new tactics, and that employs praxis-oriented experimentation with and reflection on those methods, is a movement that will stay flexible and unpredictable.

Public demonstrations

Why do movements spend so much time and effort organizing public demonstrations? Some feel that the public demonstration is obsolete—that public space no longer exists, or that power is now too fluid and dispersed to be contested by gathered masses of people. There are so many other tasks for activists: direct action, recruiting door-to-door, fund raising, lobbying, training, reflecting/theorizing/writing, building counter-institutions at the grass-roots level, and jokering TO workshops and performances, to name a few. Although this may seem a very basic and obvious question, there are many, sometimes conflicting, often overlapping motivations for the public performance of dissent. Here is a nonexhaustive list, with each item accompanied by the tactical emphasis most beneficial to further the particular goal:

1   *To collectively express dissent on a specific issue*, in order to influence the state, and/or other elites, and the larger public, or at least to embarrass the state and put mass opposition to state policy on the public record. The more important this is to the group, the more the coherence of its message matters.
2   *As an expression of strength for the movement*, both for internal confidence-building and as a general warning for opponents. If this is important to the group, then successfully organizing a big turnout is of the essence.
3   *To recruit new members and grow the movement.* If this is important to the group, then the public space they inhabit should be attractive to be in. And even if the issue is deadly serious, there should be something about the time spent and the physical movement through space that inspires desire and defiant joy. An atmosphere of serious play, of ludic experimentation with freer ways of being, may be ideal, but concerns about going past a broader public's horizons of expectations or understanding may complicate this.
4   *To define collective identity for a group, subculture, or movement.* Since demonstrations alone rarely change public policy or power structures, they arguably should serve a countercultural purpose, to build cohesion and sustain resistance. When developing a countercultural identity is important to the group, then the style of the demonstration matters a great deal. Organizers and participants may ask themselves: What is the mood at the demonstration? Is the composition of the group diverse or homogenous? What culture is being created and expressed in the space? How are people's bodies costumed/gendered and how do they move in the space? What is the dramaturgy of the space—the blocking, timing, tone, composition, design? What is the role of art and creativity? Is the emphasis toward individual identity or collective identity or toward a non-dualistic mix/interplay of the two?
5   *As a way to convene the movement for targeted direct action.* The anti-abortion movement, for example, has gathered people from all over the US to shut down abortion clinics in some localities. The pro-choice movement has responded in kind, gathering masses of activists to protect access to those clinics. The global justice movement regularly convenes to disrupt and protest the proceedings of state/corporate globalization agencies

such as the World Trade Organization. If this goal is important to the group and the target is well-defended, then it helps to have a diverse organization that is trained to implement a diversity of tactics in the space.

6   [Insert your motivation here.]

These different priorities are always in competing and overlapping play with each other. The friction between International ANSWER and Absurd Response described earlier reflects a conflict between priorities at a demonstration. International ANSWER most valued coherence of message while Absurd Response valued creativity, style, and opening up a joyful, countercultural space. These two approaches parallel two overarching models of public demonstration—"occupying public space" and "opening public space." Almost every public demonstration shows elements of both models in a tensive, dialectical mixture. When the two styles clash in the same place, the result is often an instructive disruption that reveals their underlying assumptions.

Instructive disruptions: occupying versus opening public space

Demonstrations that occupy public space typically preprint thousands of identical signs and ask people to hold them high while they stand, listen, and march together, chanting the same chants at the same time, in order to keep their message absolutely clear. However, this uniformity can be boring and uncompelling. Dramaturgically, this sort of action may have been seen so many times that viewers react to it the same way they react to any cliché—by tuning out even when they wish to pay attention. A mass of social actors fade into the background like blurry extras from central casting.

But there is something else that is unappealing about this style of demonstration in its extreme form. Generally speaking, there is no process whereby the average participant can contribute creatively to the dramaturgy of the protest. The underlying ideology of this sort of gathering is monologic, with a mass of spectators listening to a few elevated and amplified leaders. The clear division between speakers on a podium and the audience stands in sharp contrast to TO concepts of dialogism and spect-actorship. However, this sort of demonstration does occupy a public space to serve a unified purpose and a clear message. Just because it is monologic does not make it necessarily authoritarian. It requires no special effort to attend, so if one is really tired from work or life, all one has to do is show up.

In contrast to the occupying space model, with its very clear message and control of space for unified dissent, is the opening space model. This model attempts to open a space for collective and individual, Do-It-Yourself creativity, generally organized around a certain loose theme (such as Absurd Response to an Absurd War). Sometimes the group will even bring extra costume elements (e.g., plastic Billionaire top hats) to offer to people who didn't have the time or energy to bring their own.

The opening space message may get confused, lost in the fun, or there may not even *be* a central message. Far from a liability, Naomi Klein (2002) considers this desirable, at least in the case of the anticorporate movement which reflects a coalition of diverse agendas. This variation in focus is accepted in the hopes that the event as a whole will nevertheless hold together. Beyond the pleasure of the moment, these unpredictable and participatory actions can help create a joyous counterculture that can sustain long-term participation in a movement.

Some public actions have no explicit, verbal political content besides the action itself;

they are not clearly opening space or occupying space models. For example, a Critical Mass action disrupts car culture and exerts pressure for non-polluting urban public transport by the "organized coincidence" of hundreds of people riding their bikes on the streets at the same time. These actions can polarize by angering and inconveniencing car-users. However, activists have consciously accepted that polarization as a necessary aspect of directly confronting what they perceive as an unsustainable and unacceptable urban infrastructure and system of priorities that have gone unmarked for too long. While this action captures the monologic message of an occupying space model, its participatory design borrows from the opening space model (especially on Hallowe'en Critical Masses, when pirates, monsters, and superheroes of all shapes and sizes convene for the ride).

In some contexts, different motivations for demonstrating can coexist in a mutually reinforcing way. A group may decide that they can more clearly communicate their agenda if the greater public and passersby are actually compelled to stop and pay attention. They may thus make their demonstration interesting and entertaining, which, in turn, also serves the purposes of recruitment and of performing the movement's countercultural identity. A group may then feel pressure to be innovative and keep coming up with new material; interestingly, this is the same challenge that career comedians face to avoid staleness.

Both occupying space and opening space models have the option of using a variety of aesthetic strategies in their public demonstrations and performances. Next, I examine the ramifications of using the particular strategies of humor and irony as elements of protest in both models.

Humor and irony

[T]he weird and clownish forms . . . get on the nerves of the Establishment. In the face of the gruesomely serious totality of institutionalized politics, satire, irony and laughing provocation become a necessary dimension of the new politics.

(Marcuse 1969: 64)

Not only can laughter take the piss out of grim authorities, it can also help the laughers to get through the strains and tensions of everyday life and movement activity. Humor can also add to the efficacy of a demonstration as people are often more likely to stop and listen if they are entertained.

It is important to note that the opening space model has no monopoly on the use of humor in protest. The use of humor takes different forms for the two models. For opening space it means the encouragement of a festive and ridiculous theme for the event. The result may be a less organized type of humor, one that does not have a single point of focus, a sort of simultaneous and chaotic variety show. On the other hand, occupying space protests may attempt to choreograph and coordinate complex and surprising humorous performances, organizing the space to direct audience focus as desired.

Andrew Boyd (2002) argues that irony has become a tool for a highly motivated new generation of activists. Inverted meanings and sarcastic satire can surprise people and stimulate reflection. Irony, which throws several simultaneous meanings at recipients, may cause passersby to do interpretive work, puncturing their assumed frame of reference to let new light shine in. There is always the risk of losing spectators if the irony is either too simplistic or too abstruse. There is no way to control the creative consumption of irony by all individuals, but performers may nevertheless play with audiences' sensibilities, trying to anticipate possible misfires.

Here is an example of the use of irony in an opening space action: on the day after Thanksgiving, New York City's Union Square is traditionally filled with booths of people selling freshly baked goods. On this day in 2002, members of Absurd Response staged a "Bake Sale for the Military" in Union Square. While activist Kate Crane held out a tray of (delicious) missile-shaped gingerbread cookies, I called out for people to "Give 'Til It Hurts Someone Else." As concerned citizens, we hawked our wares, calling out to the passing crowd to please help our charity, to dig down deep, to do their part, because a lot of missiles were about to be expended by the government in the first few minutes of impending war, and if we could sell 1,200,000 cookies we would be able to buy one replacement missile for the rubble-bouncing second wave.

The bake-salers were accompanied by a small mob of Billionaires and a trio of joyfully ultra-rightist Missile Dick Chicks. The latter were dressed in red, white, and blue wigs, showgirl outfits, and makeup, with enormous missiles jutting out from their crotches. They performed tightly choreographed numbers remaking songs such as "These Bombs Were Made for Dropping" to the tune of "These Boots Were Made for Walking." The idea of selling cookies on the street fit in with the bake-sale context; the cruise-missile phalluses waving around in proud unison did not. The charity drive rhetoric was familiar; the premise of the Pentagon being strapped for funds and in need of volunteer help was not. People hesitated, cocked their heads, watched, listened, and walked on. Some approached us. Of those, most played along, responded wryly, and were rewarded with a missile-cookie and some antiwar mobilization literature.

However, there were three concerned, apparently antiwar people who asked, "Are you serious?!" We responded in character, playing out the irony as blatantly as possible, and while this seemed to reach them, they were still shaken up enough by the spectacle to need our straightforward assurance that we weren't serious. I stayed in character and handed them the antiwar literature, and this finally gave them the relief they were looking for. The literature served as a catch-all for anyone who wasn't comfortable with the irony, while also giving them an internet link for antiwar event schedules and locations. This was hardly an act of Invisible Theatre! Nevertheless, our choice to use irony, in the context of an opening space protest with lots of swirling, absurd signifiers all around us, did confuse a few people.

Protests that use irony and other forms of humor are engaged in a balancing act between novelty and familiarity. Public reactions to them are not predictable. They may help a movement reach people in a more engaging way, but can threaten the clarity of a movement's message. On the other hand, an emphasis on unity of message, of being "on point," can suppress the multivocality of a diverse movement.

Unity meets diversity

As noted earlier, the occupying space model has the strength of emphasizing a movement's unity. However, when the movement is composed of a coalition of various interests and identities, unity is a false and fragile façade that can ultimately detract from the movement's integrity and efficacy; unity itself must be redefined. As Kelly Moore and Lesley J. Wood argue, coalitions are strongest when they do not claim a unity of interests, priorities, or tactics, but rather acknowledge their diversity while emphasizing the spirit of cooperation for the tasks at hand (2002: 30). The US global justice movement is an example of such a complex array of loosely-coordinated affinity groups and blocs of activists who gather at non-hierarchical "spokes-council" meetings to plan actions.

The decentralized affinity group model is not just ultra-democratic dialogism for its own sake. The consensus process, by which affinity groups make decisions, can result in greater efficacy even if it takes more time than an authoritarian central committee might. Starhawk (2002) argues that the decentralized aspect of the movement made it much more capable during the "Battle of Seattle" against the World Trade Organization (WTO) in 1999. The movement nonviolently swarmed the city, the WTO was disrupted despite the violent response of the state, and the existence of mass opposition to corporate globalization in the USA was established for a global audience.

When affinity groups meet at spokes-councils, the emphasis on dialogue is not purely idealistic but vital for planning intelligent action that acknowledges the heterogeneity of the movement. At the spokes-council meeting for the massive February 15, 2003 antiwar demonstration in New York City, representatives for the Carnival Bloc made a very important negotiation with the People of Color Bloc. Both groups were planning to gather at the main branch of the Public Library, and then to move out in the direction of First Avenue where the rally was taking place. However the City of New York, with the help of a Bush Administration lawyer, had successfully banned any marching against the war that day. The rally was permitted, but there would be no legal way to march in the street in order to get there.

The Carnival Bloc, including such opening space-oriented groups as Reclaim the Streets, the Glamericans, and the Missile Dick Chicks, tends to ignore such antidemocratic rulings and demonstrates in public spaces anyway. For reasons of privilege or motivation, this bloc is mostly made up of people who are willing and able to incur some risk of arrest in this sort of situation. The People of Color Bloc, however, included many who could not afford to be arrested because of job, income, family, or legal status. At the spokes-council meeting, it was agreed that the People of Color Bloc would set out for the rally first, staying on the sidewalks and following traffic signals. After they had traveled far enough away that they would not be embroiled in any mass arrests, the Carnival Bloc would set out on its path, following its agenda of taking over a street or a neighborhood and playing music and dancing against the war despite the permit ban. In a movement that privileged a more totalizing, reductionist unity, or which took orders handed down from a central committee, this dialogue might not have occurred, and one group's needs might have been subsumed under that of the other.

Working with a diversity of tactics is more complex than having a central command, but it is also more dynamic and flexible. Organizers of occupying space protests may be more tempted to emphasize or impose unity than those that attempt to open space. However, in the planning stage of either type of event, a movement can engage in open dialogue between blocs so that diversity of interests, tactics, and identities are acknowledged and respected. Pre-action TO workshops may be of use in acknowledging and dealing with these differences as well.

Tactical carnival

> Carnival does not know footlights, in the sense that it does not acknowledge any distinction between actors and spectators.
>
> (Bakhtin 1968: 7)

Recent creative protest, with its Do-It-Yourself ethos, emphasis on collective and individual creativity, and free-flowing multivocality, is often described as carnivalesque. Kauffman asserts that:

> [T]he central idea behind the carnival is that protests gain in power if they reflect the world we want to create . . . a world that is full of color and life and creativity and art and music and dance. It's a celebration of life against the forces of greed and death . . . not unlike creating a community garden.
>
> (Kauffman 2004: 380–81)

It is instructive to see how the opening space model largely follows the practice of carnival. The global justice movement, for example, often convenes in massive, festive, creative street protests, and has consciously theorized itself using terms such as "Carnival Against Capital" (Notes From Nowhere 2003: 185). This type of engaging, ludic protest encourages people to enjoy, and to imagine other possible worlds. The attempt to remove the performer/audience divide follows Bakhtin's notion that carnival is liberatory and subversive because it "does not know footlights." Calls to action for this carnivalesque model do not only list a series of angry complaints, but solicit contributions to a counterculture fantasia, or a human community garden. The Glamericans come to protests in maximum glam-majesty to decorate public space with themselves. The Rock Stars Against the War assume alter-personas, get on their tour bus, and turn protests into hard-partying, no-sleep adventures.

Carnival is as much for the benefit and social change of the activists as it is for any spectators who will hopefully become spect-actors. The serious play is meant to inspire desire, collective stories, group cohesion, and identity formation—making a movement that has denser social networks and is more sustainable and adaptable through hard times. Even setbacks and misfires will be fed back into the creative process to help generate new ideas for the movement. As Stephen Duncombe argues,

> This is *praxis*, a theory arising out of activity . . . An *embodied theory* of mass activity is competing against the *idealized theory* of capitalism that celebrates the self-gratifying individual . . . Direct action groups . . . consciously try to create these theory-generating, lived experiences as part of our politics . . . Protest becomes a breathing, dancing example of what a liberated public space might look like. A lived imaginary.
>
> (Duncombe 2003: 15–16)

But are these protests carnivalesque in the Bakhtinian sense? Are they liberatory simply because the footlights are removed? Is this purely an opening space model? Bakhtin (1968) theorized the carnivalesque as a mode of being and as a social ritual wherein laughter and ribaldry, emphasis on the undifferentiated masses, bodily functions, and symbolic inversion of the social order created a liberatory space even in the most repressive societies. Bakhtin perhaps romanticized the power and nature of carnival a bit, and in the Stalinist context in which he was writing, who could blame him? It is questionable whether medieval carnival ever totally overrode individualism and hierarchy. Later theorists have argued that carnival is situational—that, depending on the historical moment, it can either be a liberatory moment of rebellion or a safety valve that actually serves the long-term stability of the given social order (Stallybrass and White 1986: 16–19; Kertzer 1988: 144–50).

There are important differences between modern oppositional performances that evoke the carnivalesque and the phenomenon that Bakhtin was exploring. Feudal carnival was a calendrically circumscribed event, tied to the harvest and religious schedules of Christian-agrarian societies still influenced by their pagan pasts, and the event itself was part of a commonly shared cultural and religious vocabulary. The oppositional, carnivalesque protests of today take place when and where the protestors choose: sometimes in reaction to "establishment" events, sometimes not. They may be ideologically complicated and ambivalent events, but they still tend to be more focused and specific in their social critique than most feudal era carnivals. In this sense, there is more tactical agency in contemporary carnivalesque protest, drawing on a narrower, more specialized appeal than the all-community carnival of feudal times. While those who dance, sing, and party in current street protests may share an experience of the joyous and outrageous carnivalesque, the entire village, so to speak, does not take part. Thus there is an inherent performer/audience divide in current carnival protest, and indeed the events are often framed in terms of how spectators receive them, either on the street or through the mass media. For these reasons, I would distinguish between Bakhtinian carnival and what I call the *tactical carnival* of today.

This tactical carnival is not purely participatory. It unavoidably and inherently includes an audience. It is also not purely an opening space proposition. Tactical carnival involves a dialogue and a dialectic not only between individual activist groups but between the modes of occupying space and opening space. In this sense, TO aligns with tactical carnival for Forum Theatre, in form and content, contains elements of both modes. During the initial performance of the anti-model, forum is more controlled than open space—but then the scene is opened up for spect-actor improvisatory intervention. Theatre of the Oppressed contains both strident contestation of oppressive structures and practices and a group-invented enactment and embodiment of (at least glimpses of) the future world the participants want to live in.

To be truly tactically flexible, sustainable for a diverse coalition with different interests, resources, and vulnerabilities, and to effectively engage with the ever-inventive and vigilant state, tactical carnival must negotiate and fuse techniques from various modes: a huge demonstration that scatters into a citywide radical costume ball, a creative and ironic engagement with passersby leading to earnest direct action, dozens of diverse columns converging at City Hall for an extended session of Legislative Theatre. The techniques of TO that increase the level of dialogism and spect-actorship, have already begun to take their place in the tensive negotiation that is the public demonstration.

Bibliography

Bakhtin, M.M. (1968) *Rabelais and His World*, trans. H. Iswolsky. Cambridge: MIT Press.

Boal, A. (1979) *Theatre of the Oppressed*, trans. C.A. and M.-O.L. McBride. New York: Urizen Books.

Bogad, L.M. (2005) *Electoral Guerrilla Theatre: Radical ridicule and social movement*. London: Routledge.

Boyd, A. (2002) "Irony, meme warfare, and the extreme costume ball," in R. Hayduk and B. Shepard (eds) *From ACT UP to the WTO: Urban protest and community building in the era of globalization*. London: Verso.

Brecher, J., Costello, T., and Smith, B. (2002) *Globalization from Below: The power of solidarity*. Cambridge, MA: South End Press.

Duncombe, S. (2003) "The poverty of theory: Anti-intellectualism and the value of action," *Radical Society: Review of Culture and Politics*, 30: no. 1: 11–17.

Fraser, N. (1997) *Justice Interruptus: Reflections on the "postsocialist" condition*. London: Routledge.

Kauffman, L. (2004) "A short, personal history of the global justice movement," in E. Yuen, D. Burton-Rose, and G. Katsiaficas (eds) *Confronting Capitalism*. Brooklyn: Soft Skull Press.

Kertzer, D.I. (1988) *Ritual, Politics and Power*. New Haven, CT: Yale University Press.

Klein, N. (2002) "The vision thing: Were the DC and Seattle protests unfocused, or are the critics missing the point?" in R. Hayduk and B. Shepard (eds) *From ACT UP to the WTO: Urban protest and community building in the era of globalization*. London: Verso.

Lysistrata Project website. http://lysistrataproject.org. Accessed May 26, 2004.

Marcuse, H. (1969) *An Essay on Liberation*. Boston, MA: Beacon Press.

Moore, K. and Wood, L. (2002) "Target practice: Community activism in a global era," in R. Hayduk and B. Shepard (eds) *From ACT UP to the WTO: Urban protest and community building in the era of globalization*. London: Verso.

Notes From Nowhere (2003) *We Are Everywhere: The irresistible rise of global anticapitalism*. London: Verso.

Scott, J.C. (1990) *Domination and the Arts of Resistance*. New Haven, CT: Yale University Press.

Stallybrass, P. and White, A. (1986) *The Politics and Poetics of Transgression*. Ithaca, NY: Cornell University Press.

Starhawk (2002) "How we really shut down the WTO," in R. Hayduk and B. Shepard (eds) *From ACT UP to the WTO: Urban protest and community building in the era of globalization*. London: Verso.

Tarrow, S. (1998) *Power in Movement: Social movements and contentious politics*. Cambridge: Cambridge University Press.

Wood, E.J. (2003) *Insurgent Collective Action and Civil War in El Salvador*. Cambridge: Cambridge University Press.

Social healing and liberatory politics

A round-table discussion

*Mady Schutzman with Brent Blair, Lori S. Katz,
Helene S. Lorenz, and Marc D. Rich*

The participants in the following conversation initially wrote short pieces on practices and theories merging therapeutic and political agendas that inform their work. After reading one anothers' pieces, we gathered together to have an in-depth conversation that focused on the issues that had been raised: participatory research, liberation psychology, Jungian depth psychology, ritual, and Holographic Reprocessing. The following is an edited version of that exchange held in October 2003 in Los Angeles (MS).

Schutzman: Helene, can you begin by speaking about participatory research?

Lorenz: A shift went on in the 1960s all over the world. One of the issues was how the researcher goes out in the world and gathers up information. How does the person being questioned benefit from that process? Suddenly, the neutrality of supposed scientific research was being compromised, and therefore its values were in question. At one point I got to visit a women's center in Trinidad that was doing participatory work. Ordinary women without any education, among the poorest in Trinidad, were asked to help gather information about women's experience in the community. Many of those women went on to become project leaders. There is massive evidence now that asking people to talk or write about traumatic suffering over time——or to even witness others doing it——can have important therapeutic effects. We are evolving forms of participatory research that transform the researchers as well and provide new ways of being in the world with others. Why not take the issues, or a transcribed interview, back to the subject, just as you have proposed to do with this discussion, get feedback, and ask: "What are the implications of this material?" There is a direct link here to what Boal is doing in communities with TO.

Blair: I wonder if there hasn't been a parallel process in psychology moving from an object–relations model focusing on the exchange between a definitive subject and object, toward a new model focusing more on the space in-between.

Lorenz: I would call that dialogic. Where all of the partners in the work go back and start questioning all of their assumptions. The work has to have that element of opening up into a fresh new space where everybody is invited to rethink.

Schutzman: Can you discuss the connection here to liberation psychology?

Lorenz: I think the concept originated with Martín-Baró. He was a psychologist and activist, also a Jesuit priest and provost of the University of Central America, and was very involved with the liberation movements in El Salvador and the rest of Latin America in the 1980s. He was murdered by a US-trained death squad in San Salvador in 1989. His work is rooted in participatory research, as well as in a philosophy of deconstruction, what Freire, in Brazil, had called consciencization in which we have to learn how to break open the "veil of lies" through which we have been taught to see the world. It challenges the model of psychology in which the expert comes in and makes a diagnosis without a participatory process. Nancy Sheper-Hughes (1992) writes about her experience in Brazil, where she shows that both the medical establishment and the poor have colluded to diagnose the disease "nervos"—more or less stress—never mentioning that the patients who have it are starving. Psychiatrists are prescribing medications and health drinks that cost a week's salary to purchase at a pharmacy, for patients who have no money for food. She suggests that the whole mental health establishment is collaborating with state power to cover over the reality of massive hunger in Brazil. The alternative to this form of official knowledge is to place the tools and resources of psychology in the hands of communities in need of transformation. To do this, you have to shift to an epistemology that understands psychological knowledge as something that evolves within people's representations and images of themselves and their communities as they decode and transform their own practices.

Schutzman: Might any psychological theory be appropriated for more social liberatory purposes?

Lorenz: I don't know. Some psychologies are so rooted in the ideas of individualism and of adaptation to a norm that it's hard to see how. But I'd say there is never going to be a simple construction of liberation psychology where there's a single founding school or father. Instead, there are going to be dozens of roots, a genealogy, as Nietzsche would say.

Blair: Martín-Baró indicts the psychological community's non-critical acceptance of established ways of thinking and knowing, particularly regarding disease, disorders, and dysfunction. This blind acceptance of institutional epistemologies regarding mental health is one of the basic tools of the oppressors. For example, a patient who presents with depressive disorder in New Haven, Connecticut, is not the same as the one who presents with depressive disorder in San Salvador, El Salvador. Most amazing about Martín-Baró's work is his optimism: he identifies liberation psychology as a model whose focus is future desire of the marginalized population, rather than reflecting solely on their past problem. He says, [reading] "If our objective is to serve the liberation needs of the people [of Latin America], this requires a new way of seeking knowledge, for the truth of the Latin American peoples is not in their present oppression, but rather in the tomorrow of their liberty" (Martín-Baro 1994: 27). For me, one of the greatest triumphs of the liberation psychology movement is its shift from *what* to *where* questions—its attention to location.

Katz: Internal versus external?

Blair: Intra-psychic versus inter-psychic.

Lorenz: We want both, not either/or, because what liberation psychologists want to look at is the ways in which an individual's discomfort is often echoing something in their world.

Katz: Yes, absolutely.

Rich: It seems to me that in current pop psychology trends such as the Dr. Phil Show, the primary issue can't be about context or history, it needs to be about teaching this person to think differently. It is cognitive restructuring at its most pedestrian—let's fix it in half an hour. It would be much easier to train therapists in cognitive restructuring than have therapists really consider structural oppression, structural racism. What would it take to train a therapist to be a liberatory therapist?

Lorenz: What does it take to train a Joker to be liberatory Joker? I've seen people joker where they reduce Boal's work to ten steps.

Rich: Techniques.

Lorenz: Exactly.

Rich: The Joker doesn't make any reference to either structural oppression or the racism in the scene.

Schutzman: And why do you think that happens? Do you think that Jokers haven't been trained in critical thinking themselves?

Blair: In the clinical setting, the Board of Behavioral Sciences rewards you for not engaging in a deep and critical understanding of the client's life. I had a six-year-old client who wouldn't eat fruit, and would vomit every time fruit was shown or eaten around him. He had three therapists before he came to me, and nobody was asking him about his cultural background. I found out his mother and father were illegal immigrants from Oaxaca, Mexico, the client's mother was dying of cancer, she was stuck in the US because of her legal status, and quite possibly the client had internalized all this unspeakable trauma. The traditional therapy model cares little about this level of investigation, offering instead a series of cognitive-behavioral measures to insure that he stops symptomatizing in the shortest time possible.

Liberation psychology reminds us to look deeper and wider than the internal world of the patient. In this case, the client's father said he "felt like a cockroach" because in this country he's devalued, and the kid is just vomiting out the world around him. What ways of knowing do we have besides the epistemology of positivism—of proving everything with quantitative and verifiable data? I think teaching people to recognize harmful epistemologies would be a good place to begin.

Schutzman: Brent, you seem to be interested in models that privilege non-discursive practices. How do you negotiate these with the importance in TO of social context and critique?

Blair: I'm interested in the classical Rainbow model that's looking for what psychodrama calls "surplus reality," and giving it a chance to speak and be heard.[1] What if we didn't label the unconscious image of the antagonist as the enemy, but we let it speak on its own terms? In classic Rainbow, you have this metabolized experience of exploring your desire as protagonist and identifying who is countering, or limiting, that desire. When I was visiting CTO/Rio (Centre for the Theatre of the Oppressed in Rio de Janeiro), I led an experimental dream-theatre workshop. We worked on a dream of C, a Joker who works in a juvenile hall.[2] One image was a personification of C's fear, and fear limits a protagonist's access to all the "rainbow of your desires." I became interested in what would happen if we actually treated this fear as a visitor, as an invited guest rather than a pathological force. I'm thinking of Mary Watkins' (2000) work, *Invisible Guests*. She presents all the images of the unconscious as invisible guests that actually arrive, that we can engage with. If we let fear speak, what would it say in its own words? In Jung's terms, what is our collective unconscious trying to tell us?[3] The protagonist discovered this hugely important part that had been left behind, which is her vulnerability as a Joker in juvenile hall, which I think, going back to participatory research, permeates the boundaries between what is "ego" and what is "other," or who am "I" and who are "they."

Schutzman: I hear two different points of importance to you. One is a call to bring historical, critical training into traditional practices and theories of medical science and psychology. The other is to let images speak, to leave them unanalyzed and uninterpreted. Do these contradict one another? Do you not want to engage critical dialogue about the images?

Lorenz: I'd like to put forth three different things here. One is about the subject matter itself—that dreams and unconscious material could and should come into our work. The second is Brent's questioning whether we always want to frame what arises in terms of protagonist and antagonist. There might be situations where we want to frame the work differently. The third point, I think Mady is asking whether you really mean to be saying that we can't talk with each other about our responses to what's gone on.

Schutzman: Or if you are saying that there's a particular value in not talking.

Blair: It seems to me that the genius of TO is its ability to connect the *whys* with the *whats* in order to lead us to some *hows*—that is, strategies for change. What seems missing from the equation are the *wheres*—from *where* does this voice come? And it seems to me that that's a conversation worth having, especially if some of the voices don't necessarily live in the intercultural world but also have a place of origin from outside—what is often referred to as the divine, or the dream world, what Jung calls the collective unconscious. It's something classic TO seems to rarely change.

Schutzman: So, you are saying that it is a viable choice to move away from the more pragmatic scene at hand. And you are acknowledging the mystical or spiritual dimension in therapeutic work toward social change.

Blair: Desire is still always at the center. It was at the center, I think, of Martín-Baró's work in liberation psychology, it's been at the center of Boal's work—it's called "Rainbow of Desire". But *whose* desire and from *where* does the desire come? That is still my question. "What do you want?" The Joker is still presenting this question, right? And, ultimately we're assessing, "Did you get what you want?" even if the scene shifts out of one arena—intra-psychic—and goes into another—dreamworld. I'm wondering, what does this *other* image itself want?

Schutzman: So is there another question you are proposing the Joker ask?

Blair: Instead of "What do you want?" the Joker would ask "What was that like?" A whole other world opens up that might never have appeared had the Joker gone with questions limited to personal agency and individual desire.

Lorenz: I think Boal's techniques often do what you're asking for. He speaks about undercurrents, he is naming something like unconscious images. In Rainbow of Desire, the idea of metaxis gets at what you're talking about. In one layer, you're in the ego world of every day, but you're entering into another realm. What it depends on, finally, is the genius of the Joker in charge, whether they can let those images break the conventions that the audience and the performers are trapped in, or whether the anxiety of the situation of metaxis clamps down immediately on anything new that could come out of the situation.

Katz: I think it's very different to put an image of someone's fear on stage than it is to put an image of someone experiencing oppression.

Lorenz: It's so clear in Boal's work that we're in this room doing things together for the sake of something that's outside of the room. A rehearsal for something. In what you're proposing, Brent, it sounds more like a kind of catharsis would be reached in the room. I wonder, then is that the rehearsal or is that the whole thing?

Blair: I think it's the rehearsal.

Lorenz: How?

Blair: Fear is its own voice that has been present from time immemorial and continues to be present and it speaks a language that's alien to me, a little bit. It's not me speaking. Classic psychologists call it the psycoidal or psychotic realm—leaning toward psyche. But if we call it psychotic to hear other voices as distinct or as different, then we're right back into Western medicine where it's all about you and your response. If I can let fear be an ally and not colonize it, I can then go out into the world and work in juvenile hall in a new way.

Lorenz: How?

Blair: For C, fear ruptured a façade that she had put up that in turn distanced her from her work with the kids. C said she'd always seen fear as something to be conquered. But when fear itself spoke, she let go of the physical tensions that prevented vulnerability. It's the heart of vulnerability that is embodied in the archetype of fear.

Schutzman: I hear you saying that there might be value in getting away from language and moving into what is happening in visceral space.

Rich: I also hear you saying, I want to know the desire of the antagonist, let's embrace not only the fear but let's see the humanity in the antagonist and embrace that. Let's start collapsing these binaries. And my question is, are those binaries useful sometimes? Do we want to embrace the antagonist? Or come to understand the antagonist better?

Schutzman: I'm not sure that it has to be one or the other.

Blair: Right.

Schutzman: I think that Boal would consider therapy in the service of activism. There are antagonists in the world and they do have to be confronted, and yet to do so it might be best to learn about them by exploring their desires.

Blair: [You're still thinking in terms of] Strategy. I'm interested in hearing what is typically understood as part of a binary speak as if it were autonomous. And not judge it.

Katz: Like in Gestalt therapy, where fear is put in the chair and then you have a dialogue with it?

Blair: I still hear in what you're saying, let's give it its own voice, and I believe it *has* its own voice, it doesn't need to be *given* one. It's a subtle distinction.

Lorenz: I want to go someplace else with this which is contextual. Boal's early techniques developed to address liberation movements opposing oppressive military regimes. It made sense to talk about protagonists and antagonists. The situation today is different in many locations. We could talk about this in terms of South Africa. The anti-apartheid movement has state power, and those who were enemies yesterday might be neighbors today. So the question becomes how to engage with our history so we can build a basis to live together. The Truth and Reconciliation Commission created a participatory process where everyone could come forward to talk about how they had acted in the years of turmoil with the goal of forgiveness and restoration of community. Here, no one was considered simply an antagonist. In Argentina there is a war over historical memory. Instead of a protagonist opposing an enemy antagonist, which is Boal's historical context, we have a former enemy opposing a former protagonist, still with different class interests, still with different world views, still with wounds that need to be addressed. In the United States, Germany, Guatemala, and Chile, there are children and grandchildren of victims, bystanders, witnesses, and oppressors who have never gone through any healing process together, yet may meet each other regularly at work, in neighborhoods, or in classrooms. Communities are fragmented and broken by this kind of history, and there is evidence that broken communities exacerbate public and mental health issues. The goal of TO in these places might be to allow for dialogue, historical accounting, imagination, and transformation. [Short break]

Schutzman: Let's segue to the interest some of you expressed concerning ritual.

Lorenz: Traditionally, the deep structuring of ritual works when you have a contained and historic organic social group that shares coding. In postmodern contexts, writers like Homi Bhabha are imagining the creation of new kinds of rituals in "third space," which is a kind of liminal space. Traditional rituals for organic societies don't work now in urban and diverse environments. We don't know how to create the third space, we may not be able to find each other or know each other if there is too much diversity in the way we live. I'm viewing Boal's work as one of the modalities that helps us to imagine a destructured space, or a liminal space, that isn't entered through traditional ritual, where fractured communities can be restored.

Rich: I think it depends on one's definition of traditional rituals. For a long time, anthropologists have viewed them as contained, as culturally reflective units.

Schutzman: One way of understanding traditional ritual is as a response to a breach, a shift in a person's status, say from adolescence into adulthood, that moves them into liminal space. Victor Turner (1982) comes up with "communitas" as that group of people bonded through contemporary ruptures—communitas being a temporary, intimate community formed in response to an unexpected disaster or cultural emergency such as an earthquake, 9/11, or an oil spill. Communitas does not necessarily address chronic cultural breaches such as racism. I think we're talking about Boal as a potential facilitator of communitas.

Rich: I think so. One doesn't necessarily go through liminal space and then come out the other end. I think that Boal's work provides an ongoing liminal space for finding your bearings.

Schutzman: What is the value of looking at ritual as a therapeutic model for those of us who do TO?

Rich: In Boal's work, a group of people come together with the Joker acting like a therapist, a shaman. When it works, participants see themselves in the protagonists, and see the protagonist/antagonist dynamic in their own lives. People know something has happened—in an embodied way—but frequently don't have the language to explain it. It's more felt than understood. I think the strength of Boal's work is that it starts in the body. Maybe, as we look at these archetypes of fear or look at collective traumas of slavery and the holocaust or sexual assault, Boal's work becomes a collective ritual of healing for the participants.

Lorenz: I love that. In the work around the Holocaust, there are folks who say you can't write or speak after a trauma, but there are written reports of the facts: this many people died here, that many people were tortured there, this house was used for that. But it didn't help the healing process. People didn't feel any better. People are starting to talk about rituals that open up into other dimensions of reality and spirituality. To name one of the very best examples of this is Maya Lin's monument to the civil rights movement. (See Mock 1995.) Lin always puts a reflexive membrane in her monuments as a kind of image of the world of the dead and the world of the living reflecting each other. In this particular one, there are spokes of a wheel with phrases listing events, deaths, successes in the civil rights movement, with water flowing over them. When the monument opened, a huge crowd of people were all trying to read those dates, and in order to do that, they had to begin rotating as a group around this fountain, looking in, seeing the reflection of their own faces in the names and dates of the dead. She captures what you're talking about, that need for an embodied ritual that goes beyond the here and now and the facts and the reality.

Schutzman: One question that arises in trauma theory is whether embodying trauma retraumatizes or helps us move on? What do you think?

Rich: An example is my Rainbow work on racism. One can argue that people are often in more pain after we're done. But working in images doesn't make the conflict or pain any more than it was, it's already there. Maybe collective healing, I'm not sure if it's the right phrase, maybe authentic community, means to acknowledge the existence of these conflicts. I think what the Rainbow techniques do in many ways is honor that space, they honor the collective trauma. The risk is certainly there that you can make things worse. But does ignoring the trauma make things any better?

Schutzman: Are you suggesting that witnessing the trauma prevents, to a certain extent, the potential of retraumatizing?

Rich: When I worked with Lori [Katz] at the VA hospital[4] many of the women said that they didn't feel alone after being in the workshop. In my own workshops on racism I frequently get the same response. And, yes, I think that witnessing is a part of that process.

Katz: Witnessing helps when there is a shared experience. But it also gives a viewer some emotional distance so it's less threatening to process the experience.

Lorenz: But what is the "it" that gets witnessed? In my opinion, genocide—or public terror or repeated sexual abuse—fragments the narrative and so the biggest scar of any kind of trauma is in aporia, a kind of black hole in the personality, in the organic memory of the group where things could no longer be spoken and shared in an organic way. What I think is very beautiful and very alive is that what is witnessed is that aporia, a moment when there was a break so great that this individual and this community could not go on speaking in any normal conventional way about what had happened to them.

Rich: Arthur Frank (1995) calls it "narrative wreckage," that moment when your life story, because of a trauma, gets destroyed. He argues in *The Wounded Storyteller* that the body creates new narratives in response to that trauma. If trauma *unmakes*, maybe the Rainbow techniques *reconstruct*. Maybe the images remake who we are, telling our story from the body.

Schutzman: What happens when somebody presents a rupture but it isn't one that's shared by everyone in the group? We don't always work with people who have suffered a common rupture.

Lorenz: I was teaching a course on rupture and aporia at a graduate school to a group of people that had already known each other for nine months. The first morning of the class, I laid out this theory of loss and how it breaks the narrative and so on. I asked them, "Have any of you ever experienced a moment that broke something in your narrative?" And every single person threw into the center of that circle a story that was completely heartbreaking, and it wasn't the same story, right? Childhood incest, leaving a cult, a vicious divorce, child custody issues—I mean everything. As we continued our participatory research into this process, it became clear that we were all participating in a culture of silence. How did we sit together for nine months and this story never came into our day-to-day stories? What kind of social pathology are we living where every single person in this room has a broken life and was able to pretend to be normal for nine months? In the end, the process was experienced as extremely healing because it broke open constructs of individual failure.

Schutzman: You're suggesting a very different way to ask for stories in TO workshops.

Perhaps instead of asking for moments when participants wanted something and failed to get it, or wanted to do something and failed to act, we would be asking to hear stories in which people experienced a radical shift in how they understood their lives, a breach in meaning.

Blair: The word experience comes from *ex-periri*, literally "through danger" or "through peril." We're living all these perilous lives, but that nothing gets spoken invites what Helene's been calling "non-redemptive mourning," where we have seen something traumatic and pretend it doesn't exist.

Lorenz: When Boal began his work, the enemy was fascist state power. The enemy today is corporate globalization that is uprooting every community on earth. Individuals are migrating all over the world in search of jobs at a greater and greater rate, water supplies are being destroyed, farmlands are being destroyed, ways of life that lasted hundreds of years are being destroyed. Rupture is the personal effect of the social condition of globalization.

Schutzman: Has rupture been so normalized that any circumstance is legitimate as an anti-model?

Blair: I think anything that's experienced by the person as a kind of rupture migrates to others in the room, even if the conflict is between a woman and her roommate, that is, not necessarily between a protagonist and a socially marked oppressor.

Rich: It's about being reflexive rather than reflective.[5] Reflecting back to someone an exact replica of their story between themselves and a roommate may not be necessarily performative. But being reflexive—say by doing Kaleidoscopic Image—and mirroring back multiple images of the scene may very well lead that protagonist to see something she may have not seen before.

Lorenz: Felman and Laub (1992) say that there are certain situations in the world where the transformations are so rapid that nobody at the time can grasp what's happening and create a frame large enough to understand it. I believe that we're in one of those situations now.

Rich: What is the Joker's role in all of that? Does the Joker work with [every] story or not? If we move into the realm of looking at rituals as a potential framework for collective healing of collective trauma, what is the Joker's role in the negotiation of that space?

Blair: The Joker is a kind of a liberator of the voice, free to make choices. But if the Joker's role is to restore narrative, I wonder whose narrative is being restored? And who declares that narrative valid?

Rich: Mady uses the term "image literacy." I think a Joker needs to be able to read those images and tease out those stories.

Blair: I don't know that you can "tease out" a narrative.

Lorenz: What I observe about Jokers is that they ask questions. The Joker comes into a situation and asks, "Is this a picture of it, or is that a picture of it? Is this a solution, or is that a solution?" What Jokers are modeling is a much more inquisitive and creative approach to life, and I think that could transfer into ritual-making. Once, I asked my class to bring in images of things in American history that have been broken and never repaired and in need of healing. The next assignment was to work in groups to invent possible rituals of healing that we could try out in class.

Schutzman: Jokers have a kind of oxymoronic task of *creating* ritual. We're trying to understand something about rupture and about how common ground can speak to the rupture. But first a language, and it can be nonverbal language, has to be created for a ritual space to happen, even if there are resonances across different kinds of ruptures. Maybe part of the answer to the question—what is a Joker's role within the context of ritual?—starts with understanding his or her own strengths in terms of language building.

Rich: Even the games are a way to get people to feel like they know each other well enough to risk sharing stories.

Blair: Jung said that ritual is an interpretation of the unknown, an invitation to things we share, though not cognitively. I'm interested in how to respond to crisis and rupture when there is no pre-established vocabulary for creating a ritual. When we can't make sense in a traditional way.

Rich: I'm not sure if the Joker is in the [same] space with everyone around. My sense is that the Joker is a *present absence*. In that ritual space, she or he is there and not there. They create a space *for* ritual but they are not *of* that ritual. As a Joker my body is not in it, but it looks like my body's in it.

Lorenz: The Joker has to hold the space. The priest is like that, the priest blesses others not himself. There's always that role in this kind of ritual. There are people in Candomble and Santeria rituals who for their entire lifetimes care for and serve the people who go into trance, and other people whose work it is to go into trance, and someone whose role it is to lead the whole process.

Blair: In Nigeria that wasn't exactly the case. In fact, the priests of the ritual were in trance themselves, there wasn't an organizing conscious guide, nor was there somebody outside of the unit [serving as that guide].

Katz: I would argue something different, that there's no such thing as in or out, everyone's in. They might have a different role. I would be concerned for TO participants if the Joker stepped out of the hierarchical role and participated in the same way as the spect-actors, but just because you're not sharing your story doesn't mean you're not in the process.

Rich: That's a really good point.

Schutzman: The TO Joker is not the same priest that you see weekly, that you chat with regularly at social functions and in times of trouble. In the TO context, Jokers often work with groups that are not a community at all, there is no immediately obvious connective glue. Sometimes Jokers are creating ritual space when meeting participants for the first time.

Rich: I think the glue is the body. What brings us together are the games.

Lorenz: When I was a child, I knew the ritual of only one religion and one community. I knew how to do that with all its good and bad points. But today I know ritual bits and pieces from dozens and dozens of different communities. Some of us no longer have organic traditions that we're practicing, but we do have a kind of reservoir of fragments that people recognize, and we can make use of them to rebuild new rituals.

Schutzman: And yet, since all differences have not been created equally, and since there tends to be a sort of touristic notion of engaging with other cultures and other rituals, using these bits and pieces sometimes de-contextualizes to the point of appropriating.

Rich: Coopting.

Lorenz: Exoticizing.

Blair: "Let's do a ritual!"

Schutzman: Marc, you have spoken of ethnography and fieldwork as a way to possibly understand the risks of "therapeutic damage." What do you mean by that?

Rich: Perhaps ethnography is inherently therapeutic. Maybe what we as ethnographers are doing in the field is not only searching for the Other but also searching for ourselves. Maybe, to take it even further, we are looking for what we're lacking.

Lorenz: You're saying fieldwork can be healing, but I'm saying for only one in a million so far. I think the new generation of ethnographers is recognizing what you're saying and thinking about those things.

Schutzman: Can you say more about what is therapeutic about ethnography?

Katz: I think some of the essence of what makes something therapeutic is seeing the Other, seeing points where you and Other differ. In a place where people think differently than you, you have an opportunity to see yourself.

Rich: In order to do a critical ethnography, you need people to reflect back to you. This reflexive moment can be deeply therapeutic.

Blair: If you were to do ethnography critically, thinking of the subject studied simultaneously doing an ethnography on you . . . How do you invite that?

Rich: After collecting and analyzing stories from cancer camps, I took my findings back to some of the campers. Their analysis of my analysis was illuminating.

Blair: Would you then need to take the kid from the cancer camp to your home and say: "Interview my family and see what you make of my life?"

Rich: It's also possible to have campers speak about how they see my role as an ethnographer in their community. So their interpretation of me becomes part of the whole story.

Schutzman: But then we're moving beyond ethnography. This is not what ethnography is.

Lorenz: It's what it's becoming.

Schutzman: I don't think so. The ethnographer has the grant from the university and the contract to author and publish the piece. It seems like an odd model to use for the kind of dialogic thing that you're after. In looking for a model of intercultural exchange, why ethnography, I wonder?

Rich: Because it's the most intensely embodied methodology I know of.

Schutzman: Ethnography is just as much about observation as it is about participation.

Rich: And so is jokering.

Schutzman: Interesting. I don't think we think of TO as an opportunity for Jokers to go through therapy.

Rich: I think there's room to talk about ethnography as a potential framework for therapy. If you're going to use a traditional ethnographic model then I think it doesn't make sense. If you're going to use a non-traditional, performative and reflexive ethnographic model, it becomes a much more viable therapeutic space for both Self and Other. That is, if the ethnographer is willing to run the risks that community members are running.

Schutzman: What you're seeing in the ethnographer could help a Joker understand something about this somewhat paradoxical role of being observer and participant.

Rich: Both are liminal roles.

Lorenz: Step one in ethnography was the Western fantasy that the Other had a fixed tradition. The Western observer would go and look at it and report back to the West. Step two in ethnography, starting maybe 30 years ago, people realized there wasn't a fixed tradition, there was a performative tradition going on, and ethnography was performative, too. I'm seeing a third layer now where two different groups rub up against each other on a daily basis. That dialogical work assumes that these two groupings of people are constantly in a conversation defining themselves, defining the Other. It has a direct relationship to the work of a Joker. [Short break]

Schutzman: Lori, tell us about Holographic Reprocessing [HR].

Katz: Sure. HR is a psychotherapy that identifies behavioral and emotional patterns that are replicated in people's lives. Once identified, the pattern is dislodged or reprocessed through a simulated encounter with the original oppressor. Clients revisit a scene of oppression through imagery and view it as their current self. From this observer vantage point, they are able to see more detail and expand the context of the event. And clients are able to interact with all the characters in the scene. For example, a 70-year-old client revisited a scene when he was gang-raped in the military. He remained his current age and saw that the 18-year-old could not have fought them off. For over 50 years, he thought of himself as a worthless failure, and finally, he saw that it wasn't his fault. HR encourages clients to see multiple truths of each character and of the situation.

Schutzman: Why is it called "holographic?"

Katz: The hologram is used to explain patterns of reemerging experiences in people's lives. These patterns represent unresolved intense emotional experiences. Like the qualities of a hologram, each experience is a whole experience unto itself as well as part of a larger pattern of experiences. And each experience contains information that is consistent with the whole pattern of experiences. It is termed an "experiential hologram" (Katz 2005). Once a pattern is identified, the client can reprocess it. We [at the round-table] have been talking about moving from something that might be solid into a liminal space, something that's more watery.

Lorenz: I am thinking, how can I live as a fish?

Katz: [Smile]

Blair: But a hologram is a projection.

Katz: It's a construction. It's not real, it's something that emerges.

Rich: In this therapy, clients may be projecting a very distorted image and one of your jobs is to help them refocus that image in different ways, while it seems like one of the primary aspects of Rainbow is to distort the images.

Katz: Both processes help people see novel viewpoints, they can say, "It doesn't have to be this way." It becomes more watery instead of something that's limiting them in their life.

Blair: So as that projected image starts to shift, there's a corresponding shifting in the individual, potentially.

Katz: There is no separation between the image and the person. The person is the embodiment of that image.

Blair: I'm trying to understand the origin of the projected image. It sounds like in HR there's this client-centered perspective. What is it constructing images?

Lorenz: A fixed subjectivity?

Katz: Yes, a fixed subjectivity. That's part of what gets people into therapies. They are blocked in fulfilling their desires, they keep repeating certain patterns and running into the same problems. So we look at that, and ask, does it have to be that way? A lot of the therapy is about broadening the context, what else might be going on? What other influences or possible truths could explain a situation?

Rich: One difference between HR and Boal's work is that in HR you look for patterns. It raises a value from eastern philosophy that suggests that you keep meeting the same antagonists until you deal with them. That is more difficult in Boal's work which is very much in the here and now, let's deal with this specific antagonist.

Blair: In that way, TO is kind of ahistorical.

Rich: How do you help protagonists make historical connections between multiple antagonists?

Katz: In line with holographic principles, the whole is within the parts. So, one antagonist is the embodiment of all of them. When we identify a specific interpersonal pattern, then it is easy to plug in different people who play the same role in the client's life. In some ways, it doesn't matter where you intervene because it's all connected. If we do TO and work in one point in time, that's still getting at the whole pattern. The analogy I use is a string of holiday lights. Each light represents an event of oppression or trauma. If you unscrew one of the lights, then none of them light up.

Blair: How would you work on a specific example to get them to look at the whole, at the string?

Katz: We draw a map of their pattern, the experiential hologram. Then we discuss how that same pattern has played out with several different people.

Schutzman: Have you brought HR into the TO work that you and Marc do together?

Rich: When we first started working together it was a matter of bringing together my knowledge of jokering and Lori's knowledge as a therapist. We had a marked space for our separate jobs in the workshop. Now we're looking at where these approaches come together.

Katz: In some ways, HR is like doing Boal's work with an individual.

Blair: Yes, like doing Cop-in-the-Head, only there aren't the other spect-actors in the room.

Katz: The client is the spect-actor for herself.

Blair: So not to be devil's advocate, but I wonder how do you avoid interpreting through your role as therapist when you don't have all those other elements that the spect-actors' presence affords?

Katz: It doesn't matter as long as the client gets it. If the client gets an "ah-ha," and is able to see things in a new way, then that's good for the client. If, for example, the client feels that she can't confront her oppressor and she needs some help, the therapist might ask, "Who do you want to help you?" And the client might come up with a real or a mythical figure. The client can use fantasy, whatever helps her to feel empowered.

Schutzman: How do you see a link to a more activist space, or do you at all? Is there a way to see how the technique works for a larger spectrum of people being able to respond to social pathologies?

Rich: I'm not always sure where or if those connections are made clearly. I've heard you ask about the connections between activism and ethnography, HR, and liberatory psychology. In a lot of Rainbow techniques, as well, I'm not sure if there's a clear link to activism for participants.

Schutzman: One reason I ask is that there's been an age-old debate between those pushing a process along in order to act publicly, and others who feel there isn't enough reflexivity and engagement in the interior terrain, what we sometimes call the therapeutic. One argument being that [public] action is going to be ill-informed or superficial, that even if someone else were in power, that person wouldn't know how to embrace the position of power differently than those who have embraced it so badly. I am interested in foregrounding the relationship between what we call therapy and what we call activism.

Lorenz: I think there is something in Rainbow that is directly tied to activism. In the Cop-in-the-Head or Rainbow exercise . . .

Blair: . . . the antagonists talk back.

Lorenz: Exactly. You're given multiple situations where you're jump-starting the process of rethinking, recreating, re-feeling, and watching and hearing other people respond to those re-tries. In the original TO work, people are already in motion, people are angry, people already know who the enemy is, people already know who the problem is and they're needing to rehearse different choices. But now, 10, 20, 30 years later there's kind of the opposite problem. People have been so traumatized, there's a kind of fatalism. From a distance you can say something's wrong but you don't know how to activate it.

Schutzman: Boal came up with Rainbow techniques to address people who weren't already activated and moving toward something.

Lorenz: Exactly. So Rainbow, by its very nature, is a process to reawaken capacities that have been wounded and in that way it seems to me a step toward activism. You're beginning to rehearse the situation.

Schutzman: We're rehearsing by asking the question: "Why can we not even identify the fact that there's an external force that is leading us to feel inactive?"

Rich: The distinction between Boal's work and HR, I agree, is that the antagonists talk back. In fact, their job is to make this increasingly difficult for the protagonist. But within the Rainbow of Images, or Cops-in-the-Head, it's rare that a structure is an image—you don't typically get "the military," or "patriarchy." We may not discuss structure unless the Joker moves in that direction.

Schutzman: It may happen by making a shift in perception and seeing configurations or constellations in our head. Simply in making new connections, we get glimpses of these larger categories or structures and how they work.

Lorenz: When Boal was in Santa Barbara in June (2003), the initial spark [for a story] was a problem in a personal relationship between a man and a woman. But as the work unfolded it really raised a lot of questions about the role of men, male social bonding, patriarchy, the Latino family, the role of women in the Latino family. It radiated out into the room a whole range of social issues.

Schutzman: Which technique was being used?

Blair: I think it was Rainbow technique.

Rich: I've found that when you're doing Rainbow specifically about racism, people in the audience will often shift to a different topic. "This is really about gender, this is really about homophobia." I'm wondering about the desire of people to not deal with what is on the table. In some situations, the work can move toward deeper structures, and in other cases it makes those structures more invisible.

Lorenz: But that's the skill of the Joker. Boal facilitated this in a way that opened it out to that realization.

Blair: When Boal was working in Sweden with this group of people and the Cop-in-the-Head came up, he had been using something else, and he responded to what he saw, which was these internal cops.

Lorenz: But his work always has the vector, it's always headed out toward structures of power.

Schutzman: It's often difficult to locate and communicate that vector. When I was jokering a workshop in Texas, there arose a Cop-in-the-Head issue about a young girl terrified to tell her grandmother that she was going to live with her boyfriend. At first, I wondered, "What will this be about?" And it ended up being an extraordinary debate about what respect meant. Respect for elders, what it means to sublimate something that you want in yourself in the name of someone else whose values are strong in your life. It was far more valuable and relevant socially than anyone, including myself, could have known. I have to hand it to the techniques.

Lorenz: A lot of psychologies begin with fantasy or imagination whereas Cop-in-the-Head, by its very name, suggests that the world is filled with institutions that are imprinting authoritarian fantasies. It's built right into the technique.

Blair: This issue of the location of the projection is my question about Holographic Reprocessing.

Katz: The client is projecting out, but projections are also being imprinted back in. Both are happening. People project their reality on to the world but the world responds back. Where does the hologram reside? Within a person, a relationship, a family, or a culture? Experiential holograms exist at each of these layers. I don't think there is a definitive answer to this question. Imagine an elaborate web of interconnections.

Schutzman: I see potential in HR to investigate the way protagonists tell their stories to begin with. I think there are assumptions and habituated, reductive ways of narrating what one's experience has been. What we're staging in part reflects a way one's experience has been framed. And maybe that framing needs to be blown open.

Rich: So, you have someone in the workshop who wants to tell a story about how men are oppressed in our society. What do you do with that story? Do you find other ways of getting him to tell that story? Or do you try, as a Joker, to show how the story is inventing a larger structure? Or do you hope the audience does that through Cop-in-the-Head or Rainbow?

Blair: Is there such a thing as a reduced story? Say you tell a story that's culturally uncritical and reductively stuck in your own pattern, and if we didn't do HR but just started with this blabbing out, as we usually do with Rainbow. I wonder if the work itself doesn't deconstruct it, simply in the gathering of images and then when you're actually in an image and trying to transform it. I've frequently seen people realize, once they're in the image, "Wow, this isn't at all what I had wanted or imagined."

Lorenz: Three years ago when Boal was in Santa Barbara (2001), a woman faculty member did a piece about how she was being oppressed by a male professor. I couldn't see the Cop-in-the-Head in the woman at all but several people who played various facets of her did, and were able to enact aspects of her unconscious arrogance, her insufferable behavior. It was quite shocking for me and other women faculty to have to deconstruct our notions about being victims and consider our own rigidities. The technique does blast open pieces of narrative in ways that really shake up the teller and the listener.

Blair: I've seen many times, even with an effective Joker, an effective story, an audience that's engaged, the techniques don't even move to short-term solutions. Even with the best of things aligned.

Lorenz: You could be seeing what Melanie Klein calls manic defense, where people are obsessively telling over and over because they do not want to have the "other" story emerge. Or you might be dialoging with somebody who's ability to form any narration has been virtually destroyed. For them, simply to be sitting in the room saying any sentence with the word "I" in it is a heroic victory. We can't make any assumptions about a universalized individual.

Katz: I agree. Trauma work can simply be about healing the story itself. The person may not be able to say the story, they might have pieces of it, they might have memory blocks or distortions or defensives. With Boal's work, there is an assumption that you have an intact narrative and you can use it.

Blair: That's actually really huge. Mary Belenky (*et al.*: 1997), in *A Tradition That Has No Name*, talks about her work with adolescent girls who weren't able to speak their internalized voices, many didn't even know that they had one. Sometimes we forget the complete shutting off, the memory loss, which is how we survive trauma.

Katz: Trauma doesn't reside as a verbal narrative, it resides in experience and that's why they can't access it verbally. So when we use experiential techniques and make images, they are able to see a lot more of their story, to piece together parts of it that split off. There's a lot of healing in that.

Lorenz: That's why image exercises in TO are so important. People in workshops start out [constructing] almost media images, very accessible images, and then they gradually deepen and take the challenge to show more difficult images. There's a lot of learning in that first hour that has to do with showing an analogue between what's felt wordlessly and what could be imaged in a way others can witness.

Schutzman: Before we end, let's talk briefly about TO's spiritual dimension, which has been raised but not quite named as such.

Blair: What place does the realm of the divine or, for Jung, the collective unconscious or *imago*, have in our work? I once worked with a group of trauma survivors who had lost their children to police violence. They were mostly Catholic and very religious, so all of the images of their lost children were mixed with a lot of religious metaphor. And even though they knew that the cops had killed their children and that there was real injustice, they were also aware that their children were in Heaven, and were, as one mother put it, "walking with Jesus and Mary." As a Joker, I was wondering what to do with these images. How do I incorporate this into the body of work? Another question I had was what to do with experiences of synchronicity. One woman's son awoke in the hospital from a coma and recounted a dream of dead bodies falling through the air. He was climbing this cascade of bodies and suddenly stopped and spoke with one of the falling bodies. The body gave the dreamer his first name and said, "The cops shot me 15 times in Pasadena." As the mother was telling our group about this dream, another mother in my circle gasped and said, "That's my son!" I didn't know as a TO Joker what to do with these things that I couldn't ignore.

Katz: Those things happen and they happen a lot, these bizarre synchronistic things that are so beautiful. It reminds us of a bigger context, in and out of the body. The spiritual realm is such a larger context.

Lorenz: A lot of religious ritual falls into that category. There's a moment that opens up into an unknown, like when the wine turns to blood or the spirit descends and possesses. Just as in trauma, attending to the negative and destructive aporia is part of the moment of truly witnessing what trauma does, and it is part of the healing. I think Boal's work sometimes opens up to that kind of space in a really beautiful way.

Notes

1   Tyan Dayton (1994), author of *The Drama Within*, describes "surplus reality" as that layer of narrative that exists just below the surface of our conscious understanding. A major goal of

psychodrama is to create dramatic investigations that can bring this unconscious pattern of thinking to the surface. Having a direct relationship with one's surplus reality is key to beginning to change the patterns of destructive behavior in the life of the client.

2   A juvenile hall is a detention facility to hold minors who have committed a law violation while they are processed throught the Juvenile Court and until such time as the individual is released to an authorized person or agency (other juvenile or adult jurisdictions, foster and group home placement, or short-term community assignments). In Rio de Janeiro, juvenile halls are called "closed schools" that, despite the name, are run very much like prisons.

3   In classic Jungian depth psychology the central organizing principle of the collective unconscious, manifest through dreams or dramatic play, is one of autonomous agency that falls outside the bounds of personal historical experience. Jung felt that the images that arise from dreams or dramatic improvisation are not only limited to our repressed personal past experiences as Freud might have believed (leading to the concept of "surplus reality" in psychodrama), but at times were just as likely to parallel ancient mythological stories that predate the narrow time and place of personal experience. The idea of location is significant here: depth psychology acknowledges the independent voice of the image with origins *outside* the realm of the personal unconscious. This shift in thinking invites the dreamer or actor to pay subtle attention to the authority of the "visiting voice" as opposed to projecting onto the image his/her own personal sense of meaning. The logic (*logos*) or meaning of the image may be quite other than what we would ordinarily expect were we left to analyze it within the framework of personal history.

4   Veterans Administrative Hospital.

5   Reflective images are analogous to looking into a mirror and seeing an "accurate" representation, i.e., the mirror image game in TO. Conversely, reflexive images are those conjured in Rainbow of Desire or Analytic Image, wherein multiple representations are created through deliberate distortions (such as exaggeration, caricature, resonance) and utilized for interpretive purposes. See Turner (1982).

Bibliography

Belenky, M., Bond, L., and Weinstock, J. (1997) *A Tradition That Has No Name: Nurturing the development of people, families, and communities*. New York: Basic Books.

Bhabha, H. (1994) *The Location of Culture*. London: Routledge.

Boal, A. (1995) *Rainbow of Desire: The Boal method of theatre and therapy*, trans. A. Jackson. London and New York: Routledge.

Dayton, T. (1994) *The Drama Within: Psychodrama and experiential therapy*. Deer Beach, FL: Health Communications, Inc.

Felman, S. and Laub, D. (eds) (1992) *Testimony: Crises of witnessing in literature, psychoanalysis, and history*. New York and London: Routledge.

Frank, A.W. (1995) *The Wounded Storyteller: Body, illness and ethics*. Chicago, IL: University of Chicago Press.

Katz, L. (2005) *Holographic Reprocessing: A cognitive-experiential psychotherapy for the treatment of trauma*. New York: Taylor and Francis.

Martín-Baró, I. (1994) *Writings for a Liberation Psychology*. Cambridge, MA: Harvard University Press.

Mock, F.L. (2003) *Maya Lin: A strong clear vision* (film). Santa Monica, CA: American Film Foundation.

Scheper-Hughes, N. (1992) *Death Without Weeping: The violence of everyday life in Brazil*. Berkeley, CA: University of California Press.

Turner, V. (1982) *From Ritual to Theatre: The human seriousness of play*. New York: PAJ Publications.

Watkins, M. (2000) *Invisible Guests*. Woodstock, CT: Spring Publications.

Performing democracy in the streets

Participatory Budgeting and Legislative Theatre in Brazil

Gianpaolo Baiocchi

Augusto Boal's Brazil is a country marked by deep inequities, but it is also home to many experiments with novel ways of making politics from below. Participatory Budgeting, a hallmark of Workers' Party administrations throughout Brazil, is one innovative form of participatory democracy and policy-making. Challenging the prejudice that "average citizens" are not capable of making "technical" decisions, this participatory system literally turns over most municipal budgeting decisions to citizen assemblies, where through a year-long process of learning and discussion, participants throughout the city decide on budget priorities and specific projects. Participatory Budgeting is now practiced in hundreds of municipalities in Brazil and has served as inspiration for democratic reforms throughout the world, involving thousands of citizens in each locality within which it is practiced.

Like Legislative Theatre (and Theatre of the Oppressed (TO) more generally), Participatory Budgeting revolves around critical discussion as a pedagogical process and values the voice, experience, and knowledge of a wide range of participants as it promotes dialogical problem-solving. Both share a root in Paulo Freire's participatory pedagogy, although Boal's techniques developed through theatre and Participatory Budgeting through a diffuse path of popular education, urban social movements, and experimentation by Workers' Party administrators. And instead of proposing legislation, Participatory Budgeting participants propose plans for municipal investment priorities. This chapter briefly covers the development of Participatory Budgeting and its connections to Legislative Theatre,[1] including the latter's potential to extend and deepen the reach of the Participatory Budgeting project.

The development of Participatory Budgeting and the Porto Alegre example

Participatory Budgeting in Brazil originated with the rise of urban social movements during the transition from dictatorship to democracy in the 1970s. These movements emphasized autonomy from manipulative government agencies and patronage schemes, attention to proceduralism, democracy in decision-making, and democratic access to urban services. Throughout Brazil, participants in these movements sought ways to organize local neighborhood associations and social movements into common blocs that could make demands on city and state government. With the discussion for a new constitution beginning in 1986, urban social movements made demands for more accountable forms of city governance. The meeting of the National Forum for Urban Reform in 1989, for instance, concluded with a statement of principles that called for citizen participation in the running of city affairs as a basic right of citizenship.

Several of the notable experiments of municipal reforms in the 1990s were carried out by the Workers' Party, which relied on its successes in providing efficient service delivery, especially to poorer sections of cities, to build up electoral support. Founded in 1980, the Workers' Party started to contest local elections in 1982, eventually registering significant victories in 1988.[1] The Party has evolved from close identification with its industrial working-class core to associations with a broad range of social movements, a platform of social justice, and democratization of state institutions.

But when the Workers' Party came to power in 1989, it faced the challenge of putting its vague promises about participation in government into actual practice without previous experience. There was little agreement as to what, exactly, the "Workers' Party way" of governing would look like, beyond a broad agreement on democratizing and decentralizing the administration, reversing municipal priorities toward the poor, and increasing popular participation in decision-making. One of the most successful examples of democratic reform in municipal governance has been in Porto Alegre, in southern Brazil, where Participatory Budgeting became the model for many subsequent administrations. Attending to a long-standing demand of the Union of Neighborhood Associations of Porto Alegre, which already in its 1985 congress called for a participatory structure involving the municipal budget, Workers' Party administrators developed a series of processes that extended popular control over municipal budgeting priorities. Reforms were introduced during the Workers' Party's first term, and by the end of four years, the administration had balanced municipal finances and brought in several thousand people as active participants in forums on city investments. Largely as a result of the success of these citizen forums, the administration has kept local opposition at bay and carried out a number of ambitious reforms, such as introducing land-use taxes targeted at wealthier citizens that have funded many Participatory Budgeting projects.

But Participatory Budgeting efforts in 1989 and 1990 lacked significant training periods. Participation was limited to choosing among demands and priorities proposed by governmental representatives in the absence of either an overview of municipal finances or the technical knowledge to determine which projects were actually feasible. As community activists loudly complained at the time, this limited degree of participation did not empower participants in a significant way. In addition, because of a disconnection between day-to-day decisions (i.e., what road should we build?) and longer-term processes (i.e., how much money is there for the whole city?), early attempts at Participatory Budgeting raised expectations that were not met. By 1991, however, with a more comprehensive format that allowed more participants significant input, coupled with fiscal reforms that led to increased funding for these projects, the process took off.

Participatory Budgeting has evolved over the years into a two-tiered structure of forums in which citizens participate as individuals and as representatives of various social groups (neighborhood associations, cultural groups, special interest groups) throughout a yearly cycle. They deliberate and decide on projects for specific districts and on municipal investment priorities, and then monitor the outcome of these projects. The process begins in March of each year with the first tier—regional assemblies in each of the city's 16 districts. These large meetings, with open participation of upwards of a thousand persons, accomplish two goals: first, the election of delegates to represent specific neighborhoods in successive rounds of deliberation; second, review by participants of the previous year's projects and budget. The mayor and the staff attend these meetings to reply to citizens' concerns about projects in the district.

The second tier of the process begins with delegate attendance at assemblies to learn about the criteria and costs involved in various projects and to discuss their districts' needs and overall priorities; all areas of municipal investment are eventually decided this way. Common projects range from the construction of new roads to the delivery of social services and healthcare. Nonvoting, City Hall-appointed facilitators run these meetings, which take place weekly in most districts. At the end of the yearly cycle in July, delegates vote to determine the district's projects and priorities as well as to elect representatives from each of the districts to serve on a municipal Budget Council that is responsible for the ultimate decisions over budget items, such as the allocation of municipal funds per district.[2] While the Budget Council makes decisions over the next months, delegates in the districts continue to meet, often to monitor the outcome of chosen projects.

The process draws in participants from the city's poor periphery who are seeking solutions to practical problems. Central concerns of these residents may include making their housing situation "regular" (so they are not liable to be forcibly removed in the middle of the night) and gaining access to urban services like water, sewage, public transportation, public clinics, and schools. They first come to sessions through word-of-mouth, having heard that there is a government meeting of some kind where others have received some of these services. They attend with a concerned neighbor or two and begin to get a sense of how the process works. They see other people from the district asking about results of demands made in previous years. Eventually they decide to participate and elect a delegate who represents them for the rest of the process. He or she participates in meetings once a week or more, often for months, and eventually votes on the priorities and preferences for the district, while choosing councilors from among the delegates who will make the eventual, binding budget decisions for the city. Meanwhile, back in the neighborhoods, residents continue to come to meetings at the district level, usually to follow up on the selected projects. Every year, new and previously uninvolved participants come to these meetings and become more engaged in the life of their community.

Porto Alegre's Participatory Budgeting shows how complex management of a whole city can occur through a combination of direct and representative democracy. The deliberative processes occur continuously over the years, and thus provide opportunities for participants to learn from mistakes. The local units, though vested with substantial decision-making power, do not function completely autonomously from other units or from central monitoring units. Rather, central agencies offer supervision and support while respecting local decision-making power. In Porto Alegre's case, support comes from the administration in the form of regional agents who act as non-voting facilitators. The higher tier of the participatory structures, the Municipal Council of the Budget, brings together representatives of each of the districts. They deliberate on the rules of the process as a whole as well as on broad investment priorities; they also act as intermediaries between municipal government and regional activists, bringing the demands from districts to central government, and justifying government actions to regional activists. Participatory governance has expanded beyond budget meetings to new forums that now include social service and health provisions, local school policy, and human rights. Participatory Budgeting itself has grown to include decisions concerning education, culture, health, social services, and sports.

Despite potential barriers posed by technical and time-consuming discussions, large numbers of participants representing broad segments of the population have attended Porto Alegre's Participatory Budgeting sessions, with some 20,000 participants at the first yearly assembly in 2000. The socioeconomic profile of the average participant continues to be significantly below the city's average. Over half of participants live in households earning four minimum wages or less, and over half lack education beyond the eighth grade. On the other hand, better-off citizens are under-represented, as roughly a third of all participants come from households earning five minimum wages or more, as compared to the 55 percent of the city's residents who generally fall into this category.

Porto Alegre's budgeting process is a successful instance of empowered participatory government, which Fung and Wright (2003) define as efficient and redistributive decision-making within a deliberative framework that includes participation from poorer strata of the citizenry. Nonetheless, its very success raises two important issues for the model: inequality within meetings and the question of whether or not its success requires particular political conditions. In the first instance, theorists and practitioners of participatory democracy are keenly aware that participation among unequals often means that discussions will not take place on an equal footing. This real world problem manifests itself in many ways, from the unequal availability of time and resources that favor the participation of the privileged to the dynamics of actual discussions which may be too technical, or dominated by the better educated or by men. The Porto Alegre experiment has shifted the discussion away from inequality as a problem of individuals (as if the "problem" were the lack of education of some participants) to inequality as a problem of process (the "problem" is creating a process in which the less-educated can participate on equal footing). Therefore, much of the year is spent in educational sessions so as to equalize access to the language of budgets and municipal affairs. Meetings take place after the workday or on weekends. Evidence of the efficacy of these measures is in how inclusive the process is: the proportion of low-income and less-educated participants is twice as high as the city average (Baiocchi 2003b).

But this is not enough. The participation of women at the higher tier of the process is low and there are constant discussions in Porto Alegre today about how to make the process even more inclusive. While there is a well thought-out pedagogical component that empowers participants to debate the minutiae of budgeting, full participation in the process year-round demands quite a bit of time. For those with the responsibility of a household in addition to a job, taking on a "third shift" of community activism is a burden.

The second concern, that experiments like Participatory Budgeting may not be possible save for unusual political conditions in which agents like the Workers' Party are in power, has not been borne out. Even in Porto Alegre under a Workers' Party administration, there was initial opposition to the broad participation of the new budgeting process. Many politicians in the municipal legislature felt that the process devolved too much power to the population and robbed the city council of its traditional jurisdiction. Once or twice in the early years, city council members tried to derail the process by decree, and in those instances literally thousands of participants appeared in City Hall to voice their opinion in favor of the process. The Porto Alegre story teaches us that broad participation has a way of legitimating the process itself and buffering against political opposition.

Today, Participatory Budgeting is integrated into Porto Alegre's routine, just part of the way that things work at the city level. It has grown from its social movement roots to an institution that reaches much broader sectors of the population through several years of trial, error, and experimentation. It is an institution that shows us that effective governance and broad, empowered participation can be compatible and mutually reinforcing. It also demonstrates the potential of broad-based civic engagement through an institutional arrangement that devolves power to the general populace in a way attentive to how people actually learn and communicate in a public setting. It is to this aspect I turn next as I review the importance of critical pedagogy in the design and history of Participatory Budgeting.

The influence of Paulo Freire

The work of Paulo Freire (1988) is an extremely important, if not always acknowledged, influence on the way Participatory Budgeting works today. Popular educators of the Freirean mold, sometimes as progressive clergy and sometimes as simply middle-class compatriots who moved to urban peripheries, were extremely active in the new social movements in Brazil in the mid-1980s. They influenced much of the discourse and practice of those movements through their demand for autonomy and truly democratic participation, through the way they carried out educational work, as well as through their impact within the Workers' Party itself. Some of the original texts of the Workers' Party describe a new kind of party in which popular movements could have a genuine voice and not be dictated to by a vanguard, an ideology that could have been directly lifted from *Pedagogy of the Oppressed*. In Porto Alegre itself, many of the early administrators of Participatory Budgeting came from a Freirean tradition that has left its mark.

However, in early attempts at Participatory Budgeting, intellectuals from the Workers' Party did not always have a clear conception of how to create a critical dialogue with residents of poor communities. Discussions within the Party were highly abstract and about such topics as the meaning of a socialist administration: can socialists command a capitalist state?; should it be an administration for workers or for the whole city?; should the aim be to improve services or pave the way for a national Workers' Party victory? Administrators faced crises early on, from lack of a clear conception of how to garner popular support to a romanticized vision of how popular sectors "should" behave. For instance, administrators thought that transportation should have been the principal issue for the city's poor residents (whose first priority was, in fact, pavements) and thought popular demands were "not correct, too immediate."

Community activists harshly criticized the scope of early Participatory Budgeting meetings that involved the general population only in making demands but not at higher levels of the process, such as defining the broad investment priorities of the city or discussing the city's income or personnel. As mentioned earlier, the administration was also justifiably charged with not "providing information in accessible language" (FASE 1990: 1). A letter to the administration signed by representatives from several districts and neighborhoods proposed changes including starting the process earlier in the year and holding regular meetings in each district that offered accounting of ongoing projects from the year before and clear explanations of the budgeting process as a whole.

Between the first and second year of Participatory Budgeting, administrators, interested in better applying their own Freirean philosophy, therefore introduced a number of improvements, relying heavily on Party members with experience in popular education and ecclesiastic base communities. Meetings were dedicated to informing participants about the rules, technical criteria, etc., so that they could debate municipal engineers on a more even footing. More emphasis was placed on the collective process; rather than one meeting to select priorities, the process was stretched over a year to discuss common needs and the overall city budget. A collective learning process was instituted whereby the group would find its common interests in a critical conversation over that year. A facilitator was assigned to each district to help participants find common ground, draw in new participants, help run meetings, and assist with discussions around hierarchies and priorities without directing them. Facilitators were charged with "improving the discussion of concepts of budget policy," "challenging citizens to think of problems of their district as a whole," and "establishing relationships based on values of cooperation and solidarity" (Prefeitura Municipal de

Porto Alegre 1992: 21). These moves were truly Freirean reforms. Just as TO moved away from the heavy-handed political theatre of the 1960s and 1970s that dictated what the poor ought to think, Participatory Budgeting moved to a system that was more truly open for popular input on equal footing.

The more Freirean version of Participatory Budgeting brought numerous surprises. For example, administrators who had assumed transportation would be the principal issue for workers, realized that they had been thinking abstractly about the life of a working-class person, assuming difficulties getting to work to be the central problem. People who do not live on unpaved streets might not realize how important pavements are: the health of one's family is hurt by dust as cars go by, getting dirty makes one's work life more difficult, while living on a paved street gives residents a sense of pride and respect.

Another surprise for administrators and facilitators was how difficult it became to "control" meetings once people were empowered to speak out about their concerns.

Participatory Budgeting and Legislative Theatre

The most significant link between Participatory Budgeting and Legislative Theatre (and indeed, Boal's entire TO project) is the common root in Freirean pedagogy. First, both emphasize the connection between participation and individual and collective *concientização*, or "consciousness-raising." Liberal democratic theorists advocate participation for its effect on decision-making, as well as on individual virtue. Participatory Budgeting not only seeks to bring about better decisions, but also to challenge individual and collective preferences and foster more solidarity. Its ultimate goal is social transformation—a contested theoretical point among practitioners, but it involves a transformation of individual horizons, collective horizons, and social relationships, both within communities and between communities and authorities. Participatory Budgeting is thus not only a tool for redistribution and participation, but also an instrument for social change. Similarly, while Legislative Theatre produces indisputably better legislation than other approaches, its ultimate goal is also social transformation.[3] Like Participatory Budgeting, it is a radically democratic transformation that is distinct from older leftist visions, and it takes place first in society's periphery—the neighborhood and the community—rather than at the center. This connection between participation, collective and individual learning, and social change is central to the practice of both Participatory Budgeting and Legislative Theatre and owes much to a Freirean vision.

Second, both democratize access to authority and challenge traditional conceptions of expertise. Unlike liberal versions of consultative government and participation, such as the town hall meeting, Participatory Budgeting and Legislative Theatre challenge what it means to be an expert without actually dispensing with expertise. As in the Freirean vision in which the position of the teacher as holder of knowledge and truth is challenged and the teacher, who holds specific knowledge, becomes a participant in the dialogue, in Participatory Budgeting the sovereignty of technical experts is challenged. For years, in Brazil and elsewhere, urban planners had been given wide latitude about technical decisions, thus masking elite interests—e.g., that a city should invest more resources in its downtown area in order to promote business. The participants of Participatory Budgeting challenge this habitual practice and by making it an object of explicit discussion, giving it a name, and recasting it as a political decision, they make another choice, transforming city patterns of investments and reversing old patterns.

The Pólis Institute of São Paulo, a Non-Governmental Organization (NGO) that promotes the democratization of urban governance and services through publications and workshops, and one of the principal promoters of Participatory Budgeting, also recognizes the link between Participatory Budgeting and Boal's work. One of its publications, *Dicas*, recently included Legislative Theatre in its list of municipal innovations of interest to administrators and activists.

While Participatory Budgeting and Legislative Theatre share these basic Freirean roots, one difference between the two models is the relationship of participants to governmental decision-making. As a prototypical case of empowered participatory governance, Participatory Budgeting creates direct deliberation between citizens at the local level and devolves substantial amounts of decision-making power to these local settings. These citizens are involved in pragmatic problem-solving and in monitoring and implementing solutions. Scholars of empowered participation have emphasized the importance of the direct connection between citizen discussions and policy implementation, even while citizens' decisions remain subject to expert review. Legislative Theatre also links discussion with policy, though in a different way. Its participants engage in deliberation and pragmatic problem-solving, and propose legal solutions. These are then subject to expert review and proposed by a legislator. Legislation is then debated by all legislators and either approved, modified, or rejected. While both Participatory Budgeting and Legislative Theatre rely on this technical expertise (though in both cases it is put to use by the popular mandate and not the other way around), the principal difference in the relationship to governance is that Participatory Budgeting connects popular decision-making to the executive branch while Legislative Theatre links it with lawmakers. Connecting with executive action makes a relatively direct link between citizen input and government action; in a democracy it is the executive branch's prerogative to make and carry out policies. While budgeting per se is a responsibility of both branches, in practice participatory budgets crafted by citizens are approved with minimal modification because the sheer numbers of participants make it difficult for legislators to make modifications legitimately.[4]

Both Participatory Budgeting and Legislative Theatre position citizen-participants to circumvent some of the traditional representative institutions of democracy in favor of direct decision-making but they do so to different degrees. Through Participatory Budgeting, citizens participate directly in budget decisions that are then enacted by the representatives they elect. This process, situated in the executive branch, cannot be duplicated in the legislative realm because legislators do not have the prerogative to carry out policy. Rather, they are entrusted with representing their constituents while they deliberate on legal principles and make binding laws.

But while Participatory Budgeting offers a more direct experience of democracy than does Legislative Theatre, the horizons of engagement within the former process are more bounded. Discussions are confined, for example, to the limits of budgets, technical capabilities, and municipal government action. And while in practice discussions often extend to other realms, such as national political problems, decision-making is restricted to investments and projects for one's district (and later for the city as a whole). Not only are certain standards set—e.g., a road cannot be built unless there is a clearance of so many meters, and the yearly investment for the city does not exceed a set amount—but the horizons of possible action are also limited. It is not possible in Participatory Budgeting, for example, to decide to change the type of benches at bus stops to accommodate the blind, even though people can decide to increase the number of bus stops along a certain route. In my fieldwork,

I often witnessed fights among community activists who wanted, for example, a traffic light at a particular corner when such a project was forbidden by technical standards.[5] Proponents of Participatory Budgeting argue that such limits on citizens' power are inherent necessities for the system to remain practical. Yet it is also possible that these limits introduce a rationalization into discussions, subtly colonizing them from an unchallengeable technocratic standpoint, an issue that has worried social theorists for the last century.[6]

Toward a radical governmental theatre

Given the similarities between Participatory Budgeting and Legislative Theatre, it would seem natural for there to be cross-fertilization of experiences and lessons learned between them. This dialogue exists in Brazil, though not yet in a sustained or systematic way. For those who apply the principles of these two models elsewhere, there is usually an even greater distance between practitioners of each who often have distinct disciplinary and institutional connections. By way of conclusion, I briefly consider here a means to expand Participatory Budgeting through elements of Legislative Theatre.

Legislative Theatre has been performed in the opening rounds of Participatory Budgeting (e.g., in 1998 and 1999 in Santo Andre and Porto Alegre)—largely symbolic events with often more than a thousand people present. But there is tremendous potential to include it as a regular feature of district-level meetings with the delegates as a way to improve the existing discussions, to propose changes to Participatory Budgeting itself, and even to generate ideas for government reforms. It is easy to imagine a format whereby each year's round of Participatory Budgeting district meetings would include one Legislative Theatre session with the delegates to address some of the limitations they had identified during the previous year's rounds. The workshop might result in a list of possible modifications to Participatory Budgeting and its rules themselves, as well as yield a list of possible actions by the executive or even the legislature in areas other than budgeting.

Legislative Theatre, as an aesthetic language, has definite advantages as a pedagogical tool. Theatre's ability, via role play, can address people's unequal abilities to speak verbally. It can break down technical ideas into concrete scenes that can be enacted. And it can result in less time pressure, especially important for poor participants, since the actors prepare the scenarios and thus the interaction with groups of people might be more contained, and a range of solutions/preferences communicated through spect-actor interventions more succinctly. In addition, a Legislative Theatre session could contribute to the continuous reform of the process. Regular participants are among the most astute critics of Participatory Budgeting. In my interviews, they criticized its demands on their time in meetings, the difficulties inherent in bringing information back to the neighborhood, and the gender imbalance of elected delegates. In 2001, a working group composed of participants and City Hall officials proposed changes to shorten the yearly cycle and lessen the demands on time. But the other critiques remain and are more difficult to address within the structure of the process. The problems of gender and communication between delegates and their neighborhoods could be posed in a Legislative Theatre session. No doubt some novel solution would emerge that could improve the process in a dynamic way.

Finally, a regular Legislative Theatre session within the structure of Participatory Budgeting would allow participants to come up with new solutions to local problems, new suggestions for governmental action (including new legislation, of course), and new ideas for governmental reform. The results could be forwarded to the Budget Council as suggestions for restructuring the budgeting process, to the appropriate government agency regarding suggestions for reform, or to the local legislature as support for a law. As a regular component of Participatory Budgeting, it opens the opportunity for continuity year after year. This would allow public monitoring of the eventual outcomes of these suggestions as well as important learning about the types of governmental action that are likely to produce positive outcomes.

Both Legislative Theatre and Participatory Budgeting seek to harness public creativity and energy, break down barriers between government and citizen, and challenge traditional notions of expertise and authority. Having evolved side by side from similar Freirean origins they emphasize different aspects of critical pedagogy. Participatory Bugeting emphasizes connecting critical problem-solving to tangible outcomes while Legislative Theatre places greater emphasis on the process of problem-solving itself, and is more attentive to the ways in which participants become actors in the discussions. Legislative Theatre is by its very nature more open-ended, inviting questions about what problems are on the table for discussion. Participatory Budgeting and Legislative Theatre are outcomes of differing trajectories. Comparisons and combinations of these trajectories, beyond those I have discussed here, will emerge from further practice and experimentation. If history teaches us anything, it is that practice and experimentation with participatory tools of democratic governmental action will produce unexpectedly good outcomes. Those who carry out such experiments must above all remember that the ultimate goal of both Participatory Budgeting and Legislative Theatre is not improvement of urban governance or promotion of participation for their own sake, but rather social transformation.

Notes

1   It is impossible to review here the history of the Workers' Party. See chapters 1 and 11 in Baiocchi (2003a).
2   At the time of the research, there was a formula in place that allocated these funds to each district based on the district's population, its level of "need," and its priorities. See Fedozzi (2001); Prefeitura Municipal de Porto Alegre (1998).
3   While Boal was a legislator in Rio de Janeiro, several laws originating through Legislative Theatre were passed. These include some symbolic acts, like the establishment of a day of solidarity with the people of East Timor, but also many with a great deal of impact on the lives of the less privileged in the city. One law, for example, mandates that hospitals make accommodations for companions of elderly people; another makes irreversible treatments for mental conditions illegal in public hospitals (Boal 1998: 102–3).
4   In principle, a municipal budget is crafted by the executive and then debated, modified, and approved by the legislative. In Porto Alegre and elsewhere, legislators sometimes complain that Participatory Budgeting has hollowed out the powers of the legislature.
5   For a detailed discussion of one such example see Baiocchi (2003b).
6   For a contemporary example, see Piven and Cloward (1979).

Bibliography

Baiocchi, G. (2003a) (ed.) *Radicals in Power: The Workers' Party and experiments in urban democracy in Brazil.* London: Zed Books.
—— (2003b) "Emergent public spheres: Talking politics in participatory governance," *American Sociological Review* 68: 52–74.

Boal, A. (1998) *Legislative Theatre: Using performance to make politics*, trans. A. Jackson. London and New York: Routledge.

FASE (1990) "Em discussão o orçamento municipal," Mimeo. Porto Alegre, Brazil.

Fedozzi, L. (2001) *O Poder da Aldeia*. Porto Alegre: Tomo Editorial.

Freire, P. (1988) *Pedagogy of the Oppressed*, trans. M.B. Ramos. New York: Continuum.

Fung, A. and Wright, E.O. (2003) *Deepening Democracy: Institutional innovations in empowered participatory governance*. London and New York: Verso.

Piven, F.F. and Cloward, R. (1979) *Poor People's Movements: Why they succeed and how they fail*. New York: Vintage.

Prefeitura Municipal de Porto Alegre (1992) "Processo de avaliação da gestão da frente popular," Porto Alegre: Gabinete do Prefeito: Coordenação de Relações com a Comunidade.

—— (1998) "Regimento interno do orçamento participativo," Porto Alegre: Prefeitura Municipal de Porto Alegre.

Section 2

Tropes

Activism in feminist performance art

Suzanne Lacy

Theatre of the Oppressed (TO), proclaims Augusto Boal, "is not new nor is it something that I have invented" (1978: 113). His premise that theatre is "our capacity to observe ourselves in action" links art to constructs of self as well as the social context in which those constructs are enacted. This capacity, he reasons, "affords us the further possibility of . . . combining memory and imagination—two indissociable psychic processes—to reinvent the past and to invent the future. Therein resides the immense power with which theatre is endowed" (Boal 1998: 7).

What are we to make of this prodigious and articulate artist who strives not for originality but for efficacy within a clearly defined paradigm of equality and justice? Is it possible that the values and concerns of social change themselves engender aesthetic forms common across disciplines? It is useful not only to see in what ways TO is exemplary but how it resembles other art/art practices of Boal's time—the similarities perhaps contributing to a better understanding of such work. In this article, I explore aspects of the artistic terrain of the 1970s and the 1990s, including two case studies from my own performance work, that demonstrate the common ground between the work of Augusto Boal and US feminist performance art.

Feminist performance and invisible theatre, 1970–80

In 1975 I was artist-in-residence at the Guy Miller Homes, a government-funded urban housing project for the elderly. As I made the daily one-hour journey in my vintage light blue Mazda pick-up through an increasingly devastated Los Angeles urbanscape that had not been rebuilt after the 1969 riots, I felt a gathering depression, a sense of placelessness in the withering heat. Here there was no retreat outside of one's home—no park, no corner café, no supermarket, no mall or civic center. In post-riot Watts, there was virtually no safe, shared public space.

I found my respite inside a friendship with Evalina Newman, a single and childless woman in her mid-fifties who had retired from industrial cleaning when workplace chemicals had combined in her body to produce respiratory and coronary illnesses. With only an eighth-grade education, Evalina had a creative and conceptual mind, an openness to new experiences, and a bent for community organizing that made her a perfect friend for a budding conceptual artist. Her home became my sanctuary in Watts, including a kitchen where we introduced each other to stewed greens and fresh garden salads and a living room half filled by a quilting frame upon which she worked while we talked, a Formica table at which to scheme, and a couch where I spent the night when it was too late to drive home safely. Over several years we designed and produced a series of installations and performances that grew out of our relationship. Our collaboration was co-equal but each of us contributed something different: I knew the language of 1970s' conceptual and performance art and had an audience there; her audience was her immediate community and she understood its mores and sensibilities and lived its critical issues.

Our first installation was initiated when Evalina wanted to engage her neighbors in making quilts for nearby senior homes. While they quilted, 10 women discussed fears of neighborhood teenagers who watched from behind cinderblock walls and made increasingly bold investigative forays into the complex. (Evalina, outspoken in her admonitions, was a particular target for the youth.) We created portraits of the community—its creative expressions (women there practiced gardening, home decoration, and a series of crafts), its organizing, and its security needs. To attract attention to residents' needs, we recruited politicians, police representatives, artists from greater Los Angeles, and local activists to installations in the residents' recreation hall. Alongside full-sized and lap-sized quilts, pipe-cleaner poodles, doll-head Kleenex box covers, and crocheted potholders, we exhibited quilts of photos documenting life there.

One Saturday night Evalina and I collaborated on a performance that began on a street corner in Watts. We placed a call to performance artist Nancy Buchanan at a gallery in downtown Los Angeles where an audience waited. Nancy hung up the phone and announced that the piece had begun: she showed slides of an incident where Evalina surprised a youthful intruder and held him at gunpoint for hours waiting for the police to arrive. She played a phone conversation between Evalina and me planning the performance, with Evalina explaining that recent heart problems would prevent her from undertaking the stressful bus ride. Back in Watts, Evalina walked me to a bus stop with a small pistol in her apron pocket and waited until I boarded the bus for the trip downtown.

During the 1970s—the inception of visual arts performance as we know it today—artists in the US drew inspiration from happenings and the Fluxus movement, exploring duration, minimalism, survivalism, and intervention as often invisible gestures. Gender and urban culture were frequent themes: Vito Acconci surreptitiously trailed women in New York City; the Feminist Art Workers made random calls from phone booths to talk to women about how to handle obscene phone calls; and Chris Burden told a woman art critic that if she wanted to interview him she would need to meet him alone, late at night, in an abandoned district of downtown Los Angles. In those same urban streets, I too performed an exercise in danger, at once an exploration of gendered vulnerabilities within public space and an act of affiliation with women like Evalina whose mobility depended upon public transportation. After leaving Evalina's house I rode the city streets for over an hour. At one point, a brick shattered a window but the driver did not stop. At the last change of buses it was dark and, standing on a desolate downtown street, I calculated that the mile run to the gallery was preferable to waiting for notoriously late buses. The performance was completed when I arrived without fanfare, almost invisibly, to the gallery—a party now in process—and called Evalina to let her know I had arrived safely. Although the urban theme of risk and the formal element of duration were common to that era's performance, Evalina and I were also performing our cross-cultural and cross-generational relationship within our two different communities. In this our work departed from the heritage of visual art and aligned itself, unwittingly, with that of Augusto Boal.

If there are coincidences of form and intention between Augusto Boal's Invisible Theatre and feminist interventionist performance from the 1970s, and I believe there are, there was little, if any, knowledge each of the other. US feminist visual performance art derived its sources from the explorations in the relationship of art to life that accompanied major twentieth-century visual art movements such as Constructivists' public appearances in oddly decorated formal attire and Futurists' verbal assaults on audiences who returned the favor with rotten fruit. Subtle, interventive, and invisible visual art performances gained impetus in the 1950s and 1960s when composer John Cage, dancer Merce Cunningham, and visual artists Marcel Duchamp, Robert Rauschenberg, and Allan Kaprow were influenced by technological developments, a rising consciousness of mass media culture, and Eastern philosophy. In 1952, in the dining hall at Black Mountain College, Cage's *Theatre Piece No. 1* was a seminal event from which emerged the Theatre of Mixed-Means. It involved a simultaneous and unrelated reading of poetry, dance, music, "chance action," and paintings (Kotz 1990: 76).

This Theatre of Mixed-Means (Kostelanetz 1981), with its emphasis on chance occurrences, ignored the divide between visual and theatrical arts and reinvented the time-based gesture as a visual art practice. "Once a human shadow gets into a painting for a moment, everything becomes possible and the conditions for experimentation enter the scene. Possibility, artists know, is the most frightening idea of all," wrote Allan Kaprow (2003: 73), chief chronicler and theorist of the happenings movement.

During the 1960s, life itself became irresistible as a formal element. Kaprow argued that the venues and audiences of art should take place anywhere except in galleries and museums, at any time, and possibly even unbeknownst to its audience. Compare Augusto Boal speaking about theatre:

> If you make any changes within the theatre—a theatre that has a proscenium, a stage, an arena, or a combined version of stages—this is but reformism; you are not really changing anything. We believe that you can go anyplace and make theatre.
>
> (Driskell 1975: 75)

Jan Cohen-Cruz notes that the theatrical legacy of ideas such as contingency, simultaneity, dissolution of the spectator/artist divide, and contiguity of art with daily life provoked expansive concepts in "(1) where [theatre] takes place, (2) what is considered the core of the theatrical event, and (3) how fully the actor and spectator are involved" (1994: 110–24). Visual art performance in the 1960s was against authority, but it usually focused its rebellion on cultural rather than political authority, being mostly enamored of aesthetic invention. Visual artists were more intrigued with ideas and structures than they were with virtuosity, narrative integrity, or presentation. Events, happenings, appearances, and interventions generally took place unrehearsed and only once, often performed unannounced or unwitnessed in public places. While not overtly political, at least in the sense of dealing with public issues, Kaprow's call to equalize the valuation of real life subjects and subjectivities nevertheless suited the democratic spirit of the times.

While teaching at California Institute of the Arts in the early 1970s, Allan Kaprow laid important groundwork for West Coast feminist visual artists. His "life-like art," in which the subject matters and aesthetic strategies looked like life itself, provided feminists with a rationale to explore and call art what was before considered mundane—the intimate stuff of women's daily lives. Performing life, or image-enriched versions of it, artists built a theoretical construct of gendered embodiment, a visual arts performance practice centered in the body and its actions: Mierle Laderman Ukeles helpfully scrubbed the floors of the Guggenheim Museum, Martha Rosler staged a garage sale in an art gallery to sell her "stuff," and Linda

Montano convinced a bar in San Diego to hire her as a country western singer (although her inability to remember the lyrics of more than one song cut this career short after a few weeks).

Montano began in the 1970s by assuming characters that existed parallel to her own life, enacting situations that resembled her own reality—slightly off-key. The narrative structures of these performances were shaped not by dramatic imperatives such as a story line and protagonists but by Montano's experience of living within a specific time frame. Whether they lasted a year, an hour, or the length of a song, her performances ended without fanfare and were often, to incidental audiences, invisible as art.

Lynn Hershman made repeated unheralded appearances over several years as a fictitious self named Roberta Breitmore. Breitmore was a subtle, ironic, sometimes sympathetic and sometimes pathetic working-class secretary with big blonde hair who wanted to better understand herself, find a lover, get a job, and achieve happiness. Her incidental audience—the social security clerk where she applied for her card, the therapist to whom she went for help, the anonymous date arranged through personal advertisements—was not spectator but unwitting accomplice in the dramas of Roberta's life. Hershman's performance inserted into everyday life was not about transforming audience consciousness but rather constructing an alter ego. She had little interest in theatre per se but rather in invention, subterfuge, secrecy, and experience.

In the beginning, feminist performance art focused on internalized oppression, what Boal calls Cop-in-the-Head, without structured opportunities for audience reaction. Provoking topical and focused conversation in incidental audiences, a characteristic of Invisible Theatre, was not part of the motivation, nor was there intent to inform or engage the audience. Rather these artists sought self-exploration within the material of life, framed as the art practice of uneasy outsiders. In contrast to Invisible Theatre, these invisible feminist performances were idiosyncratic and personalized, relying on the artist's real persona for what was essentially an unduplicatable form. The split between the public representation of femininity and female interiority preoccupied women of the era and was marked by a fluctuation between concealment and display. This public gendered embodiment raised questions of intimacy, belonging, exclusion, relationship, and self-awareness. Performances were based on artists' bodies functioning as visual images, on artists as experiencers subjecting themselves to social or physical situations, and on artists as provocateurs operating as lightning rods for public projections.

The polemic of this first generation of feminist performance artists was often directed toward the art world as an arena where change was possible, rather than toward a broad public audience where the goals for transformation were more difficult. The site of intervention was often the profession's exclusionary practices toward women and minorities. Adrian Piper, for example, began a series of provocative appearances in the streets of New York in 1970 (*The Catalysis Series*). She wore clothes smeared with rancid butter, dried food, or wet paint in public; carried tape-recorded burps with her to the library; and blew bubbles with her chewing gum, leaving the splattered remains on her face. She did not enter deliberate conversation with bystanders; rather, she was interested in the experience of the outsider whose visible features of identity (in this case gender and race) were themselves broader social provocations. She reported these incidents to the art world, and one would presume that this professional community was the overt target of her discourse. In another guerrilla performance, Lorraine O'Grady appeared at a 1981 art opening as "Mlle. Bourgeoisie Noire Goes to the New Museum." Wearing a gown and cape made of 180 pairs of white gloves, the artist shouted invectives against the racial politics of the art world.

Beginning in 1973, at the Los Angeles Woman's Building and th e Feminist Studio Workshop, women could for the first time study the performance art of women and invent their own. In this politicized and collective feminist environment, performances took on a distinctly populous and reformist cast, leading to the development of activist performance art, more kindred in spirit to Boal's Invisible Theatre. Students Nancy Angelo, Cheri Gaulke, Sue Maberry, and Jerri Allyn, among others, formed collaborative groups such as the Feminist Art Workers, the Waitresses, and Sisters of Survival. Leslie Labowitz and I founded Ariadne: A Social Art Network to umbrella public performances on violence against women. In New York, women organized into groups such as No More Nice Girls and Carnival Knowledge. In this work we see a clear pedagogical intent to address audiences outside the art world in politically relevant discourse. Relationships between women (such as Evalina's and mine) and to a public audience were integral to the production and meaning of this work.

Although the art was activist and dialogic, fulfilling in spirit important aspects of Boal's Invisible Theatre, its invisibility, technically speaking, varied. Influenced by Kaprow's stylistic interventions, these feminist performances reflected a flagrant lack of concern about whether the work would be seen as art, therapy, or political action, indicating that its true invisibility might be to the art world itself. In an installation by Nancy Angelo, a circle of pink chairs was available for audience seating, with six of the chairs already taken by television monitors mounted at eye level. The audience found itself in the middle of a mediated consciousness-raising group, where the close-up videotaped faces of six women talked, listened, and responded to each other about experiences of incest. At the end of the video, during which most people forgot they were listening to prerecorded confessions, a professional in sexual trauma led the audience in an emotional group discussion. This incorporation of audience experience, like 1960s' happenings but with the addition of politicized personal content, was not Invisible Theatre per se but it also softened boundaries between art and life to encourage reflection and transformation on individual and collective levels.

Derived from the historical trajectory of visual arts, feminist performance artists were nevertheless left with the dilemma of explaining the social justice intentions in their work to a largely indifferent profession. Visual art performance had evolved as a series of reactions: to the object, to the museum, to the market system, to the subjects seen as appropriate for art, and to the identity of the maker. The goal was not the emancipation of the polis per se, but of artists and even art itself. For Kaprow, the "un-artist" was a countermodel to the over-mythologized artist (e.g., Jackson Pollock) and to art as commodity. His claim was to undermine a hierarchy of ideas, to produce innovation for the sake of art.

Boal established a clear paradigm of difference between his work and traditional theatre while retaining enough of its aesthetic inheritance to clearly situate himself in the trajectory of theatre scholarship. Boal reconfigures recognizable elements of theatre with activist agendas: "The theatre has to be . . . regained, reclaimed, from the bourgeoisie which has preserved theatre in its own likeness as a closed system" (Boal, cited in Driskell 1975: 75). Thus the passive spectator is transformed into the spect-actor, the stage redefined as the focus of the gaze, the rehearsal is "a cultural political meeting" (Boal 1998: 48), and the performance is "not a catharsis but a stimulant" to real action (Boal, cited in Banu 1981: 6). His social justice goals were configured as aesthetic strategy itself, and it is here that feminist performance art finds common ground with Boal, a similarity explored in more depth in the next section.

Evalina Newman and I performed our relationship in the unstable contexts of the Watts community and the Los Angeles art world. Our theatre was often invisible, and like Boal's, it intended to provoke engagement: of the residents with their community, of local police in response to the vulnerability of Guy Miller residents, and of the art world with themes of race and class. But our performance was built upon the metaphor and reality of an ongoing relationship.

These real relationships did not end with the completion of any single piece: *Evalina and I* went on for years. Like extended family gatherings, between 1975 and 1986, Guy Miller residents participated in several performances. *Immigrants and Survivors* (1983), for example, a series of localized potluck dinners (invisible performances) throughout Los Angeles, culminated in a potluck with 150 women from amazingly diverse backgrounds, ages, and social circumstances. After dinner the performance continued, a cross between Forum Theatre and evangelistic testifying, with spontaneous stories of survival from recent immigrants, Native Americans, youth from group homes, disabled women, and several elderly black residents of Guy Miller Homes. In *The Dark Madonna* (1986), five of these Guy Miller residents took a prominent position in the Franklin Murphy Sculpture Garden, the site-specific stage for a 200-woman performance on race, racism, and healing.

Evalina was not present at these performances. In 1980, we commemorated her premature death from heart failure and celebrated her life and community work at the Woman's Building, where residents and I recreated her living room. Surrounded by photographs of Evalina, her artwork, her favorite furniture, and her unfinished quilt, an electric sewing machine chattered perpetually, propelled by an unseen foot.

Legislative Theatre and public performance art, 1990–2000

In 1992, Boal was approached by the Brazilian Workers' Party to run for *vereador* (a position similar to city councilman) of Rio de Janeiro. He was elected and immediately founded Legislative Theatre, furthering two fundamental principles of TO: "(1) to help the spectator become a protagonist of the dramatic action so that he can (2) apply those actions he has practiced in the theatre in real life" (Boal 1988b: 2).

Legislative Theatre was an ingenious use of public resources on behalf of the public through the method of theatre. Boal and the members of his theatre company, whom he hired as staff, organized populist forums to articulate and subsequently institute needed laws, e.g., disabled access and health care for the elderly. For four years, Boal and his staff worked in *barrios* with oppressed groups, holding council meetings in public squares, organizing theatre productions as civic discourse, and forming ongoing community development organizations within 19 neighborhoods.

Half way around the world, in Oakland, California, just as Boal was running his election, a team of artists led by photographer Chris Johnson and myself began a 10-year series of projects on the politics of youth. Jan Cohen-Cruz (1994) discusses how both Boal and I used performance to provide organizing tools in follow-up after the performance and as a vehicle for the voice of the powerless. She further explains that both of us drew on participants' experiences as the content of the work (1994: 117). Perhaps an even more fundamental similarity can be found in the underlying forces of urgency and opportunity that shaped our aesthetics. In the following case study, I explore how the intentional activism of Boal's theatre adds meaning to feminist performance art two decades later.

The social category of "urban youth"—a vast and disparate population facing impoverishment, dysfunctional homes, race discrimination, inadequate schooling, and stereotyping by mass media culture—first appeared as an urgent public issue in the 1990s. Throughout the decade, I collaborated with scores of Oakland artists and youth to produce performances and installations on public schooling, health care, criminal justice, and public policy issues. Our strategies included reflection on core issues (community policing, schooling, neighborhood safety, youth leadership, and civic participation), skill building (public speaking, computer literacy, writing, video, and photography), and workshops on team building, mentoring, and antiracism.

Like the several-year trajectory of Legislative Theatre, each Oakland project engaged significantly with relevant institutions and policy makers, one initiative building on the next. In *The Roof is on Fire* (1994), 120 students from eight public high schools expressed their opinions and experiences on education and other youth-selected topics before a national news audience. Youth leaders asked us to address sexuality in *Expectations* (1997), a six-week summer school program and installation on gender issues, institutional support systems, and political manipulation of teen parenting. Youth opinion also led us to focus on police–youth relations in *Youth, Cops, and Videotape* (1995), a training videotape for the police and *No Blood/No Foul* (1996), a highly-publicized basketball-game-as-performance between police and youth to support the passage of Oakland's first Youth Policy.

Then in 1999, dozens of black, red, and white cars with headlights blazing converged on the rooftop of the City Center Garage. In the spotlight of these beams, 100 police officers met in small groups with 150 local youth to talk candidly and intensely about crime, authority, power, and safety. An audience of 1,000 community members roamed freely between cars witnessing the spontaneous dialogue of youth and police exploring realities and stereotypes. Named after the police radio code for "emergency, clear the air waves," *Code 33* was a three-year performance project to explore institutional intervention through visual performance art concepts, to practically reduce police hostility toward youth, and to provide youth with a set of skills and a public context more conducive to civic inclusion.

By the time we produced *Code 33*, we had developed a model which included an extensive workshop period prior to a large public installation or theatrical event. For two years before the rooftop event, activities in different neighborhoods were constructed to serve a need but configured as "acts" within the whole "performance": weekly youth leadership team meetings; youth presentations before Neighborhood Crime Prevention Councils; art workshops for 350 probation and high school students; a prototype youth-police training series aired on local television; collaboration with non-profits and mentoring groups; and an artist team who designed the *Code 33* performance.

Our model was derived from process-based and media-critical visual arts theories and grew out of strategies that had continually evolved since 1970s feminist performance art. Here again, Kaprow's ideas were important in the transition from single event to complex and layered community performance. Kaprow emphasized art's meaning-making capacities. His focus on process could be extended such that all parts of a community-based artwork, including preparation and follow-up, were part of what I later termed an "expanded performance." Activities in *Code 33* were framed as components of (in Kaprow's terms) the entire life-like performance.

Although this work was not influenced by Boal's, and my own mentorship by Kaprow places me squarely in his visual arts lineage, *Code 33*'s deep structures bear an uncanny resemblance to Boal's Legislative Theatre. Speaking of this work, Boal suggests: "It should be understood that rehearsals are already a cultural political meeting in themselves . . . every exercise, every game, every technique is both art and politics" (1998: 48). Boal and Kaprow share this and other aesthetic ideas, particularly those having to do with expanding boundaries of art, and relate to the times from which they drew their inspiration. While Kaprow clearly gives permission to include all subject matter as relevant, it is in Boal's work that we find evidence of a highly refined aesthetic of social justice in operation, one that informs and deepens the critique of feminist performance art.

The public gaze and the politics of perception

TO and feminist art share a focus on the act of perceiving and the politics of perception. An often-related tale told by youth in *Code 33* goes like this: a black teenager is walking down a street and approaches a middle-aged white woman who involuntarily clutches her purse as she hurries past him. Knowing they are objects of a frightened, disapproving, and racially charged gaze, youth often respond with aggressive boisterousness. One youth spoke with frustrated helplessness: "They say, 'Oh, he black, he rob, he kill.' What can I do? I'm only sixteen years old. If nobody won't help me, I might as well do it."

Boal, too, gives an example of the relationship of the gaze to oppression, one he observed in the Satrouville mental hospital: "I was surprised at the expressions in [the nurses'] faces which changed according to whom they were looking at. When their eyes met mine, they were polite but when they looked at a kid, they became authoritarian, severe, and tough" (1988a: 22). He speculates on the personal impact of this intimidating intimate gaze.

> Let's assume that . . . I was taken for a sick person. How long would I have been able to stand it? . . . I am not saying that these kids became sick because of the nurses (gaze) . . . They all had their own families' histories prior to being there which included . . . alcoholic parents, poverty, overcrowded homes, dirty neighborhoods, drugs, physical abuse . . . They certainly did not need to be hurt by a simple gaze in order to be where they were. But this way of looking at people struck me in a powerful way.
>
> (Boal 1988a: 22)

When I began working on the Oakland projects, it was in part because of the image publicly projected by groups of youth who walked from high school to a bus stop near where I worked. I was curious: who were these young people with their hooded sweatshirts, baggy pants, and loud theatrical street discourse? The perceptual effect was an attractive one—textural, colorful, and sonorous, with a group synergy that clearly excluded me. I was vaguely aware of increasingly ominous images in the early 1990s' California mediascape: youth as unwed mothers, truants, dropouts, addicts, and criminals.

After a year volunteering in an Oakland high school, a shift occurred in my perceptual field. As crowds of youth walked by I no longer visually noted gray hooded sweatshirts but found myself unconsciously peering inside the hoods: was it one of the students from our class? Similarly, after a year of working as an artist with police officers, long enough to know several by name, I noticed another unbidden perceptual shift. Whereas earlier a black and white police car registered in my awareness by the pattern of its color, calling forth a furtive reexamination of my recent actions, now the car's appearance was a signal to peer into the window in an attempt to recognize and identify its occupants. My looking was refined and individuated by intimacy.

For five weeks during the development of *Code 33*, after-school sessions of intensely moderated encounters between 18 youth and 12 police officers explored their stereotypes of each other, developing an underlying fabric of relationship that carried over into their encounters on the street. In participants' evaluations, both youth and police stressed the shift in their perception of the other.

According to Mady Schutzman:

> To engage in Boal's "therapy" is to become situated in a space between the individual and the socialized category of all such individuals . . . Boal's techniques point the way to awareness of the society's politicization of gender, race, class, family, and/or psyche.
>
> (Schutzman 1994: 152)

This personal/political positioning links Legislative Theatre and *Code 33*-type works; in both there is a metaphoric situating of the individual such that his or her body, or presence, challenges stereotypical perceptions and categories. In *Code 33*, actors and spectators represented themselves as individuals in the context of social stereotypes portrayed daily in Oakland newspapers. Suspecting that my shifts in perception of youth and police might be shared, to some degree, by an audience, *Code 33* presented the community with a more intimate access to real people in the process of trying to understand each other.

Legislative Theatre, too, restages and reinvents mediated images in a public setting, forcing the audience through steps in the politics of perception toward intimacy:

> The aesthetic space is the creation of the audience: it requires nothing more than their attentive gaze in a single direction for this space to become "aesthetic", powerful, "hot", five-dimensional . . . the objects no longer carry out their usual daily signification, but become the stuff of memory and imagination . . . [E]very tiny gesture is magnified, and the distant becomes closer.
>
> (Boal 1998: 71–72)

The significance of a civic site selected as a stage is not only based on geography and metaphor (in this case, the rooftop garage overlooked City Hall, source of policy for the city's youth, and the rooftop's height represented street life elevated to theatrical status) but on significance provided by the rapt gaze of the audience. Who the audience is and what experiences they bring to the event—whether activists protesting police abuse, families of policemen, teachers, children, the elderly, African-American, Latino, white, or Southeast Asians, politicians, students, or businessmen—provides aesthetic texture and political significance to this gaze.

For an hour and a half, the *Code 33* performance oriented the attention of over 1,000 people, with another 1,000 or so unable to get in, gazing up to the rooftop. The unremarkable garage site was temporarily filled with significance: flooded with light (car headlights, stage lights, lit windows of nearby office buildings, the setting sun, and the spot of a circling police helicopter); covered with fields of red, white, and black cars; and surrounded by 30 television monitors perched on the perimeter walls. On a second stage were white picket fences and grass-covered platforms; youth video reporters, website displays, and a wall-sized projection of Oakland streets; and a large, red, X-shaped mentorship sign-up table. But it was the collective gaze of the audience that lifted the normally privatized discourse to civic relevance—a multivocal and simultaneous civic discourse spotlighting the relationship between youth and police before the media and the community.

As with Legislative Theatre, the drama of *Code 33* relied upon real people assuming the roles they played in life, with legitimate stakes in the event. Performers traversed roles: some policemen and policewomen dropped their impenetrable façade and expressed vulnerability and fear, some youth offered advice to officers. Boal discusses the importance of transitive roles:

> The frontier between the actor and the spectator is no longer impassable because there is an exchange of duties . . . It is the stable division of functions which has been trans-formed, as neither the actor nor the spectator plays the same role throughout the event . . . the double role of all theatrical work has been preserved as the action always takes place under the control of a critical gaze.
>
> (Boal, cited in Banu 1981: 6)

Of course not all performers experienced the transition between power and vulnerability. Very real power difference was always there ready to erupt at any sign of disturbance.

Code 33 began in tension with audience expectations of explosive confrontations. The narrative structure was loose, life-like, shaped by the agency of individual viewers who chose which group to listen to, whether to watch the television monitors, talk to friends they encountered on the roof, or stare out over the darkening city. There was time to take in information, reflect, and converse. In the second act community members traded places with the groups of youth and police, with 80 representatives from eight different Oakland neighborhoods reflecting on the impact of conflict between the city youth and police in their communities. The frame created by stage setting and audience gaze finally dissolved, diffusing into "life itself" as people left.

Boal distinguishes theatre as politics from political theatre: "In the latter case, the theatre makes comments on politics; in the former, the theatre is, in itself, one of the ways in which political activity can be conducted" (Boal 1998: 20). This suggests that such art must be assessed, in part, on the life-likeness of its theatrical moments, and redefined to include public actions that are lifted into art not only by the artists' techniques but also by the public gaze. This intricate psychology of perception and relationality ties Boal's theatre to that of 1990s' feminist performance such as *Code 33*. And so does his interest in demonstrable accountability toward the people with whom he works.

Both the Oakland Projects and Legislative Theatre were situated in mainstream, institutional contexts allied with governmental representatives empowered to take concrete actions. In Oakland during the 1990s, the growing population of youth of color, youth activism, and a political administration sympathetic to the needs of young people created an opportunity for artists to work with civic leaders on public agendas. Two police chiefs over five years supported (with bemusement and occasional confusion) a series of art productions and our access to officer time and equipment was considerable. Politicians were regular attendees at events and could be called on to increase media coverage with their public statements; in turn, their statements solidified their own resolve to establish policies favorable to youth. There was widespread social pressure to provide better education, more safety, and more positive opportunities for young people. In this social and political environment, in a city where one quarter of the residents are under the age of 21, we artists experienced an access to public institutions that one gains only rarely.

Visual and theatre artists working in communities struggle with a continuing quest to make their work effective and relevant. What they often cannot deliver is ongoing public policy and institutional change. At the end of three years, *Code 33* was a known community entity and there were several follow-up projects within the community and the police department. As I write, another training session is being planned by one of the officers who worked with us in the past. However, all of our efforts have not resulted in the permanent implementation of a youth-centered training program within an institutional police culture that is (the favorable disposition of its top leaders not withstanding), not prepared to do so by its mission, resources, staff, or structure.

In 1996 Augusto Boal was not reelected to his office, thus ending the first phase of Legislative Theatre. Such opportunities in artists' lives do not an art form make. But one cannot overestimate the importance of those moments, rare though they might be, when leadership and community align on important issues and welcome artists into the public sphere in meaningful ways. Such was the three-year time span immediately after the Russian Revolution, when the government made vast resources of people and materials available to artists to reenact key moments in recent history. At these times one begins to see the outline of an aesthetic of justice.

Legislative Theatre, a particularly brilliant application of Boal's entire body of theory brought into being by a particular and perhaps unrepeatable circumstance, is nonetheless inspirational. In this work we see that "the new" is not the key element of his aesthetic vangardism. Boal's quest to clarify and improve his social-aesthetic vision is an optimistic affirmation that through art life can be made better for the oppressed and underprivileged of the world. "The capacity to observe ourselves in action" is precisely what motivated the first generation of feminist performance artists in the 1970s to take to the streets, often surreptitiously, as characters and totems for public projection. More deliberately, performance artists from the Los Angeles Woman's Building combined their memory and imagination, particularly on themes of incest and violence, to "reinvent the past and to invent the future." Through their performance art they reached out to a broad audience with works that were relationship-affirming, assisting individual women's empowerment and, later, social transformation around multiple themes of oppression.

As for Augusto Boal, after a brief reorientation in the mid-nineties during which his staff of theatre artists scrambled for other forms of subsistence, he optimistically "entered a new phase: Legislative Theatre Without Legislator!" (Boal 1998: 115).

Bibliography

Banu, G. (1981) "Augusto Boal and the project of a self-managing theatre," *International Theatre Yearbook 1980*, Warsaw: International Association of Critics.

Boal, A. (1978) *Canadian Theater Review #19*, Summer.

—— (1988a) "Une expérience à Sartrouville," unpublished trans. by S. Epstein.

—— (1988b) "Three hypotheses for the cop in the head," unpublished trans. by S. Epstein.

—— (1998) *Legislative Theatre: Using performance to make politics*, trans. A. Jackson. London and New York: Routledge.

Cohen-Cruz, J. (1994) "Mainstream or margin: US activist performance and Theatre of the Oppressed," in M. Schutzman and J. Cohen-Cruz (eds) *Playing Boal: Theatre, therapy, activism*. London and New York: Routledge.

Driskell, C.B. (1975) "An interview with Augusto Boal," *Latin American Theatre Review*, 9: 1.

Kaprow, A. (2003) "Experimental art," in J. Kelley (ed.) *Allan Kaprow: Essays on the blurring of art and life*, 2nd edition, Berkeley, CA: University of California Press.

Kostelanetz, R. (1981) *Theatre of Mixed-Means*. New York: Archae Editions.

Kotz, M.L. (1990) *Rauschenberg*. New York: Harry N. Abrams.

Schutzman, M. (1994) "Brechtian shamanism: The political therapy of Augusto Boal," in M. Schutzman and J. Cohen-Cruz (eds) *Playing Boal: Theatre, therapy, activism*. London and New York: Routledge.

Redefining the private

From personal storytelling to political act

Jan Cohen-Cruz

According to Seyla Benhabib, "All struggles against oppression in the modern world begin by defining what had previously been considered private, non-public, and non-political as matters of public concern, issues of justice, and sites of power" (1992: 100). This transformation is seminal to Theatre of the Oppressed (TO), in which the sharing of personal stories is the point of departure for collective problem-solving around oppression. In what follows, I explore how and under what circumstances, in TO and other practices, the telling of a personal story uncovers a societal injustice and performs a political act.

I begin with the storyteller and the witness. What conditions allow a great range of people, even those unused to public participation, to tell personal stories in collective contexts? How does being heard play a role in the shift from the personal to the political? What does hearing a personal story ask of the witness? I then look at the larger group that identifies with the teller, especially considering where testimony overlaps with personal storytelling. Whereas some kinds of stories are so much a part of the teller's life that they need to be told for the teller to recognize their noteworthiness, testimony is a genre of stories that are often so out of the ordinary they need to be told as part of the teller's process of resuming a familiar life. According to Shoshana Felman, testimony is "the fragmentary product of a mind overwhelmed by occurrences that have not settled into understanding or remembrance . . . events in excess of our frames of reference" (1992: 5). Testimony frequently bespeaks large public horrors such as genocide and holocausts. But the line between personal story and testimony is not always obvious. The shift from story to testimony sometimes happens in the act of telling: what the teller has lived with as an everyday occurrence may become unbearable when revealed to people for whom such acts are unacceptable. Suddenly the teller has a context in which she can feel an extraordinary experience that she has nonetheless learned to live with as the breach it is. In the next section I describe three theatre artists—John O'Neal, Suzanne Lacy, and Augusto Boal—whose work with story instructively integrates the personal and political. I conclude by reflecting on balancing the needs of the individual and the group in storytelling processes.

The storyteller and the witness

The political potential of personal story is grounded not in particular subject matter but rather in storytelling's capacity to position even the least powerful individual in the proactive, subject position. For personal story draws on the authority of experience; everyone is an expert on his or her own life. It follows from the authority of experience that there are multiple views on what constitutes reality. As bell hooks writes, experience "affords a privileged critical location from which to speak" without denying others the same (1990: 29). This suggests how personal stories can be great levelers, diffusing hierarchy even in liberatory forms such as TO and other community-based performance modes. At key moments in TO workshops, participants move into small circles and the work becomes decentralized, the Joker no longer in the foreground, as people share private particulars of their lives. In much US community-based theatre, story circles happen *with* the facilitator also telling a personal story on a shared theme (the circle itself symbolic of the non-hierarchical relationships to which such work strives), she thereby becomes an equally vulnerable member of the group.

The equalizing underpinnings and collective context of storytelling support the individual bravery needed to speak out and tell a personal tale. An individual alone may feel she has nothing of interest to share. But invited to do so in a group where everyone else is doing the same makes it more possible. When Ann Kilkelly asked her Virginia Tech students for stories about being part of the various communities they inhabit, "They thought they had no experience, no stories of interest, yet as they told stories and wrote, the lives tumbled out, often in moments they tried to throw away" (Kilkelly, cited in Burnham 2001). The very act of speaking one's story publicly is a move toward subjecthood, toward agency, with political implications.

The story circle is one of the most pervasive forms of workshopping and playbuilding in community-based performance. Although there are many variations, circles typically involve from five to twenty-five people who choose a theme and then, one by one, tell a tale. Each story is welcome no matter what its style. In accordance with the Appalachia-based Roadside Theater for example, stories might recount family history, local history, folklore, ghost lore, a personal experience, or even riddles or jokes passed down through the generations. Participants in story circles typically focus on listening to the other stories and they then decide what to tell in response to what they have heard. Telling personal stories in this sense is a way to have a public conversation, to be in relationship to others. Such stories do not necessarily address oppression; they are as likely to be about cultural celebration and individual affirmation.

Stories of both celebration and oppression move toward the political but differently. Telling stories of cultural celebration is a way that members of marginalized groups express their own values and is an example of assets-based community organizing, emphasizing a group's strengths. To the degree that the teller has a strong sense of identity with an under- or misrepresented culture, the story is personal *and* political; attention to the story is attention to that culture as represented from within. Such stories often serve as counter-histories which make public points of view that were previously "hidden from history" (Rowbotham, cited in Perks and Thomson 1998: ix). Through stories that emphasize oppression, people see such occurrences as struggles in social context rather than as personal limitations: the larger inequities that underlie their personal experiences rise to the surface. Stories in TO are unresolved, because that is the opening through which spect-actors intervene with potential solutions. Participants find others with experiences of the same oppression and are both affirmed in the reality of their struggle and joined with potential allies to fight against it.

Storytelling literally makes knowledge through group interaction around hitherto private experiences. Such was the role of personal storytelling in the context of grass-roots consciousness-raising (CR) groups, one of the seminal processes of the 1970s' women's movement. In my own experience, a group of six or seven women would meet every two weeks in one of our apartments and talk about gender concerns from our everyday lives. We told personal stories to unearth their political implications. We'd hesitate; it seemed so petty to talk about our little relationships. But like women telling such stories in kitchens all across the country, we were discovering that many of our personal peeves were in fact socially structured to keep women in their place. Such knowledge emboldened us to change our everyday arrangements.

Personal stories with political implications shared in CR-like groups can become building blocks of theatrical expression with the addition of artist-facilitators. Particular techniques maximize the strengths of participants who are not necessarily trained actors. Scenes are often kept loose rather than written down and memorized. Sometimes a clear dramatic structure, such as Forum Theatre, is used to support nonactors. Other methods include director John Malpede's practices with homeless actors—calling out lines when they forget or having a more experienced actor double for a less experienced one, literally accompanying them on stage as a kind of shadow/support, simultaneously creating an interesting experience for spectators.

While artist/facilitators ought to be sensitive to people whose stories provide the basis of any enactment, this is crucial when the enactment is based on a traumatic testimony. As has been well-explored in drama therapy, if the enactment based on a personal story too literally repeats what happened, the teller may either be overcome with emotion or shut down. She may thus prefer the distance of witnessing someone else enacting her story. But if the enactment is too far from what happened, the teller may not reconnect enough. Drama therapist Robert Landy elaborates: "The overdistanced individual has blocked his ability to experience painful emotion . . . He remembers the past but detaches himself from the present feelings associated with past experiences" (1986: 99). Landy defines the ideal state as aesthetic distance, in which "one retains a piece of the overdistanced, cognitive observer and a piece of the underdistanced, affective actor" (1986: 100).[1]

Listeners, too, must balance intimacy and distance, especially in the case of highly emotional stories. Dori Laub writes, "For the testimonial process to take place, there needs to be a bonding, the intimate and total presence of *another*—in the position of one who hears. Testimonies are not monologues; they cannot take place in solitude" (1992: 70–71). Ultimately, the role of the witness is to assure that the storytelling experience serves the teller. But as Nancy Miller and Jason Tougaw assert, the transmission of testimony is "doubly complicated, first by the [teller's] own degree of temporal, spatial, and emotional distance from what is being documented, and second, by the listener's reactions" (2002: 12). These may include "a sense of outrage," "a flood of awe and fear," "foreclosure through facts," and "hyperemotionality" (Laub 1992: 72–73).

Philosopher Susan Brison, who survived a violent and life-threatening sexual attack, asserts the value of witnessing testimonies similar to one's own. She writes that group therapy with trauma survivors often leads to "greater compassion for their earlier selves by empathizing with others who experienced similar traumas" (Brison 2002: 63). Brison interprets this as "a shift from being the object or medium of someone else's (the perpetrator's) speech (or other expressive behavior) to being the subject of one's own" (2002: 68). By engaging with others who suffered the same predicament, the survivor finds her own perspective and subjecthood in the trauma, breaking the hold of the perpetrator's point of view, and defusing his power. Brison explains, "The act of bearing witness to the trauma facilitates this shift . . . by reintegrating the survivor into a community, reestablishing connections essential to selfhood" (2002: 68). This resonates with the original conception of Forum Theatre taking place in homogenous communities among people able to affirm firsthand each other's particular experience of oppression.

Even if not identifying with the story, witnesses can facilitate the survivor's mastery of the narrative. I experienced the witness' role in maintaining a balance between the teller's traumatic past and therapeutic present while co-facilitating a workshop with refugee teenagers who came to the US because of armed conflicts at home. The teenagers shared stories of some aspect of their lives in their homelands and each session, along with a team of New York University (NYU) student facilitators, we translated one of them into an art form be it photography, rap, or improvisation. But the team experienced a crisis of representation when a 17-year old told of rebels bursting into her home in Sierra Leone and before her eyes, killing her father and raping her sister. The NYU student facilitating this session, Ryan Baum, saw no value for her in illustrating these acts realistically so chose a variation on Image Theatre and simply called out words suggested by the story—fear, grief, aloneness. In response, participants constructed silent images of these words and narrated (imagistically) the story back to her. Then everyone sat in a circle and thanked her for sharing the story, acknowledging the strength that she demonstrates in her life in New York. This was intended to underline her present life and not let her slip back into the past of the traumatic story. A few months later, we presented a work-in-progress for another group of refugee teenagers, including this story and our enacted responses. In a post-performance dialogue session, she told the group that sometimes people look fine on the outside but are carrying more than they can bear on the inside. She thanked the workshop for making a space where she could move the story out. Speaking publicly in this way, she continued to be active in relation to her story while putting it at a distance from her current self.

This experience drove home the necessity yet potential harm of the witness. The refugee teenagers *wanted* to talk about the wars. Our presence made it more possible for them to take in the horror of *each others'* stories and see these experiences as political wrongs rather than private crosses to bear. We provided a safe space by at once listening empathically to their travail and not stepping over the edge into identification. Dominick LaCapra describes the role we played as "secondary witness[es]," who should "neither confuse their own voice or position with the victim's nor seek facile uplift, harmonization, or closure" (LaCapra, cited in Miller and Tougaw 2002: 6). By not merging with the young refugee, we reasserted her new life in a country on whose soil war is not raging. Through empathy, we established a human context in the present that contrasted radically with the circumstances of her traumatic past.

Philosopher Adriana Cavarero sees the central role of the witness, exemplified by our use of images with the Sierra Leone teenager, as narrating the story back to the teller. Cavarero argues that we do not see the meaning of our own life story because we live it. For that we need someone else to tell us our tale: "In the heart of everyone beats the question 'who am I?' and . . . it needs as a response one's own story narrated by another" (2000: 136). For Cavarero, we can never master our own story—it's the pattern our life has taken, only known after it has happened. In contrast, stories told in TO are self-narrated, at least initially, and are not finished but rather incomplete situations replayed in order to seek alternatives to the direction in which they are pulling the unhappy protagonist. Their unfinishedness is part of the liberating dynamic; the witness' role is to enact other directions that the story, and the teller's life, might take, not to reflect back the teller's self-narrative. Spect-actors of TO stories—witnesses in effect—classically respond from a place of identification, not difference. Both have value.

Critic Cheryl Razack raises important questions regarding what witnesses do with stories. Addressing a Canadian organization that collected and intended to publish the stories of immigrant women, Razack asks:

To what uses will these stories be put? Will someone else then take and theorize from them? Will they serve to reassure everyone that Canada really is diverse, full of folklore? Who will control how they are used? Will immigrant women tell a particular kind of story in a forum they do not control?

(Razack 1993: 84)

While the professional has the know-how to bring stories to a public, their presentational form must nonetheless benefit the teller.

Collective identification with personal story

In Forum Theatre, when the story is enacted, it is no longer just that person's tale. Each person's story is but the raw material from which the scene, with which everyone in the group must identify, is created. In testimony about social oppressions, the teller is speaking on behalf of not just himself but a whole class of people struggling against similar unjust treatment. Under what conditions are people with no social cachet individually not only listened to but treated as catalysts, their experience deemed important, and their authority to speak for a group recognized?

As Shoshana Felman writes, to testify is "to produce one's own speech as material evidence for truth—to accomplish a speech act rather than formulate a statement" (1992: 5). Testimony in a legal context refers to serious statements made under oath that may hold life and death consequences; the term also means a public declaration of religious experience. In both cases, testimony contains the notion of answering to a higher power, be it the nation state in whose realm the court is situated or the spiritual force in whose realm institutions of faith are located. One puts one's hand on the Bible and swears to tell the whole truth. The act of giving testimony unites the teller with the listeners by evoking shared values. The context of an institution whose authority is accepted renders the individual's voice within that context authoritative as well.

Political action and personal therapy are intertwined in testimony, given its "double function" of "producing social discourse and initiating individual recovery" (Miller and Tougaw 2002: 13). There is, however, a danger of relegating the individual to a secondary position in the interest of furthering the social goal. Orly Lubin describes an example of imbalance between the value for the individual and for the collective in the uses of the testimony of Zivia Lubetkin.

One of the leaders of the Warsaw ghetto uprising of April 1943, Lubetkin immigrated to Palestine and gave her testimony twice. The first time she told her story privately to two Zionist leaders, one of whom writes: "She told us—in tears, with pauses, in Yiddish, in Hebrew, in silences—what was in her heart. The story was unimaginably tragic. There was nothing in it of heroism, no glory, but it was as if she herself was bearing the entire six million" (Rabinowitz, cited in Lubin 2002: 133). The second time, two days later, she gave her testimony publicly: "Relinquishing the first-person grammatical form, she translated her personal experience into a collective narrative," embodying the "new Jew" that fought Nazism and "thus answered a collective need" to know that some Jews did not go to their slaughter like sheep (Rabinowitz, cited in Lubin 2002: 133). Lubin analyzes the expanded role of the witnesses to Lubetkin's testimony: "Lubetkin allows her listeners to do more than enable the testimony; she allows them to mold it, to determine its narrative form and its symbolic use. Making herself subservient to the group, she tells a story that they need to hear" (Lubin 2002: 134). Lubetkin's personal trauma was resituated at an alarming speed, from her own experience to a collectively sustaining image. I wonder if and how such a radical reinterpretation of the story helped her through her own despair even as I can imagine relief at having the story be so meaningful to her new community.

Despite personal costs, the teller can absolutely galvanize a community that identifies with her. Such was the case of Rosa Parks, whose story was chosen by civil rights leaders to be the symbol of bus desegregation for a large, public audience. In December 1955, when Parks transgressed Jim Crow-era laws segregating people of color to the back of the bus, she was not the first. The previous March, "a feisty high school student named Claudette Colvin . . . defended her right to the seat in language that brought words of disapproval from passengers of both races" (Branch 1988: 120). In October, Mary Louise Smith likewise refused to give up her seat for a white woman. Yet civil rights leaders decided that Smith's alcoholic father and substandard living conditions—"one of those see-through clapboard shacks"— made her "no better suited to stand at the rally point than was Claudette Colvin" (Branch 1988: 127). Parks, on the other hand, was considered so beyond reproach by people of color and whites alike that her personal story of injustice was selected for courtroom dramatization. The timing was so ripe that the Montgomery Bus Boycott was organized to protest her arrest. Parks' story became *the* story through which the community organized and drew a line: no more arresting Negroes for not giving up their seats to white people in public buses. As the Reverend Martin Luther King Jr. articulated when rallying the community to join the boycott,

> [N]obody can doubt the boundless outreach of [Parks'] integrity. Nobody can doubt the height of her character, nobody can doubt the depth of her Christian commitment . . . And you know, my friends, there comes a time when people get tired of being trampled over by the iron feet of oppression.
>
> (King, cited in Branch 1988: 138)

And yes, the crowd responded, yes, their voices rose up, yes.

A play, too, can resituate personal stories as the expression of a particular group. Boal experienced such a dynamic with a play he staged in 1962. It was based on personal stories about a metal workers' strike in Santo André and was written by one of the workers. At a performance in Santo André, the man on whom the villain was based protested vigorously, leading to interaction with other audience members upon whom other characters were based. What followed spontaneously anticipated Forum Theatre in the active audience involvement elicited: "The real people other characters were modeled upon got up on stage and each incarnated themselves in front of their actors, the scene fragmenting into explosive simultaneous dialogues with worker-models of characters pitted against actors and their characters" (Boal 2001: 203). In the ensuing mayhem, Boal tried to convince angry spectators that it was just a play, a fiction, not them. They would have none of Boal's explanation, feeling grievously misrepresented. Finally they agreed that the actors could continue to speak the script but they would correct them as necessary. This performance intrigued Boal in its interaction of the image and the reality of the same character. He also recognized the dynamizing effect on the people on whom the play was based and the level of interaction precipitated when not just an individual but a whole community gets to see performed what they themselves presumably said or did.

This production also raises the issue of intimacy and distance—i.e., the degree of closeness to or remove from what actually happened—beyond the storyteller and on to the people who identify with it. While a play is always a representation, even when based on an actual event, such recognition is difficult for an audience watching a play of and about themselves, using their very words. For the Santo André audience, this play *was* their story. That intimacy caused a problematic but ultimately productive level of engagement, resituating the play at the intersection between an aesthetic event and a documentary of their very lives.

Critical storytelling in theatrical practice: O'Neal, Lacy, Boal

Not all storytelling is liberating. One might use personal stories to come to any conclusions. Personal story risks merely reproducing dominant ideology, as with a rape narrative through which the victim blames herself: "I shouldn't have been there . . . The way I dressed was asking for it." In this section, I discuss exemplary practices of three artists whose work with story does have a liberating component.

In 1963, artist/activist John O'Neal co-founded the Free Southern Theatre as a cultural wing of the civil rights movement that used stories to promote agency in people who were at once the least powerful and most affected. Rather than telling them what to do or think, the company's performances were intended to stimulate post-show discussion. The exchange of stories proved a better way of having dialogue than argument because, explains O'Neal,

> Adversarial debates reward people who are trained in their techniques. Those tend to be people who have the largest vocabularies and largest egos and most willingness to claim ground and hold it. Which merely affirms the problem you're starting with in the first place. So instead of standing on stage and answering questions, I moved off the stage and sat in the audience and said, "Why don't you tell me a story that the experience of the theatre evoked in you?"
>
> (O'Neal 2002)

In O'Neal's current initiative, *The Color Line*, story gathering is part of an assets-based approach to dismantling racism. One artist, one educator, and one activist in each of several towns collaborate around the local legacy of civil rights. The artist gathers personal stories on the subject that are used in some way thereafter with the help of the educator and the activist. The idea is that people may have limited material resources but are rich in experience. The stories are vessels for what people have learned and what they find meaningful that can be translated into educational and activist projects.

Suzanne Lacy, who creates large scale, visually-compelling performances with nonactors about issues that concern them, is cautious in her use of personal story. While she weaves consciousness-raising processes into performative pieces, she finds that personal stories tend to distort perspective, especially when they do not move to a larger level:

> Everyone operates within a personal narrative history and present that centralizes them within a very vast world. One of the problems with race relations today [Lacy has worked intensively in cross-racial contexts] is how white people centralize the narrative. Like, "I hurt so much because you are oppressed." As a director I remove myself from any given single representative narrative, and focus on creating mass or political

perspective through the commonality of multiple narratives—the spaces between the people.

(Lacy 2002)

Over the past decade, shifting her focus from women to teenagers, Lacy has continued to problematize personal story. She is interested in what the young people's stories reveal about young people as a group. She helps young people analyze the social conditions that result in their collective behavior. The stories have become source material for performances and also for a curriculum that builds from a focus on themselves, to their personal relationships, to their institutional and familial alliances, and then to their public position: "We'd ask, 'How do people treat you on the bus?' and they began to make the links. The kids operate as beings in terms of their own personal narrative but they also operate as symbols for a culture, with a political impact" (Lacy 2002). Personal stories raise awareness of the kids as both "beings" and "symbols," real individuals who are often treated generically as representatives of a (maligned) group.

The movement of Lacy's work with young people, from their individual experience to the social implications, resonates with Boal's concept of ascesis. As Adrian Jackson describes,

> [W]e work on the case of an individual, and from that individual case we extrapolate into the group present, and then, sometimes, from that group into the larger society of which it is a microcosm or a fragment. This process Boal calls "ascesis," the movement from the phenomenon to the law which regulates phenomena of that kind; and his concept of "osmosis" enables this free play from one arena to the other, suggesting as it does that no individual consciousness can remain unmarked by societal values.
>
> (Jackson, cited in Boal 1995: xx)

With ascesis as an underpinning, personal stories in the Forum Theatre process are combined, and invented elements inserted to get to the scenario that the actors will perform. Boal writes, "All the singular elements of the individual story must acquire a *symbolic* character, and shed the constraints of singularity, uniqueness" (1995: 40). Boal identifies singularity as the domain of the psychotherapist, and generalization as the terrain of the theatre artist. He emphasizes that TO "is the theatre of the first person plural. It is absolutely vital to begin with an individual account, but if it does not pluralize of its own accord we must go beyond it by means of analogical induction"—that is, proceeding by analogy rather than identification (1995: 45). I have by and large been astounded by the significant discoveries people have made through this process. Although Boal counsels participants to make sure they feel represented in the story brought to forum, given the degree of self-assertion required, it is questionable if people necessarily do so. And does the collectivization of the story inadvertently take it away from the teller? Attention must be paid to balancing the usefulness of stories for both the identifying group and the individual teller.

Boal, O'Neal, and Lacy all fulfill what Benhabib, cited at the beginning of this chapter, calls redefining the "private, non-public, and non-political" as "matters of public concern, issues of justice, and sites of power" but they do so in different ways. Boal proposes a structured approach to illuminating the political realities embedded in personal stories. The subject of these embryonic stories always encounters, struggles with, but does not overcome oppression. Thus an opening is provided for public problem-solving. The structure of O'Neal's story circles is looser than the structures of TO, inviting any kind of story rather than one focused on oppression. O'Neal sees dialoguing through story rather than arguing as providing an accessible point of entry into a liberatory practice. Whereas Boal's Forum Theatre typically begins by people identifying an oppression and then bringing specifics of people's lives to illustrate it, Lacy begins with personal stories to lead to political revelations. For example, as long as rape was considered a private matter, it was beyond the ken of political guidelines. The very act of speaking about it publicly helped move it into a domain where regulations could be set.

All three of these artists use institutional links and partnerships with people from other professions able to concretely address inequities the stories make public, to move the insights garnered through personal story into political realms, but again do so differently. During the civil rights movement, O'Neal allied the Free Southern Theatre with a non-governmental organization, SNCC (Student Non-violent Co-ordinating Committee), and still regularly partners with activists and educators. Lacy worked together with maligned teenagers and their nemeses, police. A decade of performance work in Oakland grounded in stories and conversations between them led to better police training especially in regard to male teenagers of color, who hitherto voiced bitter stories of their treatment at the hands of "Oakland's finest." Boal became a city counselor of Rio de Janeiro and used the revelations of personal stories gathered through Forum Theatre as a dossier pointing the way to needed legislation. Indeed, over a dozen laws were passed on that basis.

It is worth noting that institutionalizing the movement from personal story to political act does not require artists. There is a history of national commissions following traumatic periods using personal stories of trauma as the starting point for moving on. The Truth and Reconciliation Commission hearings in South Africa, for example, helped put closure on apartheid through the public telling of personal accounts of transgressions during that terrible period. For some people, the hearings at least uncovered what happened to loved ones who had "disappeared" after military roundups. For others, there could be no reconciliation without justice, i.e., the very conditions of amnesty that gave people the safety to speak also cancelled the project's efficacy.

Reflections on the political master swimmer

Philosophically, personal story at the service of political action relies on a relationship between the individual and the larger category of human being. Boal and philosopher Adriana Cavarero understand the role of story in that relationship differently. Cavarero recognizes the limitations of her own métier, philosophy, which is concerned with "the universality of Man," whereas biographical knowledge "regards the unrepeatable identity of someone . . . The first asks, *what* is Man? The second asks instead of someone *who* he or she is" (2000: 13). Boal is also sensitive to the interplay between Man and man. But whereas man in Cavarero's discourse is not knowable except posthumously and then only by a narrator, it is the man, in person, in his struggle to live, with whom Boal is most concerned.

Boal addresses the absurdity of privileging the *idea* of a person over actual individuals, universal Man over specific people, in an allegorical story (Boal 1994: 134). A much beloved master swimmer, who had saved many people from watery deaths, was walking by a swimming pool when he heard the cries of a drowning man. The master swimmer told the drowning man that as soon as at least 20 people were drowning he would save them because he was a *political* master swimmer. Boal thus captures how the abstract notion of the political can obscure the needs of actual people. The grounding in people's stories concretizes abstractions and focuses on people's lived experience, so relevant to why personal stories are such sturdy building blocks for collective ideas and actions.

A related danger is an overly-simplified notion of a man or woman resulting from overly-fixed narratives. Here the risk is reducing tellers to a singular identity, be it "the oppressed," "the oppressor," or any other fixed self. Take the woman from a caregivers support group a friend of mine was facilitating who came to him after a year and said, "I don't want to come to this group anymore. The only time I feel really bad is when I'm in this group." He accepted her departure but asked her to come one last time and tell the others why she was leaving. In fact, she eventually returned, having opened the group to the need to expand the parameters of their discussions beyond their hard lot as caregivers. As this story suggests, while people have much to gain by investigating solutions to their oppression, constantly telling such stories can inadvertently reinforce oppression rather than liberate from it. A similar dynamic occurred in our teen refugee group where a solution was also found by a group member. After a period of very heavy stories, one of the teenagers exuberantly created a fashion show featuring marvelous clothing from her native Sierra Leone. In its affirmation of cultural riches, the fashion show did as much for the group negotiating past and present as did the works coming out of their traumatic histories.

Theatre-maker Jerzy Grotowski calls the best kind of disciple the unfaithful one who adheres to the principles of the work if not its letter. In that spirit, I am an unfaithful disciple of TO, and don't always elicit stories that position the protagonist as oppressed. Working with women who had recently been released from prison, I found them uncomfortable with Forum Theatre structure. They wanted to be appreciated for their good traits; they'd been all too in touch with their oppressed selves in prison. While their response to Forum Theatre was luke-warm, they were quite energized during workshop breaks, singing a cappella together, dancing routines they all knew. They sought a collective pleasure rather than a collective identification with oppression. We hence developed a hybrid of Image Theatre and "girl group" song and dance. We'd sculpt images of their current struggles and then write pop songs about them. The choreography that accompanied the songs was adapted from the images. Each woman got a turn in front, doing a verse, but was always backed up by the others and grounded in the comfort zone of the cultural expression they knew they were good at, pop song and dance. The agency of the people with whom we are working trumps adherence to any one specific technique. As facilitators who may fancy ourselves political master swimmers, we must be ready, nonetheless, to join participants in the dances they propose.

Note

1   See also Julie Salverson (1996) and her chapter in this volume.

Bibliography

Benhabib, S. (1992) *Situating the Self: Gender, community and post-modernism in contemporary ethics*. New York: Routledge.

Boal, A. (1994) "The political master swimmer," in M. Schutzman and J. Cohen-Cruz (eds) *Playing Boal: Theatre, therapy, activism*. London and New York: Routledge.

—— (1995) *The Rainbow of Desire: The Boal method of theatre and therapy*, trans. A. Jackson. London and New York: Routledge.

—— (2001) *Hamlet and the Baker's Son: My life in theatre and politics*, trans. A. Jackson and C. Blaker. London and New York: Routledge.

Branch, T. (1988) *Parting the Waters: America in the King years 1954–63*. New York: Simon and Schuster.

Brison, S.J. (2002) *Aftermath: Violence and the remaking of a self*. Princeton, NJ: Princeton University Press.

Burnham, L. (2001) "Telling and listening in public: Factors for success," in D. Cocke, L. Burnham, and E. Kohl (eds) *Connecting Californians*. San Francisco, CA: James Irvine Foundation.

Cavarero, A. (2000) *Relating Narratives: Storytelling and selfhood*. London and New York: Routledge.

Felman, S. (1992) "Education and crisis, or the vicissitudes of teaching," in S. Felman and D. Laub (eds) *Testimony: Crises of witnessing in literature, psychoanalysis, and history*. New York: Routledge.

hooks, b. (1990) *Yearning*. Boston, MA: South End Press.

Lacy, S. (2002) Unpublished interview with the author, Oakland, CA.

Landy, R. (1986) *Drama Therapy: Concepts and practices*. Springfield, IL: Charles C. Thomas.

Laub, D. (1992) "Bearing witness, or the vicissitudes of teaching," in S. Felman and D. Laub (eds) *Testimony: Crises of witnessing in literature, psychoanalysis, and history*. New York: Routledge.

Lubin, O. (2002) "Holocaust testimony, national memory," in N.K. Miller and J. Tougaw (eds) *Extremities: Trauma, testimony and community*. Urbana and Chicago, IL: University of Illinois Press.

Miller, N.K. and Tougaw, J. (2002) *Extremities: Trauma, testimony and community*. Urbana and Chicago, IL: University of Illinois Press.

O'Neal, J. (2002) Unpublished interview with the author, California.

Perks, R. and Thomson, A. (1998) (eds) "Introduction," in *The Oral History Reader*. New York and London: Routledge.

Razack, S. (1993) "Storytelling for social change," in R. Bannerji (ed.) *Returning the Gaze*. Toronto: Sister Vision Press.

Salverson, J. (1996) "Performing Emergency: Witnessing, popular theatre, and the lie of the literal," *Theatre Topics*, September, 6:2.

Tougaw, J. (2002) "Testimony and the Subjects of AIDS Memoirs," in N.K. Miller and J. Tougaw (eds) *Extremities: Trauma, testimony and community*. Urbana and Chicago, IL: University of Illinois Press.

Metaxis

Dancing (in) the in-between

Warren Linds

To better understand the significance of metaxis in Theatre of the Oppressed (TO), we need to return to the word's origin in Plato: "All spirits occupy the middle ground between humans and gods. As mediators between the two, they fill the remaining space, and so make the universe an interconnected whole" (Plato 1994: 43–44).[1] "Middle ground" in this passage is translated from the Greek μεταξυ (*metaxu*) meaning "between + in, in the state of in the middle, betwixt, between, between-whiles, in the interval, neither good nor bad" (Liddell 1996: 1115). Plato underlines that *metaxu* is a dynamic space between two separate things where mediation keeps the universe together. Eric Voegelin calls this the tension "in-between the poles of man and of the reality he experiences" (1989: 72). In Voegelin's view, human existence takes place in tension in the space between, not at the poles. Rather than seeking to move to one pole or the other we should explore this in-betweenness.

For Boal, "theatre is born when the human being discovers that it can observe itself; when it can . . . see itself seeing" (1995: 13). He speaks of metaxis as:

> [T]he state of belonging completely and simultaneously to two different, autonomous worlds: the image of reality and the reality of the image. The participant shares and belongs to these two autonomous worlds; their reality and the image of their reality, which she herself has created.
>
> (Boal 1995: 43)

Participant and audience belong completely to both these worlds. Through the process of metaxis, theatre becomes the space for interplay between the actual and the imagined, the tangible and the ephemeral. "The scene, the stage, becomes the rehearsal space for real life" (Boal 1995: 44). Protagonists practice in this second world (the aesthetic) in order to modify the first (the social). Boal calls this "aesthetic transubstantiation" (1995: 43). Yet metaxis does not just occur at the border between the real and the fictional; it also exists as an encounter between participants and their role in the play or image, between spect-actors and actors, and between the actor's meaning of the play and how meaning emerges throughout the workshop process. Here multiple circles of metaxis interact.

The notion of embodiment is central to understanding this in-between state because meaning emerges through our bodies acting in a metaxic space. Embodiment refers to the double sense of the body as living and the experiential structure or context of cognition where living is embedded. The body is not an object, but a grouping of constantly changing lived-through meanings. Self-observation through metaxis allows us to see knowing as it is enacted in each moment of the present, not as something which already exists. We begin to understand Boal's "rehearsal for reality" (Jackson, cited in Boal 1992: xxi) as a reworking of "real acts" (Boal 1979: 141) in a constantly shifting *as-if* world. Performance, whether in play or in presentation, enables continuous disruption of the taken-for-granted, necessitating questioning of the binary distinction between body and mind. Through metaxic action, our bodies become generative sites of knowing; learning is tangible and available for future exploration.

To expand our understanding of metaxis as an embodied phenomenon emerging in physical and social space, what follows is an exploration of in-between space as it manifests in contexts very different from TO—that is, in the biology of cognition, systems theory, complexity theory, and phenomenology.

The biology of cognition

Expression always goes beyond what it transforms.

(Merleau-Ponty 1969: 69)

Cognition is not the representation of a pre-given world by a pre-given mind but is rather the enactment of a world and a mind on the basis of history of the variety of actions that a being in the world performs.

(Varela *et al.* 1991: 9)

According to Francisco Varela, Evan Thompson, and Eleanor Rosch, cognition does not happen in the mind of the perceiver/actor, but rather between the perceiver/actor and the world he/she inhabits. The perceiver does not live independently (in a vacuum) and construct meaning about the world, since "what counts as a relevant world is inseparable from the structure of the perceiver" (1991: 13). We know the world because our bodies interact with/in the world through the structure permitted by our senses that coevolved with the world. In the enactive view, "cognition has no ultimate foundation or ground beyond its history of embodiment" (1991: xx).

Inspired by the Buddhist philosophy of a middle way (a nondualistic approach which proposes codependence between self and world), Varela *et al.* propose a path of being-in-the-world in which we are open to change and motivated by compassion. As contrasted with a worldview that locates knowing in minds, and knowledge as a relatively fixed and permanent commodity, an enactive approach engages us in experiencing the everyday world with more than a desire to ground, objectify, fix, and reify. If there is a location for the in-between, it is not an objectively precise space. Varela *et al.* refer to that awareness which is not attached to any one body, event, or concept as "groundlessness" (1991: 144). If knowing is understood as anchored, it is anchored within the unfolding of events and is perpetually adrift in the movement of relationships. Groundlessness welcomes the unexpected. Whenever we find ourselves holding tightly to being in a certain place, or seek to control outcomes, the in-between invites us to step into "another domain where coexistence takes place" (Maturana and Varela 1992: 246), a both/and rather than an either/or space. When knowing and experiencing are located in the shifting terrain of in-between-ness, new possibilities emerge for action and knowing.

In TO, we work together to dramatize collective stories activating the whole body through nonverbal and verbal expression. Participants can see themselves in the nonverbal images based on stories by others. The stories are not explained. This emphasizes showing over telling; it also invites spect-actors to "write" themselves into the stories of others.

Through activation of images using our bodies we move from a nonverbal static picture of an experience to a story in movement. We move back and forth in time and space, providing actors with opportunities to investigate, through their interacting bodies, the characters they have been given by the storyteller. Their only resources for those characters are their interpretations of the stories, their own bodies, their own perceptions of themselves through their bodies, and their interaction with others in the scene.

The Forum Theatre performance extends this process. Boal (1995) links the question of self to the transformation of action in Forum Theatre:

> Who is the "I"? . . . It is very easy for us to decide—in fatalistic fashion—that we are the way we are, full stop, end of story. But we can also imagine—in a more creative fashion—that the playing cards can be re-dealt.
>
> In this dance of potentialities, different powers take the floor at different times—potential can become act, occupy the spotlight and then glide back to the sidelines, powers grow and diminish, move in to the foreground and then shrink into the background again—everything is mutable. Our personality is what it is, but also what it is becoming.
>
> (Boal 1995: 39)

Groundlessness, the very condition revealed in common sense, is "knowing how to negotiate our way through a world that is not fixed and pre-given but that is continually shaped by the types of actions in which we engage" (Varela *et al.* 1991: 144). The value of this living cognition consists in being able to select, within broad constraints, the relevant issues that need to be addressed at a given moment. What is relevant to the moment is contextually determined by the sense of what is needed and not needed. To draw attention to the reciprocal and dialogical relationships in which organism and environment, self and other, are intertwined, Varela *et al.* call this process of cognition through everyday experience "co-emergence."

Humberto Maturana and Francisco Varela (1992) describe the process of co-emergence as it occurs in biological systems. A self-organizing system like a cell has a set of relations among its components that characterize the system as belonging to a particular class; whether sunflower, cat, or human being, the function of each component is to participate in the production or transformation of the set of relations. "The product of its operation is its own organization" (Maturana and Varela 1980: 80). Examples of this form of organization include the way ants self-organize into ant-hills, birds into flocks, and humans into social and political collectives. Although control of a complex system's organization (or dynamic structure) is distributed (or decentralized) among its parts, the system as a whole both adapts (or learns) and maintains a coherent identity. Within this systemic conception of cognition, component structures are interconnected, adaptive, and constantly changing in response to fluctuations within and among other aspects of the system.

Shifts within systems or structures are evidence of learning through adaptation. Reciprocal "perturbations," or slight changes or shifts in the system, trigger a kind of coevolution, as other aspects of the system also change in response. A perturbation itself does not determine how the organism evolves, but it triggers the organism to change its structure. Maturana and Varela (1980) call this phenomenon "structural coupling."

If I have a living system . . . then this living system is in a medium with which it interacts. Its dynamics of state result in interactions with the medium, and the dynamics of state within the medium result in interactions with the living system. What happens in interaction? Since this is a structure determined system . . . the medium triggers a change of state in the system, and the system triggers a change of state in the medium. What change of state? One of those which is permitted by the structure of the system.

(Maturana 1987: 75)

This process and these relationships constitute knowledge and cognition which Varela *et al.* elaborate further as involving embodied action whereby "sensory and motor processes, perception and action are fundamentally inseparable" (1991: 172–73).

Varela *et al.* exemplify this notion of experiential and enacted cognition through a discussion of color (1991: 157–71). Claiming colors are neither out there independent of our perception and knowing, nor are they inside us, independent of the world, Varela *et al.* see cognition encompassing both—color is both experienced and belongs to the world in which we live. Echoing Boal's notion of the birth of theatre, this middle path resolves the classic inner versus outer, mind versus body debate by looking at knowledge not as representation but as embodied enaction:

How can we talk about the seer of the sight who is not seeing its sight? Conversely, how can we speak of sight that is not being seen by its seer? Nor does it make any sense to say that there is an independently existing seeing going on somewhere without any seer and without any sight being seen.

(Varela *et al.* 1991: 222)

Another example of structural coupling in the realm of biological cognition is illustrated by this metaphor:

To draw a carp, Chinese masters warn, it is not enough to know the animal's morphology, study its anatomy or understand the physiological functions of its existence. They tell us that it is also necessary to consider the reed against which the carp brushes each morning while seeking its nourishment, the oblong stone behind which it conceals itself, and the rippling of water when it springs toward the surface. These elements should in no way be treated as the fish's environment, the milieu in which it evolves or the natural background against which it can be drawn. They belong to the carp itself . . . The carp must be apprehended as a certain power to affect and be affected by the world [emphasis added].

(Morley 1992: 183)

Understanding oneself in this way is to sense the space of possibility as being constantly coenacted and reenacted in our encounters. The space of metaxis is thus a moving in-between to which we belong, of which we are a part, and in which we participate. Our task as enactors then becomes awaiting, performing, testing, noticing, listening to choices and options that keep the space of possibility alive.

This is exemplified by a simple series of exercises called The Space Series (Boal 1992: 116–17) which develops an awareness of the space in which we work and interact. Participants walk around the room, trying to fill empty floorspace:

Whenever anyone sees an empty space, they go and fill it with their body, but they can't stay there, so a moment later it is empty again, except that someone comes to fill it, but he can't stop there either . . .

(Boal 1992: 116)

Play creation and performance in TO is a dialogical and social process; it is also a complex system in which people are continually finding, filling, and releasing spaces for dialogue and interaction.

Systems approach and complexity theory

Cyberneticist Norbert Wiener coined the term systems theory (1948). Under the systemic view, ecosystems, human beings, and cultural spaces are viewed as whole systems characterized by flows of energy and materials between, and among, component parts. The emphasis in a systems perspective is on how the whole arises from the interrelations among the parts. While the concept of feedback is not new, interpretation of its function has been revised with the finding that minute changes, operating in feedback loops, evoke systemic changes. Feedback loops maintain recursive self-regulation: an initial change affects the last element of a cycle of changes and the last element affects the first.

Wiener gives the example of the action of a boat's steersman as an instance of feedback.[2] When the boat deviates from a preset course, the steersman compensates by moving the rudder in the other direction, sometimes continuing to a point of over steering in the other direction. Within the continual feedback from the direction of the boat's journey through the water, the skill of steering consists of keeping the oscillation as smooth as possible. Examples abound in nature, where the principle of feedback and self-regulation characterizes ecosystems, and feedback loops form networks of interdependent interactions. Tendencies for species to undergo exponential population growth are self-regulated through a balance of interactions within the system such as the relationship between fluctuating food supply and population size, and the terrain upon which the species depends for shelter or warmth.

Against classical understandings of physics where the magnitude of change is directly proportional to the applied force, in complex systems small changes can produce large effects. Known as the butterfly effect (Lorenz 1979) or "sensitive dependence on initial conditions" (Gleick 1987: 23) in the field of meteorology, a small change arising from the flapping of a butterfly's wing can theoretically create a disturbance that will eventually change atmospheric conditions. Since small changes are amplified as they feedback on each other, this produces complex patterns of unanticipated consequences which make it impossible to forecast long-term behavior.

This idea is not new. Ben Franklin's folk poem illustrates far-reaching consequences indicative of the notion of the global effects of a minute factor:

For want of a nail, the shoe was lost;
For want of a shoe, the horse was lost;
For want of a horse, the rider was lost;
For want of a rider, the battle was lost;
For want of a battle, the kingdom was lost!
All for want of a nail.

(Franklin, cited in Gleick 1987: 23)

These insights have a social counterpart. In accordance with systems theory, the relationship between social systems and human beings is environmental. The individual reacts, adapts, and engages within a complex process of response and change amplified by self-reinforcing feedback related to the sudden emergence of new forms, emotions, and ideas. This iterative process can produce complex patterns of reaction, where each aspect of feedback has a compounding influence on the next iteration. According to systems theory, just as we cannot understand how an organism interacts with its environment by dissecting its parts, we cannot understand social systems by only examining the bodies within them.

In Image Theatre, the images that participants create crystallize an issue, story, or experience so that meaning emerges in the doing and seeing. As an aesthetic landscape emerges, doubling for the social, the theatre practice becomes a form of text—a weave of potential meanings—that extends beyond the workshop space. This structured language serves as a bridge between the image of the world and the world of the image. The image as symbol requires us to make a leap both into it and out of it. Simultaneously, individual experience gets subsumed into the collective through the collaborative forming and re-forming of the image. The frozen image becomes the prelude to action, "which is revealed in the activation of the image" (Boal, 1992: xx), bringing the images to life and discovering the directions and intentions in them. Boal (1995) maintains that the smallest cells of social organizations, and the smallest experiences in our lives, contain all the values of society and all the structures of power. That is, general themes pervade all human experiences and our bodies and our relationships express them.

Similarly, complexity, as theorized by biologist Jack Cohen and mathematician Ian Stewart (1994), focuses on the dynamic, rather than static, relationships and patterns among phenomena. Complexity is interested in life forms that live and learn, and those life forms extend beyond individuals to social groupings like classrooms, bodies of knowledge, macro phenomena—like our immune system and the brain, and global forms like species and biospheres. "We are beginning to discover that complexity has its own laws—but we don't understand them terribly well, not yet . . . What we really want is an understanding of broad questions like, "Why did vision evolve?" [or] "What causes stock market crashes?" (Cohen and Stewart 1994: 219).

One approach to these questions is to reduce evolution to one rule—winners win. Cohen and Stewart maintain that reductionist science over-simplifies. While scientists believe DNA controls biological development, they have yet to piece together how an organism works. While they can recognize a tornado, they still cannot accurately predict what it's going to do over the long term. Drawing on complexity to explore how change occurs in living phenomena, Cohen and Stewart have proposed the complementary concepts of "simplexity" and "complicity" (1994: 414–20). They theorize that simplex systems are characterized by rules which determine subsequent interactions of the parts; by contrast, in complicit systems, the rules of interaction may themselves change, based on what the system learns from the history of part-to-part interactions. For Cohen and Stewart, the word "complicity" emphasizes relations that are intertwined, complicated, and fluid. Put differently, complicity—being implicated in/with—moves us from managing a simple system of human-designed input/output-based interactions to engaging with a dynamic, evolving one.

Cohen and Stewart assert: "Simplexity explores a fixed space of the possible. Complicity enlarges it" (1994: 417). The malaria parasite demonstrates how complicity occurs when complex systems interact. For example, malaria is caused by a parasite that lives in human blood. Mosquitoes suck our blood and, along with it, ingest the parasite. When they bite another human, the parasite is passed on. There can be no malaria without the intersections of several subsystems of blood, the mosquito and the human body. When systems interact, they open up new (in this case, negative for humans) possibilities. As Cohen and Stewart argue, "the flight of mosquitoes wasn't invented to transmit malaria; when flight evolved the malaria parasite didn't exist, because people didn't. Blood wasn't invented as food for mosquitoes" (1994: 415). Bloodsucking insects evolved because there was blood to suck; put all these subsystems of insect, flight, multiple human hosts, blood and the tropical climate, together and a new interactive dynamic called "malaria" emerges.[3]

Fritjof Capra's distinction between designed and emergent structures can be viewed as parallel to Cohen and Stewart's notions of simplexity and complicity. While a designed structure is based on rules and procedures, an emergent one enables the continual emergence of new structures through innovation. While designed structures are formal and based on official blueprints, emergent structures represent an informal network of relationships that "continually grows, changes, and adapts to new situations" (1998: 47). Balance is desired: overly designed systems cannot adapt to changing conditions, overly emergent ones lose sight of goals.

In *The Web of Life*, Capra (1996) critiques the binary either–or perspective, suggesting that it is incapable of addressing global, ecological, and social problems. To understand our interactions in this world, we must think systemically. As we engage in a continuous dialogue with the world, we engage in continuous dialogue with each other through our behavior, relationships, and conversations. This web is the space of possibility, the metaxic in-between (Linds 2001). This in-between is not empty but alive with intentions, responses, and actions arising from the system's prior history. Complicity holds each of us responsible for the good or bad of the whole and bids us perceive and pay attention to the in-between.

Embodied perception

> Because we are in the world, we are condemned to meaning . . . We witness every minute the miracle of related experiences, and yet nobody knows better than we do how this miracle is worked, for we are ourselves this network of relationships. True philosophy consists in relearning how to look at the world.
>
> (Merleau-Ponty 1962: xx)

Maurice Merleau-Ponty is one of the few Western philosophers "whose work is committed to an exploration of the fundamental entre-deux [in-between] between science and experience, experience and world" (Varela *et al.* 1991: 15). Merleau-Ponty studied patterns of interacting and described relationships as "action-à-deux" or dialogue.[4] The idea of dialogue suggests something new is generated when two (or more) people come together in conversation (from the Latin con versare, to turn together) or, for that matter, in any kind of shared action, even those unfolding far below the level of conscious awareness. For Merleau-Ponty the dialogue refers to the triple sense of the body:

> The body is our general medium for having a world. Sometimes it is restricted to the actions necessary for the conservation of life, and accordingly it posits around us a biological world; at other times, elaborating upon these primary actions and moving from their literal to a figurative meaning, it manifests through them a core of new significance: this is true of motor habits [sic] such as dancing. Sometimes, finally, the meaning

aimed at cannot be achieved by the body's natural means; it must then build itself an instrument, and it projects thereby around itself a cultural world.

(Merleau-Ponty 1962: 146)

Philosopher Hubert Dreyfus and engineer Stewart Dreyfus echo this three-way distinction through their three conceptions of the body—what is biologically innate, what is acquired, and what is cultural:

> Because we have the sort of bodies that get tired and that bend backwards at the knees, chairs can show up to us—but not for flamingos, say—as affording sitting [innate]. But chairs can only solicit sitting once we have learned to sit [acquired]. Finally, only because we Western Europeans are brought up in a culture where one sits on chairs, do chairs solicit us to sit on them [cultural]. Chairs would not solicit sitting in traditional Japan.
>
> (Dreyfus and Dreyfus 1999: 104)

Perception is what lies in and creates the in-between. It is not a means of representing a reality external to us but our primary means of interacting with a world we are part of. David Abram, who drew on Merleau-Ponty's work to explore language, ecology, and perception, writes,

> [P]erception . . . is precisely this reciprocity, the ongoing interchange between my body and the entities that surround it. It is a sort of silent conversation that I carry on with things, a continuous dialogue that unfolds far below my verbal awareness—and often, even, *independent* of my verbal awareness.
>
> (Abram 1996: 52–53)

Each situation requires a series of tactical decisions, in which we adapt what has worked in the past to a new situation in the present. We don't consciously think about what to do at each moment; rather, we experience the situation that in turn draws our "doing" out. Our experiences build upon each other over time and we draw on past sequences when a similar situation occurs. This use of common sense in responding to the needs of a particular situation is known by multiple terms: skilful mindfulness (Varela *et al.* 1991), ethical know-how (Varela 1999), or spontaneous coping (Dreyfus and Dreyfus 1999).

Common sense, in fact, teaches us to become intuitive regarding the development of those skills wherein "the body takes over and does the rest outside the range of consciousness" (Dreyfus and Dreyfus 1999: 114). By continually cultivating an embodied common sense and wisdom, we move beyond observation. Our expertise is not just a set of tools; rather, our experience of the work draws the expertise out of us. It is difficult to commodify this expertise as these skills are "largely a matter of readiness to hand or 'knowledge *how*' based on the accumulation of experience in a vast number of cases" (Varela *et al.* 1991: 148).

Dreyfus and Dreyfus note that expert chess players depend on immediate intuitive responses, distinguishing between 50,000 types of positions without comparing alternatives. Similarly, when driving a car, we constantly discriminate between a large number of possible situations:

> The expert driver, generally without any awareness, not only knows by feel and familiarity when slowing down on an off-ramp is required; he or she knows how to perform

the appropriate action without calculating and comparing alternatives. What must be done, simply is done.

(Dreyfus and Dreyfus 1999: 110)

Merleau-Ponty's concepts of the "intentional arc" and "maximum grip" help us understand how skillful mindfulness might be developed for working in an always shifting metaxic space:

> The intentional arc names the tight connection between the agent and the world, viz. that, as the agent acquires skills, those skills are "stored," not as representations in the mind, but as dispositions to respond to the solicitations in the world. Maximum grip names the body's tendency to refine its discriminations and to respond to solicitations in such a way as to bring the current situation closer to the agent's sense of an optimal gestalt that the skilled agent has learned to expect.
>
> (Dreyfus and Dreyfus 1999: 103)

When we want to pick up something, we try and grab it in such a way as to get the best grip on it. To do this, we activate one of the stored skills or dispositions that respond to situations we have faced previously. This dialectical relationship between the individual and the situation constitutes the intentional arc. However, when there is a time, say, when a workshop game suddenly turns into something else because of the involvement of participants, there is a gestalt of heightened energy, a sense of balancing between what we have experienced and the as yet unknown possibilities inherent in this new situation. The dynamic involves paying attention to an ever-evolving landscape of possibility and of selecting (not necessarily consciously) those actions that are adequate to maintain one's fitness within that landscape. The environment creates boundaries for that fitness but does not prescribe what is viable or not viable. In this instance, we try and develop maximum grip, employing and adapting our skills and abilities within relatively indeterminable circumstances.

Conclusion: the dance of possibility

> The image of the real is real as image.
>
> (Boal 1995: 144)

Looking at TO through the lens of embodied perception, complexity and systems theory, and the biology of cognition, enlarges the potential of the in-between as an embodied space. The space of dramatic metaxis occurs in the moments questions arise, when we ask, what if things could be different? This space is informed by, and respectful of, a complex world, and it helps those who occupy it discover different, unknown, and unrecognized spaces within their world, selves, or community. Rather than treating these spaces as objects to be grasped intellectually, the theorists investigated in these pages suggest that we experience them as vibrant, living, creative spaces providing opportunities for dialogue and movement. Understanding their concepts potentially expands our understanding of metaxis in TO and particularly in the role of the Joker.

The Joker in TO mediates between the worlds of performers and audience, the worlds of performance space and beyond it, and the workshop world and the external world. S/he is the wild card: sometimes director, sometimes referee, sometimes facilitator, sometimes leader. The Joker is not neutral, merely passing messages from one side to the other. The Joker enables metaxis to occur by constantly stretching the space to engage in a discourse of embodied critique and possibility.

An Image Theatre exercise called *Zoom in/Zoom out* illustrates this notion of stretching space. When spect-actors are instructed to make a scene, the characters are often presented in limited view. In order to see a widened view of the world and all that has an impact on the given story, we *zoom out* to include elements previously unseen. At other times, the image involves such complex characters and relationships, that it is difficult to understand the key relationships within it. In these instances, we need to *zoom in*, narrowing our view to focus on a particular conflict or relationship.

The Joker as facilitator is aware of the need for such different views. One instrument of that viewing is the Socratic "midwife" (Boal 1992: 234) who is in a process of maieutics (the birth of ideas), but "a maieutics of body and spirit, not simply cerebral" (1992: 234). Like the midwife, the Joker enacts and enables the conditions of metaxis so that stories can emerge into and from the world. This task enables different voices, worldviews, value systems, and beliefs to converse with one another. Through this process, knowing is an unfolding, dancing metaxis into being.

Notes

1   I am indebted to Tor-Helge Allern (2001) who underlines that Plato and Aristotle only write of *metaxy*, *metaxu*, and *methexis*, and not *metaxis*, a word commonly used to describe the theatrical process but which does not exist in Greek. The word's etymology and history, however, do help us understand its potential.

2   Wiener, Rosenblueth, and Bigelow needed a new word to describe a new discipline that was apart from, but drew upon, electrical engineering, mathematics, biology, neurophysiology, anthropology, and psychology. They created the word "cybernetics" from the Greek word *cybernetes*, meaning steersman, "in order to involve the rich interaction of goals, predictions, actions, feedback and response in systems of all kinds" (Pangaro 1994).

3   We could add the associated dynamic of the effect of the ecosystem and colonialism as scientists began to look for a cure for malaria by exploiting the quinine from the bark of the cinchona tree which grows in the Andean highlands of South America.

4   Merleau-Ponty describes the communicative act as "one system with two terms (my behavior and the other's behavior) which function as a whole" (1964: 118). Our ability to perceive, to observe, to hear, to sense the other enables this phenomenon: "In perceiving the other, my body and his are coupled, resulting in a sort of action which pairs them (action à deux)" (1964: 118).

Bibliography

Abram, D. (1997) *The Spell of the Sensuous: Perception and language in a more-than-human world*. New York: Vintage Books.

Allern, T.-H. (2001) "Myth and metaxy, and the myth of 'metaxis,'" unpublished manuscript prepared for the 4th World Congress for Drama/Theatre and Education, Bergen, Norway, July 2–8.

Boal, A. (1979) *Theatre of the Oppressed*, trans. C.A. and M.-O.L. McBride. New York: Urizen Books.

—— (1992) *Games for Actors and Non-Actors*, trans. A. Jackson. London and New York: Routledge.

—— (1995) *The Rainbow of Desire: The Boal method of theatre and therapy*, trans. A. Jackson. London and New York: Routledge.

Capra, F. (1996) *The Web of Life: A new scientific understanding of living systems*. New York: Anchor Books.

—— (1998) "Creativity in communities," *Resurgence*, January–February, 186: 46–47.

—— (2002) *The Hidden Connections: Integrating the biological, cognitive, and social dimensions of life into a science of sustainability*. New York: Doubleday.

Cohen, J. and Stewart, I. (1994) *The Collapse of Chaos: Discovering simplicity in a complex world*. New York: Penguin Books.

Dreyfus, H.L., and Dreyfus, S.E. (1986) *Mind Over Machine: The power of human intuition and expertise in the era of the computers*. New York: Free Press.

—— (1999) "The challenge of Merleau-Ponty's phenomenology of embodiment for cognitive science," in G. Weiss and H.F. Haber (eds) *Perspectives on Embodiment: The intersections of nature and culture*. New York: Routledge.

Gleick, J. (1987) *Chaos: Making a new science*. New York: Viking.

Hocking, B., Haskell, J., and Linds, W. (eds) (2001) *Unfolding Bodymind: Exploring possibility through education*. Burlington, VT: Foundation for Educational Renewal.

Liddell, H.G. (1996) *Greek–English Lexicon*. Oxford: Oxford University Press.

Linds, W. (2001) "A journey in Metaxis: Been, being, becoming, imag(in)ing drama facilitation." PhD dissertation. Vancouver: University of British Columbia.

Lorenz, E. (1979) "Predictability: Does the flap of a butterfly's wings in Brazil set off a tornado in Texas?" Address to the annual meeting of American Association for the Advancement of Science, Washington, December 29, 1979.

Maturana, H. (1987) "Everything said is said by an observer," in W. Thompson (ed.) *Gaia: a way of knowing*. Hudson, NY: Lindisfarne Press.

Maturana, H. and Varela, F.J. (1980) *Autopoeisis and Cognition*. D. Reidel: Dordrecht, Holland.

—— (1992) *The Tree of knowledge: The biological roots of human understanding*. Boston, MA: Shambhala.

Merleau-Ponty, M. (1962) *Phenomenology of Perception*, trans. C. Smith. London: Routledge and Kegan Paul.

—— (1964) *The Primacy of Perception: And other essays on phenomenological psychology, the philosophy of art, history and politics*, trans. M. Edie. Evanston, IL: Northwestern University Press.

—— (1973) *The Prose of the World*, C. Lefort (ed.), trans. J. O'Neill. Evanston, IL: Northwestern University Press.

Morley, D. (1992) *Television, Audiences and Cultural Studies*. New York: Routledge.

Pangaro, P. (1994) *"Cybernetics"—One definition*. Online. Available: <http://www.pangaro.com/published/cybermacmillan.html> (accessed May 14, 2004).

Plato (1994) *Symposium*, trans. Robin Waterfield. Oxford: Oxford University Press.

Varela, F.J. (1999) *Ethical Know-How: Science, wisdom and cognition*. Stanford, CA: Stanford University Press.

Varela, F.J., Thompson, E., and Rosch, E. (1991) *The Embodied Mind: Cognitive science and human experience*. Cambridge, MA: MIT Press.

Voegelin, E. (1989) *Autobiographical Reflections*, E. Sandoz (ed.). Baton Rouge: LSU Press.

Wiener, N. (1948) *Cybernetics, or Control and Communication in the Animal and the Machine*. Cambridge, MA: The Technology Press.

Aesthetic spaces/imaginative geographies

Shari Popen

> Theatre of the Oppressed creates *spaces of liberty* where people can free their memories, emotions, imaginations, thinking of their past, in the present, and where they can invent their future instead of waiting for it.
>
> (Boal 2002: 5)

> So theatre does not exist in the objectivity of bricks and mortar, sets and costumes, but in the subjectivity of those who practice it, at the moment when they practice it.
>
> (Boal 1995: 19)

Augusto Boal originally developed Theatre of the Oppressed (TO) to address a world of oppressions and forces exterior to us, an environment of cops on the street. But during his European exile, Boal tells us, "there also appeared oppressions which were new to me: 'loneliness,' 'fear of emptiness,' the 'impossibility of communicating with others'" (Boal 1995: 8). Deciding to "work with these new oppressions and to consider them as such" (Boal 1995: 8), his task became to find out how these cops got into our heads and to find ways to remove them. This gave rise to Rainbow of Desire techniques and to a different notion of struggle against power. When the cops in the street become the Cops-in-our-Heads, forms of opposition require new categories and analytical frameworks. These new forms of oppressions require interventions of a different sort because they attack epistemological foundations themselves, the spaces of our thoughts and imaginations. In Rainbow of Desire, it is common sense itself, as it has been constructed, that must be escaped and reinvented. But because our common sensibilities, or the tools of our reason, are fully encoded in our lives and languages, there is no full escape. We are at risk of becoming dispossessed of the ability to venture beyond proscribed limits of thinking and acting. The task then is to find openings, slippages, fissures, spaces that can provide footholds onto different ways of thinking and acting. As TO practitioners, we seek aesthetic spaces to conjure alternative images and possibilities for those of us who are *in* the world but not *of* it in many ways.

The notion of transitivity in Boal's work, relevant but in no way limited to Rainbow of Desire, is central to understanding how aesthetic space restores vitality to social practices. In TO, the space of theatre is brought out of abstraction and reclaimed as an embodiment of human imagination. For Boal, this is a space of transitive learning in which people are actively engaged in multiple ways of problem solving. Boal opposes this to intransitive learning—what Paulo Freire calls a "banking model"—in which codified knowledge and conduct are reproduced and come to govern people's cognitive apparatuses. Transitive learning requires a space in which active engagement of the imagination can be realized.

Within aesthetic spaces we can dramatize our fears and practice our actions in spaces of relative safety. Children are wonderfully adept at this. In their play, they overlay material objects and places with highly imaginative and creative constructions. In their quest for defining boundaries, both physical and symbolic, and testing their permeability, children seek opportunities for expression. Trees become rocket ships, streets become ball fields, abandoned spaces become treasured sanctuaries. These aesthetic spaces make possible imaginative geographies, in which opportunities for transitive knowing are freed up, rather than over-determined by highly structured contexts and places.

Boal (1995) combines three epistemological properties to make aesthetic space transitive. First, plasticity is the property that draws on the human qualities of memory and imagination, anchoring our knowledge in a flow of human events. Just as children remake the world into their theatre, plasticity helps create a space in which things can be other than they seem. The property of plasticity allows time and space to become flexible, manipulable. "All combinations are possible there, because the aesthetic space *is* but *doesn't exist . . .* [A] battered old chair will become a king's throne" (Boal 1995: 20).

Second, aesthetic space in TO is telemicroscopic. "Like a powerful telescope, the stage brings things closer" (Boal 1995: 27) where they can be better observed and known. The practical appeal of this is that theatre in TO remains closer to the grain and detail of human existence, truer to the drama of human life, to the stuff of human hopes and fears. And because theatre is removed from the site of actual struggle and oppression, it is also critically distant from the forms of surveillance that encode that site.

A third property of aesthetic space in TO is its self-reflexivity: it is dichotomic—a space divided—and it creates dichotomy—a space within a space. "The people and the things which are in this space will be in two spaces" (Boal 1995: 23). It has the capacity to allow us to observe ourselves in action, and so imagine ourselves as actors, not spectators. Theatre of the Oppressed is a "mirror which we can penetrate to modify our image" (Boal 1995: 29), not only the image that we carry of ourselves, but also the images that we have constructed of the world.

Space matters: Michel Foucault

The struggle against cops on the street can be made known through realistic forms of dramatic representation. But the struggle against mental policing—what Michel Foucault calls "governmentality" (1991: 102)—requires different strategies and different models of knowing. Foucault has taught us to fundamentally rethink the exercise of power and the nature of the space in which it functions. He described what he called a "micro-physics of power" (Foucault 1977: 26) as a systemic network of disguised controls that produces and normalizes our thoughts and actions. In significant ways, Foucault connected the pervasive practices of disciplinary technologies, of panopticons and administrative procedures, to the ways that violence and fear colonize our social relations from within. How we understand the space that is within is critical to the emancipatory promise that Foucault provides.

In a 1967 lecture entitled "Des Espaces Autres" (later retranslated and published as "Of Other Spaces"), Foucault helped to usher thinking about space and spatializations into critical social thought. We are in "the epoch of simultaneity . . . of juxtaposition, the epoch of the near and far, of the side-by-side, of the dispersed" (Foucault 1984: 22). We have been taught by the phenomenologists, says Foucault, that we do not live in homogenous and empty space. On the contrary, the space in which we now live is heterogeneous space. In other words, "we live in a set of relations that delineates sites which are irreducible to one another and absolutely not superimposable on one another" (Foucault 1984: 23). Foucault calls these heterogeneous spaces "heterotopias" (1984: 24). Opposed to utopias, which are sites with no real place, heterotopias have material presence—they are real places. But they are also countersites in that they reflect, like mirrors, on the social spaces we inhabit.

Heterotopias are spaces of difference, of othering. They are literally the Other place, the place of the Other, who is both simultaneously excluded and included as the Other. For Foucault, heterotopias take two primary forms—crisis heterotopias and heterotopias of deviation (Foucault 1984: 24). Crisis heterotopias are places human societies set aside for people whose lives are lived for a time in a state of crisis. Boarding schools, for example, are places set aside for adolescent difference to be played out. Heterotopias of crisis, however, are disappearing in modern society, and Foucault's work has described the history of that shift. They are being replaced by heterotopias of deviation in which difference is increasingly normalized. Heterotopias of deviation are, for example, "rest homes and psychiatric hospitals, and of course prisons" (Foucault 1984: 26). No longer places that are merely transitional, heterotopias of deviation function to assign abnormality and are held in place by Cops-in-the Head. In this shift, whereby crisis becomes marked as social deviance, opposition to the workings of power and its disciplinary apparatus is tricky. Opposition must be imagined through strategic displacements rather than as exits.

Heterotopias have a function "in relation to all the space that remains" (Foucault 1984: 27). That is, they are either "spaces of illusion" (1984: 27) that expose relations in real space (carnivals function as this kind of heterotopia in which a certain festive freedom creates a mild resistance to disciplinary power) or "spaces of compensation" (1984: 27) that are more perfect than our untidy world (Foucault's example here is Puritan colonies). But the heterotopia par excellence for Foucault, the greatest reserve of the imagination, is the ship. It is "a floating piece of space" (1984: 27) constantly presenting new horizons of possibility. It tacks to and fro across the infinity of the waters, in search of exotic places, places of difference and treasures that seduce and inspire imagination. "In civilizations without boats, dreams dry up, espionage takes the place of adventure, and the police take the place of pirates" (Foucault 1984: 27). Perhaps that is why Truman (in the 1988 film *The Truman Show*) escaped the artificial place of constant surveillance that imprisoned him in a boat.

Following Foucault, there are major writers who have each developed a body of work that aims to transform the ways that we think about space. What they have in common is that they insist on the materiality of space. This notion runs counter to the idea of space that has been held by the dominant culture—that space forms a background, a setting, often rich and interesting but abstract and relatively immaterial, what others have called architectural or abstract space. Space, framed in this way, is an empty field waiting to be filled, named, colonized. Fundamentally, the new claim is that space shapes sociality in powerful and substantive ways. It acts on us; it is performative. Changing the dominant structures of power requires unpacking the ways in which space performs or acts on us.

What Rainbow of Desire techniques share with this emerging theoretical model is a critique of the oppositional play of binary dualisms. The new spatial logic that comes into play allows the materialization of a third space, the space of possibility, the space of multiplicity and practical actions. It is the dialogic space of both/and—not the dialectic space of either/or. "I wanted to retain all possible meanings, not reduce them to merely one" (Boal 2001: 149). Similarly, Foucault states that "the heterotopia is capable of juxtaposing in a single real place several places, several sites that are in themselves incompatible. Thus it is," he continues, "that the theater brings onto the rectangle of the stage, one after the other, a whole series of places that are foreign to one another" (Foucault 1984: 25). People who are imaginatively rendering this notion of third space in their writings have claimed Foucault as foundational to rethinking spatial logics. In what follows, I map the spatial imaginations that they develop and the new metaphors that they offer to reframe the notion of transitivity in TO.

Henri Lefebvre: spatial triad

The ideas of Henri Lefebvre, put forward almost thirty years ago in *La production de l'espace*, remain a vital reference point in the quest for a counterspace, or what he calls "differential space" (1991: 52). The key concept in his work is "production," a quintessentially Marxist term. His project is to rethink how space is produced, to describe its form and content in the terms of a political analysis. Space for Lefebvre is not a dead, inert, empty field, but is organic and alive. It moves, it collides with other spaces and overlays them. "We fall into the trap of treating space 'in itself,' as space as such" (Lefebvre 1991: 90). To avoid this trap, he warns, it is necessary to rethink how space enters our imaginations and constructs our worldviews. He is proposing that we examine the setting in which we live, and how our social spaces and social practices are produced. And reproduced.

This is a metaphilosophical project whose purpose is to rethink dialectics spatially by rewriting the categories that constitute spatiality, exposing the hidden contradictions within them and the will to keep them hidden. Disclosing the contradictions dialectically creates the possibility of a new space, "differential space" (Lefebvre 1991: 52) that, not unlike the space of heterotopias, "accentuates differences" (1991: 52). Differential space is, perhaps, the space of TO that holds the promise of liberation from self-imprisoning categories and from social repression. The dialectical figure at the center of his analysis is what he calls the "spatial triad." For Lefebvre, space is a product, and results from the relationships among the following three forms: abstract or conceptual space, perceptual space, and lived space. Abstract space is the codified and commodified space conceptualized and created by architects, engineers, and urban planners. According to Lefebvre, every society produces its own kind of space; capitalism and neocapitalism have produced abstract space.

> Abstract space, which is the tool of domination, asphyxiates whatever is conceived within it and then strives to emerge . . . This space is the lethal one which destroys the historical conditions that gave rise to it . . . in order to impose an abstract homogeneity.
> (Lefebvre 1991: 370)

It produces symbols that become the structure and tools of power and domination, and that homogenizes not only by putting cops on the street to police our actions, but by putting cops in our heads to police our thoughts and imaginations.

To complete the triad, the space of perception and the space of lived experience are configured by Lefebvre as spaces of practice, not structure. In a world in which production is total, they are brought into service to legitimate this dominant space. Perceptual space exists in our minds. As a result of repeated, dominant patterns of thought, places designed especially for the sensory activities of work or play are reduced into places of continued production. Lived space, the actual spaces of everyday experience—Lefebvre includes among them "ego, bed, bedroom, dwelling, house . . . square, church, graveyard" (1991: 42)—

also contributes to the reproduction of codified movement and practices within the triad. Lefebvre notes, in particular, how lived space "embraces the loci of passion, of action and of lived situations, and thus immediately implies time" (1991: 42), which in turn suggests the production of continuity and habit.

But perceptual and lived spaces also involve the pleasurable consumption of space. Human perception and lived desire or pleasure are neither determined by an existing system nor fully adapted to any system. For Lefebvre, in perceived and lived spaces, disorder and desire, the sensory and sensual always overflow the power structure's appropriation of space. Lefebvre's project then is to find ways to return space to "ambiguity, to the common birth-place of needs and desires" (1991: 391): essentially, to reclaim it as aesthetic space. "The more one examines space," Lefebvre asserts, "considering it not only with the eyes, not only with the intellect, but also with all the senses, with the total body, the more one becomes aware of the conflicts at work within it, conflicts which foster the explosion of abstract space and the production of space that is *other*" (1991: 391). What Lefebvre calls the "explosion" reflects the inability of abstract space to contain human desire.

Aesthetic space can arise because abstract space, in fact, harbors contradictions and ambiguities—it carries within itself the seeds of differential space. These contradictions are immanent in the abstract representational space because there can be no single, all-inclusive, system of representations. Rather, there are always several, on several levels of production and consumption, pleasure, and desire included, and these clash with the abstract apparatus of homogenization. To draw from the metaphor of language, linguistic structure makes communication possible, but speakers nevertheless use language as they see fit. These human practices are extra-social, strategic, in the sense that they escape by evading social norms and forms. They constitute heterogenous knowledge. "Such a know-ledge is conscious of its own approximativeness: it is at once certain and uncertain. It announces its own relativity at every step, undertaking . . . self-criticism" (1991: 65). Lefeb-vre himself understands differential space as aesthetic space, when he says, it is "thanks to the potential energies of a variety of groups capable of diverting homogenized space to their own purposes [that] a theatricalized or dramatized space is liable to arise" (1991: 391).

Gilles Deleuze and Felix Guattari: nomads and smooth space

Gilles Deleuze and Felix Guattari speak of overlaying spaces, striated and smooth spaces, textured like muscle groups, and offer new metaphors for understanding spatial dimensions and movement among them. In their often-quoted book, A *Thousand Plateaus*, they describe the difference between striated and smooth spaces. In striated space, the actor's possibility for movement is governed. Striated space is Euclidean space, walled and ordered. It is adult space from the perspective of the child, and it is dominant space from the perspective of the subaltern or oppressed. It is the "straight" space the drag queen theatricalizes and the carni-val parodies.

Smooth space, on the other hand, is analogous to what Boal calls the "oneiric" dimension of aesthetic space—the dimension of imagination, in which "the observer is drawn of her own volition into the vertigo of the dream" (Boal 1995: 22). Real space is shifted, direct rep-resentation is epistemically replaced with imaginative possibilities, and things become what functionally they are not. Down the rabbit hole, in this oneiric space, "the dreamer does not observe: here she penetrates into her own projections, she passes through the looking-glass:

everything merges and mixes together, anything is possible" (Boal 1995: 22). Smooth space is aesthetic, deterritorialized space, opening striated space onto imaginative dimensions of serious play and transgressions.

Smooth and striated space do not cancel each other out so much as overlay each other. They permit a transition, a two-way passage between order and difference. "The smooth spaces arising from the city are not only those of worldwide organization, but also of counterattack . . . sprawling, temporary shantytowns of nomads and cave dwellers, scrap metal and fabric, patchwork, to which the striations of money, work, or housing are no longer even relevant" (Deleuze and Guattari 1987: 481). There are openings in striated space, however narrow and occluded, for dodging into smooth space. This shifting brings dissymmetrical or perhaps Boalian dichotomic movements into play—it is transitive space. Actors do not transcend one space into the other so much as they slip in-between them.

The aesthetic human symbol for Deleuze and Guattari is the nomad, constantly translating striated space into smooth spaces of play. This translating is a kind of traveling that is simultaneously a mode of thinking in place. To voyage, they say, is to think. The nomad is not the migrant who leaves one place behind and enters another, but a nomadic traveler who "voyages in place" (1987: 482). "We can say of nomads that *they do not move*. They are nomads by dint of not moving, not migrating, of holding a smooth space that they refuse to leave" (1987: 482). Thus, voyaging smoothly is a becoming—a difficult, uncertain becoming.

We can compare the figure of the nomad to the Joker function in TO. Boal has identified the Joker as a wild card figure, able to jump in and out of the performance, but never fully leaving—he is "magical, omniscient, polymorphous, and ubiquitous" (Boal 1979: 82). The Joker, as midwife, can deliver transitivity between striated and smooth space, the shifting tectonic movement of the surface of space. "All the theatrical possibilities are conferred upon the 'Joker' function," says Boal (1979: 182). The Joker System that underlies the contemporary practice of TO provides a "structure that is absolutely flexible, so that it can absorb the new discoveries and remain at the same time unchanged and identical to itself" (Boal 1979: 177).

Deleuze and Guattari warn, "smooth spaces are not in themselves liberatory. But the struggle is changed or displaced in them, and life reconstitutes its stakes, confronts new obstacles, invents new paces, switches adversaries. Never believe that smooth space will suffice to save us" (Deleuze and Guattari 1987: 500). It can, however, provide a safe place within which we put a mirror up to the world and playfully improvise.

Michel de Certeau: tactics and stories

In his major work *The Practice of Everyday Life* (1984), Michel de Certeau offers a philosophy of sinking into the world. In many ways, his work is an answer to the verticality of planners from on high—those who conceive of and construct what Lefebvre calls the abstract space of representations. He intends to offer a counterpractice to panoptic ordering, one that takes place on the ground of everyday practice among people who live there.

The planners' or administrators' view of the concept city—not necessarily the view from inside the cityscape itself—is one of destruction and decay, a city that has become blind and lost to a vast array of things. De Certeau's work is meant to provide ways to transgress this blindness by enabling people to regain a sense of doing and knowing that does not put our imaginations in service to the fixed maps imposed by others. He proposes to find ways to take over the fixed places defined in advance by the planners, and convert them for the pur-poses of ordinary people. De Certeau's logic for doing this is what he calls the "art of the weak" (de Certeau 1984: 37)—the spatial practices of people, tactics, and stories.

To describe this conversion, de Certeau distinguishes between strategies and tactics. Strategies are the top-down tools of the planners and social engineers. They impose power by disciplining and ordering space, placing boundaries and normalizing codes of movement to construct proper knowledge. Tactics, on the other hand, are the weapons of the weak. They are designed intentionally to mislead and redirect, and to deflect lines of movement onto unprogrammed detours. They constitute the art of improvisation, using *what is* in unorthodox, counterproductive, often playful ways.

Traveling without a destination, tactically, becomes for de Certeau, a set of social prac-tices that engage people with a different mode of reading their environment. They are practices without an end in view that purposefully substitute process for an end product. But this process is not merely the unfolding of a plan or series of stages. He replaces the instru-mentality of product with movement as an embodied human practice in which the senses are actively engaged. According to de Certeau, space is a "practiced place" (1984: 117); the street as stage, "defined by urban planning is transformed into a space by walkers" (1984: 117). Smooth space is created by the spatial practice of nomadic walking, moving more ran-domly across places that have hitherto been sites of destination, of the finality of arrival.

This tacking about in the city suggests a mode of thought that is itself constructed through itinerant movement; it is about a mobile engagement with space. For de Certeau, language itself is structured like a city. But he refuses the linguistic model of orderly grammar, which he sees as an administrative strategy for taming thinking. "In present-day language, nothing is as fundamental . . . as spatial organization, according to which every-thing 'that happens' is classified, distributed, and conceived" (de Certeau 1997: 56). He replaces that with the messier tactics of language *use*—narrating and speaking, suggesting a role for stories that is about seeing urban space as a fluid arena of narratives. Stories in motion.

For de Certeau, stories are transformative. They are not merely *about* movement, they *create* movement. Space is perceived anew, differently, from encounters with others and contact with daily life. The city becomes a stage or theatre of possibility and interaction, enchanted with a randomness that is not chaos and a serendipity that is festive and spirited.

> In a festival, as in an artistic creation, something exists that is not a means, but that is sufficient unto itself: the discovery of possibilities, the invention of encounters, the experience of these departures for "other places"—without which the atmosphere becomes stifling and seriousness amounts to everything that is boring about a society.
> (de Certeau 1997: 118)

Several examples of this mobile practice and the ways in which we transform it from within appear in current literature. Walking, says Lucy Lippard, "offers an unparalleled way to open oneself to the 'spirit of the place' and to its subterranean history. Motion allows a certain mental freedom that translates a place to a person kinesthetically" (1997: 17). Rebecca Solnit agrees:

> Walking allows us to be in our bodies and in the world without being made busy by them. It leaves us free to think without being wholly lost in our thoughts . . . Moving on

foot seems to make it easier to move in time; the mind wanders from plans to recollections to observations.

(Solnit 2000: 5)

This vernacular, spatial practice of walking is a way of creating habitable space. Jill Lane writes, "walking the city is a textured, bodily practice of rehearsing its social life and memories. The aim of such pedestrian storytelling is not just to invent or retell the good stories of old, but to reveal their ghosted presence in things as they are" (2004: 303). These stories, she continues, offer countermemories of the silencings that tame and commercialize urban space.

Likewise, TO creates movement at a pace in which everyday life is brought closer and noticed. "This is theatre," says Boal, "the art of looking at ourselves" (Boal 2002: 15). Once we begin to take seriously the performative and material qualities of space, the art of looking at ourselves shifts to an analysis of the total environment: we can take it all in and it becomes the theatre that expands our minds. It teaches us to recognize that in society power itself is never fixed and closed, but rather is exercised along a grid that is an endless and strategic game that we must continually learn to imaginatively and tactically outwit.

Bibliography

Boal, A. (1979) *Theatre of the Oppressed*, trans. C.A. and M.-O.L. McBride. New York: Urizen Books.
—— (1995) *The Rainbow of Desire*, trans. A. Jackson. London and New York: Routledge.
—— (2001) *Hamlet and the Baker's Son: My life in theatre and politics*, trans. A. Jackson and C. Blaker. London and New York: Routledge.
—— (2002) *Games for Actors and Non-Actors*, 2nd edition, trans. A. Jackson. London and New York: Routledge.
De Certeau, M. (1984) *The Practice of Everyday Life*, trans. S. Rendall. Berkeley, CA: University of California Press.
—— (1997) *Culture in the Plural*, trans. T. Conley. Minneapolis, MN: University of Minnesota Press.
Deleuze, G. and Guattari, F. (1987) *A Thousand Plateaus*, trans. B. Massumi. Minneapolis, MN: University of Minnesota Press.
Foucault, M. (1977) *Discipline and Punish: The birth of the prison*. New York: Pantheon Books.
—— (1984) "Of other spaces," *Diacritics*, Spring: 22–27.
—— (1991) "Governmentality," in G. Burchell, C. Gordon, and P. Miller (eds) *The Foucault Effect: Studies in governmentality*. Chicago, IL: University of Chicago Press.
Lane, J. (2004) "Reverend Billy: Preaching, protest, and postindustrial flanerie," in H. Bial (ed.) *The Performance Studies Reader*. New York: Routledge.
Lefebvre, H. (1991) *The Production of Space*, trans. D. Nicholson-Smith. Oxford: Blackwell Publishing.
Lippard, L. (1997) *The Lure of the Local*. New York: The New Press.
Solnit, R. (2000) *Wanderlust: A history of walking*. New York: Viking Penguin.

Joker runs wild

Mady Schutzman

The roots of Theatre of the Oppressed (TO) lie in carnival and circus, Brechtian theory, and the pedagogical philosophy of Paulo Freire. In carnival and circus Boal found public engagement and merriment, a myriad of voices and interpretations, inversions and reversals, clowns, irreverence, and popular forms of satirical and comedic resistance. In Brecht there was outrage, critical disengagement from and analysis of the roles we play as socialized beings, a call to exploit our alienation, and an invitation to live in the fertile terrain between thought and action, reality and illusion, the ordinary and the strange. In Freire, Boal located dialogue, the belief that the marginalized are not marginal but central to the structure of society, an elaboration of the transitive and dialectical roots of social existence, and a pedagogy predicated on an ever-changing, performative reality. Boal shared with Freire an understanding of praxis—the inseparability of reflection and action, theory and practice—in pursuit of social change.

In the spirit of all of the above influences, Boal designed the Joker System with Teatro de Arena in São Paulo, Brazil, which he (among others) directed between 1956–71. The genre (an aesthetic style for staged performance, not a body of workshop techniques) is characterized by the mixing of fact and fiction, the shifting of roles during the play so that all actors played all characters, separation of actor and character, and deconstruction of habits to foster disorientation. It also introduced the figure of the Joker, both a narrator who addresses the audience directly and a wild card able to jump in and out of any role in the play at any time. This Joker, *curinga* in Portuguese, has a polyvalent role as director, master of ceremonies, interviewer, and exegete, representing the author who knows story, plot development, and outcome as no individual character can. Through all his various roles, the *curinga* was responsible for performing a commentary on the performance within the performance. [1]

While aspects of the Joker System are evidenced in Rainbow of Desire techniques—particularly the employment of imprecision, ambiguity, and indirectness as aesthetic strategies and as strategies of resistance—I glimpse in the Joker System a remedy for what I believe Forum Theatre (and perhaps a great deal of theatre activism) lacks. Forum Theatre relies on clear distinctions between protagonist and antagonist and a language of oppressed and oppressor. While Boal sees the critical potential of the original *curinga* role now in the hands of the spect-actors (Boal 2003), the structure of Forum (and of all TO techniques that rely on this duality), nonetheless, tends to dictate the kind of interventions into the anti-models likely to happen. Boal explains that before he founded TO, he (as *curinga* of the Joker System) had to "do it all himself"—that is, enact interventions and interject disorientation and incongruity into the stories being told. Spectators did not have the agency to intervene in the story through the protagonist (although Arena actors rotated roles); as yet there were no spect-actors. Thus, only with the advent of TO and the virtual end of the Joker System per se did the role of the *curinga* shift to spect-actors.

Yet, I find something is lost in this apparent transference of the *curinga*'s role to the spect-actors. The Joker of the Joker System was a live theorist and pattern detector with a paradoxical vantage point. He was a trickster of sorts, consciously wielding a strategy of re-articulation to obscure easy answers and to discourage fixed identities. When reenacted stories of oppression lapsed into reductive "us" versus "them" representations of oppressed and oppressor, Boal, as Joker, would intervene to interview a character, or shift the style from realism to melodrama, or ask each character to interpret each of the other characters, or lecture the audience on aspects of the political environment that the protagonist (or, perhaps, everyone in the scene) was unaware of. Spect-actors do not, singularly or as a group, enact interventions from these critical perspectives or loyalties; they do not know what the *curinga* knew (or might know) by virtue of being an outside observer, director, and exegete. And contemporary Jokers—working in an embattled terrain, the most practiced expressing uncertainty about their role—similarly do not embody the *curinga*'s multivalent, critical, and poetic role. (Boal called the Joker System "the poetics of the oppressed" [Boal 1979: x]). We are more likely to order and direct participants' attention to problem solving in its most traditional form—as a focused, argumentative, and intellectual challenge to oppression—than to engage the disorienting and wild card strategies that characterize the Joker System. When looking at TO facilitation and structure (particularly forum) through the radical potential of the Joker System, it appears less revolutionary in design than the theories and cultural practices that inspired it.

What would happen if we revitalized the basic tenets of the Joker System within contemporary TO practice? What would happen if the TO Joker was more like the *curinga* of the Joker System? What if theatre activism itself took a cue from jokes and jokers of all kinds including clowns, tricksters, and jokers in playing cards and tarot decks? In turning to the structure of jokes and jokers who embody the joke, *live* a joke (as compared to *tell* a joke), I am searching for an alternative approach to oppositional politics, an indirect form of resistance; I am searching for an approach to oppression that first registers, and then lands, the punch of humor.[2]

Word play as resistance: from Ganserians to Gracie Allen

I came upon the Ganser syndrome while doing research on hysteria. One of the goals of my research was to recast hysteria as a cultural and relational phenomenon rather than a disorder belonging to women's bodies (Schutzman 1999). I was particularly stirred by how the performative aspects of the hysterical narrative—an incomplete, simulated, and highly irregular narrative—suggested strategies of protest, even of healing itself. The gestural language, the dramatic modes of exaggeration, the spectacle of discontent, all expressed the hysterics' underlying insubordination, how languages marked as deviant contained within them forms of counter-discourse. I wanted to bring hysterical performance and its "deviant language" into critical consciousness as a trope of resistance.

The Ganser syndrome—one of several related to and representative of the hysterical dilemma—called out for a similar cultural recasting. In 1898, Ganser hypothesized that the syndrome was a result of an unconscious effort by the subjects to escape from an intolerable situation. The subjects of Ganser's research were prisoners awaiting sentencing and the intolerable situation was prolonged incarceration.

But it was the offering of approximate answers, or what Ganser referred to as "talking past the point," that particularly intrigued me. "How much is two plus two?" the doctor would ask. Answer: "Five." "How many legs does a horse have?" Answer: "Which horse?" Circumstances of awaiting criminal sentencing are laden with enough fear and distrust to understandably inspire strategies of benign falsification. The extremely simple and obvious questions that were asked must have seemed extraordinarily suspicious, some sort of trick (Whitlock 1982: 202).

Similarly, when asked to identify a glove, Ganserians would say it was a hand. In so doing, Ganserians slipped the perceived trap of the questioner by altering the frame of reference from specificity (glove) to concept (hand). In identifying a glove as a hand, the Ganserian becomes a pattern detector; that is, he names an underlying design (*hand*) of which *glove* is a derivation, a circumstance. While the answer is wrong explicitly, it is correct, implicitly. It is a kind of joke that refuses the logic that is apparently being used to evaluate (and imprison) those being questioned. In answering *vis-à-vis* another paradigm of symbolic thought, the Ganserian changes, or at least challenges, the rules of the game.

The overtly indirect answers offered by the patients struck me as both clever and funny, savvy more than hostile. With further musing, the discourse of doctor and Ganser patient seemed more and more like the banter of stand-up comedy teams or the cunning wit of a trickster. My imagination took me swiftly from medical science to vaudeville:

Doctor: How many noses do you have?
Patient: I do not know if I have a nose.
Doctor: How many fingers am I holding up?
Patient: I can't be certain that those fingers are yours.
Comic 1:   What is the height of dumbness?
Comic 2:   About six feet, aren't you?
Comic 1:   Do you know how rude you are?
Comic 2:   No, but if you hum a few bars, I'll tap my foot.

The joke in the above repartee relies upon "getting the point" just at the boundaries of the point—that is, it is about side-stepping the point, taking the literal and tweaking it, bending it so that we are made precisely aware of what was expected from the vantage point of the unexpected. (A master of this form of comedic repartee was Groucho Marx: "Outside of a dog, a book is man's best friend. Inside of a dog, it's too dark to read." Or, "Time flies like an arrow. Fruit flies like a banana." "When is a car not a car? When it turns into a garage.") The "right" answer—the unmarked ordinary—within the frame of the Ganserian joke is always in sight of where the joker takes us; as listeners we remain within range of the intended response. The answers are near misses, not shots in the dark, and we must attend to the uncomfortable disparity between the obvious and the odd. It is a speculative space, a place of instability. It is also a potential place of dissent. In refusing the predictability of "the point," we wonder, what is the point anyway? Is it deserving of our trust? How did it come to be taken as truth? Who benefits from our complicity with it? "Talking past the point" is a compelling, albeit subtle, way of questioning the reliability of "the point" and the apparatus of submission to it. In its use of metaphor over literalness, difference (however slight) over sameness, innuendo over exactness, and imperfection over correctness, it performs a critical resistance.

Gracie Allen, like Groucho, mastered punning and word play to wriggle out of, or at least recast, positions of submission. The following routine (from the film, A *Damsel in Distress*) between Gracie Allen (GA) and George Burns (GB), her real-life and on-camera husband, illustrates her technique.

GA: (*Entering office*) Hello.
GB: You should have been in two hours ago.
GA: Why, what happened?
GB: What happened? If you're not here on time I'll have to get myself another stenographer.
GA: Another stenographer? Do you think there's enough work for the two of us?
GB: Look, I mean I'm gonna fire you!
GA: Fire me? Why if it wasn't for my father . . . you wouldn't be here in London now.
GB: If it wasn't for your father, you wouldn't be working for me for two weeks. You wouldn't even be working for me for two days. Not even two minutes.
GA: Well, a girl couldn't ask for shorter hours than that.
GB: Did you type that letter I dictated last night?
GA: Well, no, I didn't have time so I mailed him my notebook. I hope he can read my shorthand.
GB: You mailed your notebook? You know, Gracie, I'm beginning to think that there's nothing up here. (*GB points to his own head*)
GA: Oh, George, you're self-conscious. (*Phone rings*)
GA: (*To George*) It's a Hawaiian.
GB: A Hawaiian?
GA: Well, he must be. He says he's brown from the morning sun.
GB: Look, the man's name is Brown. *The Morning Sun* is the newspaper he's working on. But tell him I'm not here.
GA: He's not here. I tell you he's not here. Ah, you don't do you, well you can ask him yourself if you don't believe me. (*To George*) George, will you tell him you're not here, he doesn't believe me.

(Wodehouse 1937)

I have made a shift from the private and power-laden dyad of doctor/patient (in the case of the Ganserian) to a far more public and generalized sphere of performance. The power of the doctor over the patient is real, immediate, and privatized. And while the patient may challenge the doctor's need to categorize, the doctor does not experience the system of classification to be undermined. The doctor, the sole spectator in this case, does not get the joke because the doctor is disinterested, from the perspective of authority, in experiencing the kind of fracture of order and rational reasoning that the joke initiates. He is intent upon the act of diagnosing, recognizing something he already knows. In the case of public performance, the jokers on stage are removed from any urgency and audience members (now in the role of the listening doctors) experience the often disquieting space between common sense and uncommon sense, between assumed values and transgressive behavior. Under no particular mandate to diagnose or evaluate, they oscillate in the uncharted territory between them, reconsidering their own boundaries of propriety, questioning whether their long-held moral codes are disputable, wondering whether something is, in fact, funny or offensive:

An elderly man was at home, dying in bed. He smelled the aroma of his favorite choco-late chip cookies baking. He wanted one last cookie before he died. He fell out of bed, crawled to the landing, rolled down the stairs, and crawled into the kitchen where his wife was busily baking cookies. He crawled to the table and was just barely able to lift his withered arm to the cookie sheet. As he grasped a warm, moist, chocolate chip cookie, his favorite kind, his wife suddenly whacked his hand with a spatula.

"Why?" he whispered. "Why did you do that?"

"They're for the funeral."[3]

There is ample room for performers and audience to explore such repositionings sitting in a dark crowd at a public performance with nothing immediate or personal at stake. Possibili-ties for activist appropriation are considered in relative safety. Resistance is far more difficult to actually embody in the face of potential injury; it will likely be cloaked in trepidation which necessarily distorts the performance itself. In considering joking as a critical strategy, we need to closely consider context, audience, and the potential risks involved.

In making the rhetorical leap from medical science to staged performance, I have also made a leap from an arena where joking is unauthorized to one where it is authorized. How can we theorize and entertain certain kinds of behavior that are sanctioned deviations in certain circumstances (comedy on stage), and dystopic and pathologized deviations when performed in anomalous situations (outside the circumstances of recognized social humor, e.g., with your prison doctor)? When behaviors move beyond their socially authorized realm—past their designated point—they are subject to institutional shaming: that which is deemed threatening is rendered impotent (e.g., resistant prisoners become Ganserians, stig-matized by a new syndrome). This tends to foreclose an exploration of their most potent cultural meaning and value. Similarly, we may tend to overlook the radical potential of "being a joke" even in the sanctioned realm (on stage), because in being declassed as the-atrical (i.e., labeled illusory) its real effects tend to be voided.

Physical jokes: taking a lesson from clowns

A clown holds a huge canister with various foods that he has thrown into it to blend. He separates his legs widely and places his feet carefully and evenly apart to get a solid grounding before he begins to shake. He extends his buttocks out behind him and extends his arms equally forward, his elbows extended out to each side. He's ready. And then he shakes and shakes and shakes, but not his arms. The canister remains perfectly still as the clown shakes his bum uncontrollably.

In terms of redressing power hierarchies, this clown routine hardly hits the spot. But it does illustrate the notion of approximating in corporeal terms. To joke, or rather to be a joke, is to be an expectation thwarter, taking an ambulant approach to knowledge and fact, putting the values of precision and clarity into doubt. What do we compromise in our obsession with correctness? Do not jokers and clowns—commenting from the vantage point of either the inchoate (not-yet-formed) or the queer (unwilling to form as prescribed)—demand that we question the righteousness of the straight man, the one who always seems to know?

A clown stands on a stage with a broom. He can't seem to sweep away the pool of light that he is standing in. A boss-character enters and points up to the stage light that is casting the circular light on the floor. The clown sees no connection between the glaring bulb above and the stain on the floor. He keeps sweeping, enjoying the gentle sway of the bristles against the puddle of light. The boss becomes more and more frustrated. His attachment to cause and effect in the face of the clown's playful deviance turns him into a deviant as well: his face contorts with rage and disapproval, anger bloats his body as if about to explode, his attachment to logic hurting him far more than the clown who simply continues to wonder with delight about the strange phenomenon of a perfectly round pool of light hugging his feet no matter what he does to whisk it away.[4]

In the physical wisdom of clown behavior, we can decipher the apparatus of a joke, of emphatically missing the mark. Generally speaking, clowns fall short of normalcy both in language and body; whether they like it or not, they embody an act of alienation. And yet normalcy is always pointed to: we see clearly what it is that they will not or cannot be (as we saw in the Ganserian, in Groucho, and in Gracie Allen). They resist—but do not directly oppose—codes of propriety. The white-face or boss-clown comments on normalcy by embodying it in excess—with immoderate elegance, hysterical control, and grotesque decency. Through his body, normalcy is worn like a suit of armor and rearticulated as tyranny. The audacity of the white-face clown appears frighteningly similar to the cloak of conceit we see performed by our political leaders. We get to see this fine line between dictator and clown, for instance, when Charlie Chaplin plays Hitler in the movie *The Great Dictator* (1940). Chaplin juggles a huge balloon representing the world with a perversely infantile delight and cruelty. He mimics madness until his naivety and playfulness slip into uncontrollable ugliness. He becomes the mask of dictator while simultaneously relaying the actor beneath, convulsing in the seduction of power (Manea 1992). Interestingly, Chaplin plays another role in the film, that of a poor Jewish barber, thus indicating a likeness (or codependence) between the two characters that would have otherwise gone unnoticed.

Over the last century, clowns have evolved into two distinct types—he who slaps and he who gets slapped (Lee 1995).[5] Each provides a commentary on sanity and reason in their own right. But when they appear in tandem, albeit as figures of apparent deformity, the nature of human conflict itself is given form. The discord between the two clowns is highlighted and exaggerated in such a way that we cannot comfortably define right from wrong; grossly overstated boundaries give way, ironically, to the messy space in-between dualities. We laugh at clowns because we recognize both slapper and slapped in ourselves; we are, in fact, committed to both. The bundle of endless humiliations that we both dish out and suck up every day is mirrored back to us. Just as the Fratellinis, perhaps Italy's greatest family of clowns, showed us the nature of materiality by exhibiting its mutability—guitars that exploded expelling sausages and hams, bicycles that deconstruct with a touch but defy reconstruction (Lee 1995: 161)—white-face clown slapper (straight man, tyrant) and Auguste slapped (comic foil, hapless brunt) reveal the highly unstable and irresolute nature of communication by performing the human penchant for dualism and combat. As they each refuse each other, their joke lies in precisely how they create each other.[6]

As the clown makes seemingly harmless social commentary, this double construct reminds us that his or her incompetence, clumsiness, imprecision, and nonsense are by no means frivolous. It also reminds us that the clown—in embracing both naivety and fiendishness—points to a paradox that plagues social space, particularly the notion of community.

Embodying a joke: the paradox of community

What is the difference between using the lessons of jokes and joking *ideologically* (i.e., as a way to be in the world, to question "truth," to remain open to difference), *actively* (i.e., performing concrete acts in the face of direct oppression), and *pedagogically* (i.e., as a form of leadership, teaching, directing)? What would it mean, what would it look like, to *embody* a joke (not merely *tell* a joke) in each of these cultural domains? Borrowing from James English (1994), what does it mean to think of humor as a social practice, as an event, not just an utterance? In other words, what do jokes do? And how might we—in theatre, in cultural performances of all kinds—do the same?

While we all may celebrate difference ideologically, there is something about jokes and punning that immerses us in the precarious, and not always funny, effects of taking difference seriously. The joker and the clown make our comfort zones—e.g., common sense, identity, and community—uncomfortable. They wake us up to our definitions of "us" (versus "them"), and, in the best scenario, keep us always vigilant against the hardening of our positions.

For many of us involved in theatre and social change, community is the base of our discourse (and the site of much of our actual practice). Community, however, is itself a shifty thing. English writes that "community is not a solution to the political problem, but a problem in its own right" (1994: 21). While community acknowledges and inscribes, names and defines, it simultaneously expresses the impossibility of itself as a unified voice, desire, or consciousness. Community, according to English, has an "unavowable character" (1994: 21). Its rough and porous edges, its inability to know its own constituents or boundaries, its disappearing and reappearing acts—these are its promise, not problems to be corrected. In fact, what community teaches is that paradox can be lived, endured, and offered up as an action not an object. The obvious action would be to commune—to talk together, to be in close rapport. But for English, community performs a joke. It fails to conform to a structure of inside/outside; it allows for stranger, more complex politics than do systems dependent on opposition. In community, English sees the potential for what humor and laughter *do*, how they create paradoxical social space, something Mikhail Bakhtin recognized decades earlier. "Humor and laughter," says English, "have no politics—that is to say, they have no automatic hegemonic or oppositional trajectory" (1994: 17). Community is thus flexible, humorous, capable of accommodating what challenges it without breaking.

For joke theorist Henri Bergson, "our laughter is always the laughter of the group" (1956: 64) allowing us to distinguish an in-group from an out-group. It is true that jokes function on many levels, and some clearly reinforce prescribed cultural boundaries—insult jokes, for example, that intensify or humiliate our allegiances. English contends, however, that while all jokes have a social and relational quality, when we laugh at jokes,

> [W]e do not know what we are laughing at . . . While humor seeks to shore up identifications and solidarities, it does so by working on those very contradictions of society which assure that all such identifications and solidarities will be provisional, negotiable, unsettled.
>
> (English 1994: 10)

Jokes, he continues, would cease to exist if we could clearly delineate lines of identity and difference. It is the combined pleasure and discomfort of something being unresolvable that makes us laugh.

A lot of people say to me, "Dave, how can you, an Orthodox Jew, use a Braun razor made in Germany?"

And I say, "Hey, give credit where it's due: Those people know how to take the beards off of Jews." [Pause, very little laughter]

"So I guess you don't think the holocaust is funny. But I gotta tell you, it killed them back in Poland."

(David Deutsch, cited in Neuman 2003)

Often when we laugh, we are not certain who the "we" is. The joke above elicits laughter from people with a vast array of ideological beliefs. What English emphasizes is that "humor often makes us laugh with those whose psychical organization is radically irreconcilable with our own" (English 1994: 14). Community is the result.

If laughter resides in the dangerous in-between, in the place of conjugality with those we don't necessarily agree with, it seems that laughter might be understood as a place where ethics—notions of relational decency, social laws that must address wide differences—are born, and where "new cartographies of social space" might be drawn (English 1994: 18). Jokes suggest a stranger politics than the frameworks of inside/outside, antagonist/protagonist, oppressor/oppressed can accommodate.

Trickster

What happens when we use notions of joking as a way of responding directly to authority? Will it make our enemies laugh? ("If your enemy is laughing, how can he bludgeon you to death?" Mel Brooks once asked.) Will it confuse them (as it does George in relation to Gracie)? Will it infuriate them in a way that reveals their absurdity (as with Avner's effect on the white-face clown)? Or will it aggravate them in a way that intensifies their authority over us, as it does the doctors who use their power to then pathologize the patients? In any of these actions, has there been any change in the structure of power? Maybe not immediately; neither artistry nor activism often effect desired change in the moment they are performed. But our political actions, those that employ the aesthetic strategies discussed here, could save our lives. How might our goals be fostered through a touch of trickery?

According to Lewis Hyde, the trickster does "joint work" (1998: 252–80); in the active spaces between things, he or she embodies the principle of motion and activates a process of interpretation that inevitably discloses resemblances where they were previously hidden. If the doctor, abiding by the categorical logic of diagnoses, was taken symbolically as a boundary keeper, the Ganserian would be, respectively, the boundary dweller and boundary mover, or trickster. Tricksters connote both stability (the boundary that defines) and vulnerability (the boundary that is being refused); they signify both identity and the shifty nature of identity-formation. While we see trickster behavior on all sides of the contemporary political equation, in myth and literature traditional tricksters reconstitute power on behalf of those without power by moving the boundaries between the haves and have-nots. The very nature of the new constitution is transiency; it is not intended to withstand time but rather to respond to its vicissitudes.

Through their antics, tricksters highlight rational standards precisely as they violate them. This violation happens in lots of different ways including lying, deceit, imitation, and magic, making the trickster figure an ethically complex one.[7] The trickster does not hesitate to use most any means available to right the wrong, to reclaim for the disempowered their legitimate position whether in the family of gods or human beings. For the trickster, the ends always justify the means (Lee 1995: 54).

> It was the final exam at a university. The instructor was very strict and one student arrived thirty minutes late. She came rushing in and asked the instructor for an exam booklet.
>
> "You're not going to have time to finish this," he said as he handed her a booklet.
>
> "Yes I will," she replied, and then took a seat and began writing.
>
> At 2 p.m., the professor called for the exams, and the students filed up and handed them in. All except the one student who had arrived late. A half-hour later, she approached the instructor who was sitting at his desk. She attempted to put her exam on the stack of exam booklets already there.
>
> "No you don't, I'm not going to accept that. It's late."
>
> The student stared incredulously at the instructor. "Do you know who I am?" she asked.
>
> "No, as a matter of fact I don't," replied the instructor.
>
> "Do you know who I am?" she asked again, this time angrily.
>
> "No, and I don't care," replied the professor with an air of superiority.
>
> "Good," she said, and she lifted half the stack of completed exams, stuffed hers in the middle, and walked out of the room.[8]

Hyde (1998) turns to tricksters to answer the question, how do we stay in motion when the world puts barriers in our path? The modalities employed by trickster figures demand that we consider the virtues of being crooked: that is, unlawful, not straightforward, bending, indirect. The trickster is agile in body and mind. When faced with intransitive structures, the trickster changes the rules of the game, stepping outside the framework of understanding itself; in the face of radical differences in values (as we are currently experiencing between those aligned with the Left and the current Bush administration), understanding is not a viable goal. Thoughtfully conceived and executed trickery, or the paradigm-altering enforcement of a living joke, may be far more effective in shifting power.

Hyde also poses the dilemma of what a society can do in the face of its wild cards: "Groups can either expel or ingest their troublemakers. The most successful change-agent avoids either fate and manages to stay on the threshold, neither in nor out . . ." (1998: 224). They teach us how to avoid doing what is expected of us without getting caught.

Jokers and fools in playing decks

Anthropologist Victor Turner (1983) uses the phrase "joker in the deck" to characterize the subjunctive mood of play:

> Play can be everywhere and nowhere, imitate anything, yet be identified with nothing . . . Play is the supreme bricoleur of . . . transient constructions . . . Although "spinning loose" as it were, the wheel of play reveals to us the possibility of . . . the restructuring of what our culture states to be reality.
>
> (Turner 1983: 233–34)

The joker, or wild card, of playing decks has always been pictured as a jester or as a harlequin, with the exception of a few decks in which a fantasy subject is used. In all cases, the joker does not signify pure play but rather the merging of play and game—paidia and ludus—by defying the rules while exploiting them (Landay 1998: 25). Of particular note is that the joker in playing cards (as well as the fool of tarot, originally a card game as well) are worth nothing unto themselves; their paradoxical power emerges only in the case of a challenge with another card against which they always triumph (being the highest trump).

In tarot decks the numerical designation of the fool card is zero—a designation that suggests a vast philosophical and mystical tradition. In tarot rhetoric, nought represents that which is beyond the sphere of the intelligible, the infinite outside the finite. As the first card of the 22 major arcana (depicting allegorical scenes that refer to principles and lessons as well as events), the fool—typically pictured as a young, brightly clad vagabond stepping off a cliff without the slightest concern (or even attention)—references potentiality, innocence, curiosity, trust, and the first necessary and risky step of turning nothing into something. The fool (called the joker in several decks) is said to not belong to him or herself, but rather is always possessed; he or she is without wisdom until moving through each of the remaining 21 major trump cards—each representing a way of being in and responding to the world. In an Indian Tantric deck, the joker (zero card), is represented as an eleven-headed creature wearing the sign of the labyrinth. According to accompanying commentary, this joker is, in fact, the enlightened player of the game, representing the possibility of movement in multiple directions simultaneously. The joker in this system reminds us to not get caught up in destiny, or fixity, or positions, and calls for humor in all situations as a way of maintaining perspective. It also harkens back to the *curinga* of Boal's Joker System.

The original Italian name of the zero card was Il Matto; rather than fool, the better translation is madman or lunatic. When Italian tarot was first introduced in the fifteenth century, lunatics were entitled to express themselves freely, to say things that others could not, and of course many of their seemingly crazy insights bore truth. Their insanity acted, in part, as a sort of shield or privilege. On the one hand, the fool or madman was unabashedly mocked and scorned; on the other hand, he was a vehicle for many profound ironies. The Renaissance jester, often a hunchback or dwarf, though of least social rank in the court, was the only subject officially entitled to play with the ruler, to tease him, to tell him things that others could not without enduring serious consequences. He was the personage viewed as both ridiculous and outstanding, grotesque and quick-witted.

The zero card holds a space—a kind of empty space (the word "silly" means empty, but also holy)—within the panoply of obligations and social conventions where nothing sticks, nothing remains, where identity will not cohere. It speaks crazy sense from that extraordinary vantage point of nought—nowhere and ever-becoming. The lived imperfections that alienated the historical fool and joker, simultaneously proffered them metaphysical authority unreachable by others. It is this very paradox that constitutes the winning power credited to these characters and the playing cards that invoke them.[9]

To use the joker in cards and the fool in tarot (as well as the trickster) as resources, is to attend to a spiritual as well as political dimension. These figures are constellated within divinatory systems; they point to that which our intellectual comprehension cannot fathom (the realm of unseen forces) but are "real" all the same, in the way images, dreams, magnetic fields, and inexplicable coincidences are real. They function between the mundane and the sacred, the known and the mysterious, and ultimately confuse the two. It is not a spirituality of apolitical disengagement that is invoked but something quite the opposite—a spiritual dimension of political engagement itself. The trickster, working (traditionally) for the have-nots, lures the haves deeper into their own disastrous psychic landscapes, makes mazes of their own spin, living nightmares of their own fears, and prisons of their own false privilege. The success of trickster, joker, and fool relies upon an ability to survive, even evolve, in ruptured landscapes and negative space (the nought)—that liminal space where stable positions unravel. As change-agents, we are summoned to embrace disidentification, and practice, in a sense, "nothing." This is not to be confused with passivity. Jokers, as sociospiritual teachers, remind us that in politics, as in everyday life, right action is guided not only by oppositional logic and rational thought but by intuition, body-knowledge, guesswork, and faith; instead of being stuck on a resolution of contradictions, jokers are bent on a playfulness among the irresolute. Consequently, paradox, inconsistency, approximation, ambiguity, and nonsense wreak their divine (and amusing) lessons into the labor of social change.

Putting the joker back in the (TO) Joker[10]

What dimensions of joke structure, clowning, and tricksterism suggest valuable directions for TO facilitation? It would be equally valuable to explore how the TO Joker might design exercises that translate joke/joker theory into new techniques for spect-actors—the site in which Boal himself says that these qualities are enacted.[11] But, for now, how can we translate the lessons of jokes and jokers to deregulate and decentralize (without forgoing necessary responsibility) the work and authority of contemporary TO Jokers?

Given that jokers and tricksters undo hierarchies, the joker as leader—as any kind of authority figure—is something of an oxymoron. Thus, it is precisely something about being an oxymoron that the new TO Joker embodies; one could say that joker as leader frustrates the notion of leadership itself. Many of us who refuse the banking model of education are acutely aware of the resistance that arises when students, however Freirean ideologically, are invited into a more democratic model. The invitation challenges their notion of knowledge itself as they question what they have to offer in relation to their teachers. The newly imagined TO Joker would make leadership a joke in the best sense of the word. While, of course, providing opportunities to explore TO techniques, the Joker would be asking participants to seriously consider what they are looking for in a leader (information? new skills? a space in which to practice their own skills? modeled behavior? explicit directions?) and what their own needs and expectations are when they imagine themselves as TO Jokers.

Tricksters and jokers do not belong to any community; as outsiders, they are loyal only to their own will. Following this directive, the TO Joker might privilege the artistic imperative over explicit political advocacy. Such a Joker would be a communicator not seeking *common* ground so much as maximizing possibilities for the articulation (and re-articulation) of *uncommon* beliefs, working toward a vision of community that thrives on constant reformulation. This kind of Joker works for the sake of *artus*.

While on the one hand, the wild card character belongs nowhere and stands outside the community of participants, the *artus*-driven, mercurial, TO Joker is an articulator (from *articulus*, the diminutive of *artus*). He or she is everywhere, standing in-between, keeping things as fluid as possible, and inevitably serving as a translator, an interpreter. The Joker, regardless of how he or she exercises her authority, is in the position of authority and must take responsibility for how much he or she affects the workshop process. While the spect-actors intervene for one another in various anti-models, the Joker intervenes in structure (less obviously, but just as significantly), continually revising the context within which spect-actors are working. This Joker walks the fine line between providing a container (being responsible) and refusing authority (hesitant to answer any questions definitively).

The TO Joker, as a trickster-like boundary dweller, would link TO with all its borders. Standing on the margin of even that which he or she facilitates, this Joker reminds us that the system we are working within cannot be understood in isolation from that which it is not. Thus, the Joker would be the first to disassemble any chart/template, including that of TO itself. One promise of jokers as pedagogues, as leaders, is that they do not let us forget that we are a composite of characters, ideals, and fantasies, of complex emotions about ourselves and the world around us, including our apparent enemies. Without jokers we run the risk of assuming that our identities are our own, and of the attendant trap of self-propriety. Interestingly, through jokers we reacquaint ourselves in the lessons of performativity itself.

Performativity is founded on mutability, embodiment, play, rehearsing, improvisation, illusion, liveness, and nonreproducibility. It is founded, in large part, on the inevitability of difference (each performance is always necessarily new no matter how rehearsed to be the same). The joker, as embodiment of performativity itself, keeps spect-actors and audience aware that we too are in a performance, making meaning over and again in the here and now and across time. While we regularly face obstructive and reductive forces of fixity—in ideology, belief, role, identity—we recognize fixity to be a performance as well, and thus changeable.

Jokers—performing their double entendres, inciting confusion and incongruity, validating the unseen, even lying and stealing—are not spoilers; their strategies are applicable, perhaps essential, to social change. Jokers animate the complexities of being both subject and object every day on the stage of our various struggles. They endorse the mobius-like twists of logic and tranform seeming handicaps (being of two minds, speaking from all sides of one's mouth) into multipurpose tools. Jokers do, and teach others to do, what Yogi Berra suggests we do in moments of uncertainty: "When you come to a fork in the road, take it."

Notes

1   See Boal (1979: 167–97) in the section "Development of the Arena Theater of São Paulo" and the Appendices for a thorough discussion of the Joker System.
2   According to Boal, the term *curinga* does not carry the diverse connotations that the term "joker" does in English, and the Anglicized meanings are not at all what was intended when Boal used the word *curinga*. Nonetheless, both *curinga* and the Joker System seem to embody the very structure of a joke and to exhibit in action what a critical pedagogy of jok(er)ing has to offer.
3   In terms of structure, this is clearly a different kind of joke than ones we have referenced thus far whereby an approximation ensues from purposeful word play. An approximation happens here, all the same, in the realm of logic. A version of this joke can be found online at http://www.afunworld.com/retirement-jokes/joke-519.htm
4   I saw this routine performed by Avner the Eccentric at the Magic Castle, Hollywood, 1994. It is derivative of a routine made famous by Emmet Kelly.
5   Lee sees these types as trickster (he who slaps) and fool (he who gets slapped), both of whom will be discussed later in this chapter.
6   A similar kind of instructive doubling occurs within classic ventriloquist routines. The dummy can tell dreadfully off-color jokes, curse and blaspheme, sing off-key, whine, and interrupt and yet be absolutely adored by the audience. As the voice of the repressed, the dummy can be everything the ventriloquist—the socialized self, the well-behaving audience—cannot be, and consequently steals his power. The joke is all the more effective as the ventriloquist is literally scripting and vocalizing his own demise, linking his fate with his very personal antagonist. As the ventriloquist attempts to maintain moral decorum, the dummy, who can do no wrong, mimics the ventrilo-

quist's controlling voice as if obscenely tyrannical, thus animating in the audience popular revolt against all oppressive voices.

7 Concerns regarding deceit are common when engaging in Invisible Theatre actions. Tricksters argue for deceit as a valid aspect of "heroic" activity.

8 A version of this joke can be found online at http://www.funnypart.com/funny_jokes/exam.shtml

9 See Andy's playing cards, online at http://a_pollett.tripod.com

10 The various cultural jokers (Ganserians, tricksters, clowns, jokers in card decks) discussed in this chapter are designated in the following pages as jokers (lower case) while the TO Joker per se is designated as Joker (upper case) in order to elucidate the potential effects of the former on the latter.

11 See the section entitled "Workshop" in an earlier version of this chapter online (Schutzman 2003) for techniques that do just that. For example, a new technique, called "Be Your Own Dummy," explores the double nature of jokes, clowns, and ventriloquist routines. After presenting the anti-model, a spect-actor replaces the protagonist while the protagonist moves through the scene as an irrational, obscene "dummy" expressing all she feels about herself and each of the other characters in the scene. This dummy is encouraged to speak nonsense, indulge feelings, express conflict, exaggerate, mock, and be childish.

Bibliography

Bergson, H. (1956) "Laughter," in W. Sypher (ed.) Comedy. Baltimore, MD, and London: Johns Hopkins University Press.

Boal, A. (1979) Theatre of the Oppressed, trans. C.A. and M.-O.L. McBride. New York: Urizen Books.

—— (1995) The Rainbow of Desire: The Boal method of theatre and therapy, trans. A. Jackson. London and New York: Routledge.

—— (2003) Private conversation, June 11, Los Angeles.

English, J.F. (1994) "Introduction: Humor, politics, community," in Comic Transactions: Literature, humor, and the politics of community in twentieth-century Britain. Ithaca, NY, and London: Cornell University Press.

Hyde, L. (1998) Trickster Makes This World: Mischief, myth, and art. New York: North Point Press.

Landay, L. (1998) Madcaps, Screwballs, Con Women: The female trickster in American culture. Philadelphia, PA: University of Pennsylvania Press.

Lee, J. (1995) The History of Clowns for Beginners. London: Writers and Readers Limited.

Manea, N. (1992) "On clowns: The dictator and the artist—notes to a text by Fellini," in N. Manea (ed.) On Clowns: The dictator and the artist. New York: Grove Press.

Neuman, J. (2003) "Schticky situation: Are we still funny?" Heeb: The New Jew Review April, no. 3. Online. Available: <http://www.heebmagazine.com/magazine/mag_3_feat_1.php> (accessed September 14, 2004).

Schutzman, M. (1999) The Real Thing: Performance, hysteria, and advertising. Hanover, NH, and London: Wesleyan University Press.

—— (2003) "Joker runs wild," American Communication Journal 6: 3. Online. Available: <http://acjournal.org/holdings/vol6/iss3/schutzman/index.html> (accessed February 8, 2004).

Turner, V. (1983) "Body, brain and culture," Zygon 18: 2: 221–45.

Whitlock, F.A. (1982) "The Ganser syndrome and hysterical pseudo-dementia," in A. Roy (ed.) Hysteria. New York: John Wiley and Sons.

Wodehouse, P.J. (1937) A Damsel in Distress (screenplay). G. Stevens, dir. RKO Radio Pictures.

Witnessing subjects

A fool's help

Julie Salverson

In 1996 Augusto Boal took a seat in the legislature in Rio de Janeiro running under the curious platform, "The Courage to be Happy." Happiness, for Boal, is both a personal and a social task that is always difficult and involves making things better: more generous, more ethical, more just, more alive. It also involves holding in tension what in every private or public relationship are contradictory dynamics: those that generate and nourish, those that violate and tear down. "What would happiness be," asks Adorno, "that was not measured by the immeasurable grief at what is?" (cited in Cornell 1992: 17). This concept is neither sentimental nor nostalgic. Playwright David Hare writes about the challenge of trying to perform a tragic musical on Broadway. He says that much of America is plagued with a fantasy of wish-fulfillment where artists are asked to tell people that everything turns out well in the end, that no matter what is suffered, what is lost, "everything is all right really" (1991: 148). I am interested in the importance, even the ethics, of a courageous, tough kind of happiness that is based not in avoidance, but in contact with others and oneself. Is there a relationship between happiness, suffering, and the capacity to bear witness, to be present to both the losses and the capabilities of others? This chapter looks at possibilities for witnessing generated by Boal's work in the context of the pragmatic ethical philosophy of Emmanuel Levinas, and asks what the notion of a courageous happiness might bring to the ethics of witnessing a tragic world.

The challenge to witness

"Witnessing" is a term used across discussions of solidarity and justice in arenas including the courtroom, the sanctuary, the classroom, the therapist's office, and the performance space. What is consistent across these different terrains is the notion of coming upon something unexpected and being impacted by the encounter such that one is compelled to respond to the address. To become a witness is to be exposed, vulnerable, to have something at stake. The nature of the risk will vary, as will the negotiations of acceptance or refusal. Philosopher Emmanuel Levinas, a Lithuanian Jew and the only one of his family to survive the holocaust, speaks of ethics and responsibility from the heart of twentieth-century European genocide. As early as 1934 he was attempting to understand the rise to power of National Socialism as something constituent to the philosophy and culture of the West, which he described as a closed system unable to know, and not wanting to know anything beyond the self.

His solution to this interiority was to explore radical ways of engaging with the Other. His writing has both grounded and challenged my theatre work with survivors of violence, has extended the range of what I imagine possible when listening and responding to difficult stories, and has provided me with a way to deepen my understanding of where Theatre of the Oppressed (TO), as practice and conceptual framework, may lead. Levinas defines ethics as the calling into question of the self through its infinite obligation to the other and by that Other's absolute alterity.[1] In other words, whatever I think I understand, there remains something beyond my ability to know, to sense, to imagine, something that will surprise me and which comes from outside myself. It is my ethical obligation to remain vigilant, ready to receive that *something* and to put myself at its service. For Levinas, the call to witness is not about prescription; he does not offer a model. Rather, ethics is prior to politics, prior to working out the *how* of doing it.[2]

Over the past few years, witnessing has become the trendy term when it comes to talking about loss. Across the literature on witnessing, I suspect a kind of thrill of the chase, a disturbing enthusiasm, a sense that writers on witnessing have discovered pain. But in the philosophy of Levinas the tragic self is challenged to become the ethical self. That is, beyond the hopeless, self-enclosing indulgence of a tragic response to existence, there is an alternative: the encounter with the Other. Witnessing, in these terms, has both personal and political consequences. For the artist working with the testimonies of survivors of violence and trying to pass on accounts that bear witness to the remains that honor the dead, the challenge to respond with integrity—honestly, fully, with one's entire being—is a challenge to witness. As a witness I announce myself publicly, and I commit myself to the consequence of response. But how can we understand what makes possible the "I" capable of either engaging with or responding to the call of another? According to Levinas, the very thing that makes me an "I," is found in my capability to respond to the Other's need of me: "I am he who finds the resources to respond to the call" (1985: 89). The answer to the question lies in the other person through whom we become not a mastering subject of, but, rather, *subject to*. Thus ethics and witnessing are about relationship.

This does not mean we become one with the other. Levinas is responding to a phenomenon he suspects to be the inevitable outcome of a Western philosophical tradition in which meaning lies in a false totality through which everything might be understood, and thus mastered and controlled. For Levinas, Western philosophy's love affair with totality reaches its logical conclusion in the terrors of fascism. He is talking about what happens when ideas of unity and discourses of oneness are taken to extremes, and when any idea or person who does not fit into the desired whole is erased, figuratively or literally, by the mastering subject. In the face of a totality that expresses itself in the world as totalitarianism, Levinas insists that the ethical alternative is only possible when I declare that I can never know (and thus erase through my assuming to know) the Other; I can only respond, attend, and remain willing to hear beyond my own conceptions.[3]

This call to ethics has implications for solidarity work, for theatre activism, for teaching, and for personal engagements. If the challenge to witness asks us to attend to another, and to attend to how we are implicated by and invested in what we are hearing, what in our practice gets in the way of such witnessing, and in the way of our being the "I" capable of responding to the call? I'll turn now to examples of two difficulties I see in attempts to witness. The first involves a culture and aesthetic of the sentimentally tragic, the second a kind of politically correct paralysis in the name of ethics.

Tragic witnesses

What is the cultural moment in North America within which testimony is performed, and what kinds of images are desired, approved of, funded? Alisa Solomon describes an American public "glutted on sentimental empathy for the proper victims" (2001: 9). What does this look like in practice? Not long ago I saw a performance piece that was advertised as being about teenagers in crisis. The show was developed with young people who have experienced violence and risked taking their own lives. It was performed by students and professionals, and was written and staged by professional artists. Before I attended the performance a colleague of mine, a director and playwright who doesn't work in the area of performing testimony, saw the piece, and I asked her about it. She paused. "It's politically incorrect, really, not to like a show like that." "I know, but tell me anyway," I said. Her remarks—as a mother of a teenage boy—were very interesting. First, she said it seemed to her strange that the performers were all so gorgeous. "Gorgeous bodies writhing about in agony on stage," she said. And, "it's kind of passive-aggressive. I'm not sure it is so good for my son to be in touch with how he hurts, *this* way." Also of interest to my friend was a kind of call and response she observed in the talkback session afterwards: "A person says, 'I suffered this too,' and everyone claps." "Confession," I said. "Baptist church healing ritual," she said.

Then I saw the show myself. It seemed familiar, and I realized I was seeing a perfect, professionalized English Canadian TO forum. I read in the program that the play had been developed through a series of theatre workshops based on TO processes. Pedagogically, these workshops are structured to serve the experience of the participants who share a common problem. The process typically begins by the Joker asking people for images of individual violation and then building a play through an analysis of those moments. In many of the projects I have seen and participated in, there is great excitement, laughter, and discovery generated through the making and animating of the images and the questions explored inside the workshop. The pivot point of the work, however, is always the protagonist's pain, and the resulting story and analysis emerges from the orientation of the subject as the victim. When it comes to forming the material into a performance aesthetic, the Jokers tend to do little more than arrange images into sequence, make sure people can be seen and heard, and theatricalize, in a limited way, the images and fairly crude skits that were the basis of the workshop. These images and skits, however evocative for personal development within a process, read in performance as simplistic regarding notions of structural and political oppression. The challenge for artists and educators, it seems to me, is to walk the delicate balance between honoring the stories of the group members while not withholding the political, theatrical, and pedagogical expertise that brought them to the workshop in the first place.

What are facilitators, as potential witnesses, withholding from the encounter with participants? Many Jokers of TO will say "we do not influence the process, it is all about the group." But the questions asked by the Joker, both inside the workshop and during the performance, shape the range of the experiences and ideas generated. The Joker usually asks, "What is your experience of hurt?", which is followed by questions about cause and effect: "Who did what to whom? How can you fight back? Who can help you?" The discussion reduces itself to injury and blame, and claims to complex analysis that move the personal into the political— the dynamic relationship between psychological, social, and political factors—are rarely fulfilled. The plays look the same, the audiences respond in the same ways, the victim is rewarded for her pain, the person who displays the most pain gets her story featured. I was once told by a teenager working with me on a project like this, "You are paying me to be a kid in trouble, aren't you, you don't want to hear about my good day."[4]

In the case of the production discussed above, what unfolded before me—to my extreme discomfort—was a morality play. It had a number of relevant TO tropes: authenticity, confession, oppressors. According to the production, teen problems are caused by divorce, stupid parents, or ignorant teachers. There were no intelligent adults and few resourceful young people. Only the lost and the losing. Going down, and proud of it, they seemed to declare. Accomplished artists who normally would exercise their considerable skills seemed to be shackled by the workshop and silenced by the enthusiasm of their encounter with these vibrant teenage sufferers. It struck me that a theatrical form I helped disseminate in Canada had become a genre I now deeply distrusted. I told my friend afterwards, "I feel like someone who helped develop a drug and now thinks it is dangerous." Or is it? Drugs are powerful. Sometimes they ease pain. Is this eroticized anguish or a stage in the process of bearing witness? Arrested melancholy or a key moment of infantile experience (that some psychoanalysts consider a part of the process of mourning)? If so, it is important to think about how elements of mourning and melancholy may be operating when encounters with violence are engaged with pedagogically, and translated into aesthetic forms.

Through the lens of Levinas' ethics, representation must always leave room for the other to breathe, and artistic interpretations need to engage a mimesis that is "impossibly double, simultaneously the stake and the shifting sands" (Diamond 1997: v). This is not to suggest only one model of theatrical language, but to draw attention to tendencies in both pedagogy and aesthetics to reduce the Other to the explainable, as in the case of the performance described above where victims are *explained* as terminally tragic. This approach to witnessing is more an attempt to entrap the Other through the crudest of representational strategies, mimesis as capture. Scholar Richard Kearney, who has interviewed Levinas, points out that Levinas is "deeply suspicious of the enchanting power of images once they cease to answer to the Other" (2002: 87). What this looks like in practice is either an almost hysterical adoration of the victim, or a self-congratulatory finger pointing at the oppressor. The subject of the testimony (the young person whose story is on stage, who has suffered the violation) and the potential witnesses (the actor who portrays her, the director who stages her, the audience who attends her) are excluded from more than the most superficial engagements which are structured, ironically, in terms of a feel-good kind of empathy.

The act of translating accounts of violence is situated within vital debates about the capacity of history, art, and education to convey the urgency and complexity of what James Young calls "the afterlife of memory" (2000: 3). The title of Young's book, *At Memory's Edge*, evokes the moment when first-person testimony gives way to secondary translations, confounding the problem of witnessing with the challenge of engaging not only what happened but how the event is passed to us and through us. It is precisely at this moment of giving way that the artist or storyteller appears, charged with the problem of representation. The cultural dynamic that turned Boal's call for "the courage to be happy" to what Vancouver TO educator Victor Porter calls "the danger of theatre of the depressed," is a complex problem.[5] On the one hand, there is the conscious desire to relieve pain and admit the historical injuries perpetrated; on the other hand, the perhaps less conscious need to make the legacies of damage disappear. One way to reduce damage is to try to fix it. Perhaps an element of the tragic approach to witnessing, albeit a seemingly contradictory element, is the need to make the tragedy go away. The quick-fix mentality stages a reduced version of the tragic that does not account for complexities, contexts, and strengths of either those who are injured by injustices or those struggling to address them. Critical to witnessing is the ability to allow for the evidence—what we see in front of us, the person in pain, the material remains—together with an attentiveness to what is not knowable, both the excess and the silence out of which all testimony speaks.[6]

For Levinas, the problem with tragic representation is that it is "never tragic enough" (Caruana 1998: 33). In its efforts to give voice to the marginalized, an aesthetic of injury risks enacting narratives of suffering that reduce testimony to the interpretive frame where all otherness is sentenced to loss.[7] The problem for the witness seeking to represent accounts of violence, then, is the danger of fixing trauma in presumed configurations of how loss looks and sounds. Presumptions and preconceptions about pain and how to recognize it restrict the ability of a potential witness to perceive strength and resilience in a survivor and the possible vulnerability or damage in oneself as a listener to stories of violence.[8] This returns me to the question, who am I as the one preparing to listen, and how well do I attend myself as I listen? Encounters with the difficult knowledge of trauma have the potential to set in motion dynamics of identification and defense that play out the uneasy negotiation between one's own experience of loss and another's account. Educator Deborah Britzman reminds us that when education—and, I would add, theatre—engages testimony, what gets opened up is the territory of psychic trauma and the internal conflicts the listener brings to hearing (1998: 117). To be available as a witness, then, is to disturb our own sense of ourselves, and to risk bringing that shaken self to the table.

Paralyzed witnesses

What is the alternative to a tragic response to a world that is, itself, tragic? A friend and former teacher of mine, Deanne Bogdan (2002), has written about what happened during the first meeting of a graduate arts and education class she was teaching at the University of Toronto on September 12, 2001. She wanted to start the seminar with a recording that would be an appropriate tribute to the victims of the tragedy in New York the day before, and tried to decide what piece of music would best suit this group of students. After considering carefully the prediscursive representational content of music, she chose Fauré's *Requiem*. When she got to the class, however, she was so worried about the overwhelming potential for unpredictable responses from her students that she ended up playing nothing. Bogdan writes a rather brave article asking if in fact she might have been wrong in this default of a choice. She asks: "Could the ethical imperatives (of the moment) supersede what may appear as surface considerations of an audience's timidity and/or vulnerability? To what degree might my hesitancy to play anything have been a failure of nerve?" (2002: 127–28).

I am not suggesting that paralysis in the face of catastrophe (or even acute distress) is necessarily the problem. It is the source of this paralysis as Bogdan explains it that interests me. There is a long list of concerns she worries through in making her decision to play no music, and in her article all of them start with "I": "Who was I, anyway?" "How could I know?" "I could not presume." "How could I have anticipated?" Again we are confronted with the I, but an I more paralyzed than prepared for difficult engagement. This is by no means to fault Bogdan, her candor in exploring this moment in writing is admirable. She describes a dangerous tension many will find familiar between the desire to help and the desire to respect the integrity of the Other. There is a fine balance to be negotiated between putting ourselves in the picture and making the picture about ourselves. Yet in this case, Bogdan was not completely removed from the situation at hand. She, too, was affected by the events of September 11, and so why did this not give her some license to offer her response through the piece of music she would play? As a teacher, did she feel she had to keep a professional distance? If the teacher and student are both to learn, and to recognize violent acts as social and not merely individual events, must they perhaps bear witness to each other? Might it have been a relief to the students to find that their teacher was also uncertain, conflicted and living out her own relationship to both the events of the previous day and the challenge of how to respond, publicly, with the class?

The other side of rushing in to *fix it*, is to be too afraid to rush at all. It is a curious irony if we find ourselves weaving a web of distance in the name of contact and engagement. Of course there is reason for caution: years of missionary zeal, imperial conquest, invasion of lands and bodies, the real presence of trauma in people we meet and work with, and our own damage and trauma. Witnesses driven by unconscious needs—legitimate in themselves but potentially confusing if not damaging to others—run the risk of acting the role of the tourist. When my inner conflict takes an upper hand, the impulse toward caution might direct not only toward protection of others—at least not initially—but also toward self-protection. The challenge to witness is complex. There are questions to be asked about how we act and how we hesitate. I do not mean to say that this is easy, or that complete self-understanding must precede the approach to another. Becoming a witness is a process, and sometimes we err not on the side of intrusion but of paralysis. The result is theatre, pedagogy, and scholarship that fails to risk the dangers of sitting together in practices of engagement. When does responsible listening become a monologue due to a listener's silence or paralysis? How do we avoid either unconscious investments and attachments we have never fully acknowledged, or, its counterpart, a pedagogy that is really about ourselves?

Witnessing subjects

Levinas challenges us to pay attention to the absolute alterity of the other, and Boal asks that we engage in the tough and courageous act of contact. But a witness who can't navigate the difference between herself and another is probably not only conflicted but also untrustworthy. One of the reasons for this problem of approach is the difficulty of how to include the witnesses' own relationship to violence in the transaction of witnessing. For example, how does a Joker who has suffered some kind of violence in his own life bear witness to other abuses, those of the participants in his workshop? This is a structural as well as an individual problem. The framework of victim and oppressor recognizes the witness only as he exists in relation to the oppressed. Within this structure, how does Deanne Bogdan witness her own response to September 11 when she is in a classroom with survivors of other violences—say, chronic racial violence—that make their relationship to the deaths in New York City significantly different from hers? She will be perceived—and continue to perceive and present herself—as an outsider as long as the structure of the analysis does not address the violence explored as a social event that somehow includes her. If she can find no structural place in which to bring this to speech in her own work, she will *speak* of this experience otherwise.

What frames of reference might help articulate the mechanisms that prevent the witness from being a witnessing subject? One might be to consider the fear of doing the wrong thing a sign of moving outside the sayable with what Judith Butler would call "impossible speech":[9]

The question is not whether certain kinds of speech uttered by a subject are censored, but how a certain operation of censorship determines who will be a subject depending on whether the speech of such a candidate obeys certain norms governing what is speakable and what is not. *To move outside the domain of speakability is to risk one's status as a subject . . .* The question is not what it is I will be able to say, but what will constitute the domain of the sayable within which I begin to speak at all.

(Butler 1997: 133)

I think it is possible that witnesses do not consider themselves subjects, and that this erasure is as much a cultural problem as it is a psychological one. If, where social change is concerned, there is a kind of structural myopia at work that makes us lose sight of the impact the witness makes, it would help to allow the symptom—the behavior—to give us permission to explore the cause. We might be surprised, even shocked, at the response we would get from the people we consider oppressed. Rosemary Jolly, a white South African writing about her work on rape and gender violence with women in Soweto, describes how the women refused to meet her in person until she explained why she was interested in their lives. "This statement did not take the form of telling them why their stories were important to the oral, historical record" (Jolly 2004: 24) because "they knew that, and had had enough of white people coming into Soweto and getting information from them without giving anything back, even money" (2004: 25). Jolly nervously writes to them her own life-narrative, forcing herself not to omit incidents she fears they will think are trivial. The women used her story

[T]o judge whether they would enter into a relationship with me or not. They responded sympathetically to parts of my narrative, parts that they saw as a testimony to a somewhat difficult life, and *I was amazed, for I had never thought I had the right to see my life in that way* [emphasis mine]. In other words, they were quite willing to grant me the subject status that had eluded them, almost all their lives, in the society in which they live.

(Jolly 2004: 25)

Another framework helpful to the problem of the tragic or paralyzed witness is that of hysteria. For Jean-Martin Charcot, hysteria was "a physical illness caused by a hereditary defect or traumatic wound in the central nervous system" (Showalter 1997: 30). According to Showalter, "Throughout history, hysteria has served as a form of expression, a body language for people who otherwise might not be able to speak or even to admit what they feel (1997: 7)." Although hysteria marked a particular gendered and medically pathologized response to oppression in the late nineteenth century, it might be understood, in a very different context, as a way to witness others' experiences and representations of violence and oppression. If we find ourselves as witnesses overwhelmed by the magnitude of the story we are hearing, and unable to locate ourselves within that story, we might become people unable to speak or admit what we feel, resulting in a kind of hysterical witnessing. Mady Schutzman (1999) suggests that hysterical performances employed consciously and strategically could be resources for resistance or healing. Perhaps hysteria, utilized as a deliberate ploy, offers a way to consider conflicted responses less as pathology and more as positive tension between our own anxieties and the call of the Other. Might the multiple influences that shape our encounters with others be put to the service of an approach that is more humble than heroic, more generous than guilty. How can we reimagine our own hysteria, and mobilize ourselves for engagement, not just with concepts of loss, but *with people who lose*?

Foolish witnesses

In a letter to Gershom Scholem about Kafka, Walter Benjamin wrote:

> This much Kafka was absolutely sure of: First, that someone must be a fool if he is to help; second, that only a fool's help is real help. The only uncertain thing is, can such help do a human being any good?
>
> (Benjamin, cited in Handelman 1991: 40)

There followed the famous phrase: "There is an infinite amount of hope, but not for us." For years I have been fascinated by this image. It suggests risk, engagement, failure. The context is the inevitable pain of ongoing loss in the midst of an almost ridiculous insistence upon life, and a hope that is different from messianic hope, that does not offer reassurance or certainties. I'll conclude with a glimpse at an alternative to a tragic or paralyzed approach to testimony by turning to the absurd, the ridiculous, the clown. What potential could be offered by a fool's help, a foolish witness?

The idea of clown I am drawing on is not the stereotypical circus clown, but one characterized by truthfulness and a willingness to engage in the face of failure. This clown begins with nothing, is in fact ridiculous but is innocent of this fact, innocent of the impossibility of hope. To be ridiculous is normal, ridicule and loss is part of life, flopping, messing up, is inevitable. "In the face of this, let us begin," says this clown. This clown always needs a playmate, someone to begin with. This idea of needing to be engaged, having to engage, suggests a new approach to witnessing.

French artists Jacques Lecoq and Philippe Gaulier teach that the clown refuses consolation, including the consolation of forgetting.[10] In their approach to teaching and performing clown there are a number of key elements: a world from which there is no escape; an audience, implicated and present; clowns on the stage, constantly seeking to love and be loved, and above all offering their naked selves, and; the tyrant clown, stronger than the rest, louder than the rest, in charge. The tyrant runs the show and the game is to play anyway, to live anyway. "Amusez-vous, merde!" ("For God's sakes, joy!") says Gaulier to his students. Having fun in this context is not spectacle or escape, but rather the deadly game of living with loss, living despite failure, living even despite the humiliation of trying endlessly. It is this idea of "amusez-vous, merde"—live and love in the shit—which I understand as Boal's approach to happiness: a tenacious, nonsentimental insistence on life within loss that is honest, ready to risk failure, and absolutely courageous. As witnesses, we inevitably fail. But how do we live? What are we like to have tea with?

I have found the most potent image of the foolish witness in a story from another twentieth-century philosopher. In his challenging work *Fear and Trembling*, Kierkegaard paints an intriguing portrait of several knights. These knights behave as all knights do: they fall in love and woo a princess. What intrigues me is the distinction Kierkegaard makes between two aspects of impossible love, which I think of as two aspects of witnessing: the Knight of Resignation and the Knight of Faith. The Knight of Resignation knows he can't have the princess. He is not in denial; he not only accepts his loss, he embraces it. And despite his life and his very self being stripped of meaning, he renounces the everyday world and turns his life toward God. This is a man worthy of admiration. Perhaps he leaves people close to him feeling guilty: they don't do nearly as much as he does to help others. And he has a "good attitude," he is not wallowing in confusion and pain, he embraces a higher purpose. This might be the witness who forges ahead while declaring to all that witnessing is an impossible task and is ultimately confounded by loss. But Kierkegaard tells us that there is something beyond loss that exists in this world.

The Knight of Faith also knows he has lost the princess. He completely renounces his claim to the finite world, and, at the same time, embraces its possibilities. The wonderfully, or perhaps dangerously, paradoxical move that this knight makes is to turn in two directions at once: toward the infinite and toward the world. This witness will risk what might come from another cup of tea. The Knight of Resignation is so busy loving God: "I shall find joy and repose in my own pain" (Mooney 1991: 54); he is using all his strength just to be resigned. He would not notice if, by some miracle, the princess should return. He is not available to this world. The Knight of Faith, however, knows he has lost everything. He knows it is impossible to gain the princess' love, but he remains available to the option of the impossible. How does he do this? "By faith, says that marvelous knight, by faith, [he shall] get her by virtue of the absurd" (1991: 54).

I take this to mean that it is absurd, even ridiculous, to risk answering the call of another. It is absurd to think that my availability as a listener, a witness, might contribute anything in the face of another's violation, another's loss, yet I step forward all the same. For Deanne Bogdan, what could her choice of music lend to anyone in the class that day? For Rosemary Jolly, what could her story give to the women in Soweto? Witnessing, I suggest, is about the absurd and yet honest offer. It is curious that another word for "offer" is "tender." Witnessing is also about impossible tenderness. To approach another, says Levinas, is to be drawn and destabilized, compelled and invited in such a way that I "lose my place radically" (1998: 185). Levinas calls this "an enormous response" (1998: 185) that causes a shudder, a trembling: "This weakness," he adds, "is needed" (1998: 185). Adorno asks what happiness would be that is not measured by the immeasurable grief at what is. But what, I wonder—turning his comment slightly—is grief that is not measured by the astonishment of living, the awakening from death that continues to surprise?

Within the terms of the witnessing encounter, I find a fascinating meeting place between Levinas and Boal, fertile points of contact and places of divergence. Boal made a crucial discovery early in his work: the spectator who steps on stage is no longer an observer but enters a kind of subjecthood which Boal calls spect-actorship. This individual and yet political engagement became central to Boal's pedagogy, essential to facing one's own and one's community's liberation and something no actor could do in the protagonist's place. While at first Boal asked the artists in his company to play the role of the oppressed subject on stage, when the subjects themselves took to the stage the actors discovered a new role. Instead of the stand-in, the actor became an implicated listener, a witness, an "I" willing to be available to the call.

How does this availability look in practice? Levinas refuses to answer that for us. This is frustrating, we want answers, we want to know *how*. This frustration is natural, the desire for guidance reasonable. But perhaps the answer to the question lies not in any particular strategies, but in the act of being available itself. Central to Jacques Lecoq's teaching about clown—and, perhaps, Boal's teaching as well—is the willingness to offer ourselves, something he called having *quelque chose à dire* (something to say). If we do not bring who we are, including our skills and our vulnerabilities, to the encounter with others, then we are not truly available. Approaching and witnessing another has far greater implications than we might imagine. Approaching, in the context of contemporary events, is a game we had best learn to play, and the stakes are high. Will we approach tragically, or not at all? Or will we, perhaps, approach foolishly?

There is a rule in Gaulier's clown work that one of his actors describes:

> When anyone felt they were *acting* playing the game rather than *playing* it, they had to go to the front of the stage, jump ten times, face the audience with "nothing," and then, with that mood, start playing the game again.
>
> (Martin 2002: 64)

Clearly it is important to take seriously how little we know of another's loss, perhaps even of our own, and to engage with others despite that lack, sometimes even because of it. To remind ourselves, it can be useful to jump 10 times. But beyond the "nothing" we must stand in, the seeming emptiness of how little we offer, there is also the "something" we bring in our efforts to listen, to teach, to engage, and to change things. It is frightening, there is a nakedness in this kind of clownish contact. But it offers another way through the victim/hero polarities, another way through the tragic appropriations of pain.

The tragic victim needs an oppressor. How many options does that configuration, that image, allow us? Does it leave scholar Deanne Bogdan in the curious position, that bewildering day in September, of having no evident oppressor to protect her students from, and so—since the logic of the image insists they need protection—protecting them from herself? How does such logic position, perhaps infantilize the adult students in her class? Caught in this meta-dramatic configuration, where is the space to engage with some kind of mutuality, and where is the possibility to witness? The destabilized position of the clown offers a place to consider relationships across difference—relationships of attention without resolution, of respect without capture—that allow for peaceful engagements. Levinas says, "it is not a matter of peace as pure rest that confirms one's identity but of always placing in question this very identity, its limitless freedom and its power" (1996: 167). In being foolish witnesses, we allow ourselves to fail while remaining always alert, ready, and willing to try.

Notes

1 The notion of responsibility to the Other is tricky, and can suggest a kind of pathologizing of victims of injury as needing rescue. This dynamic is predominant in fundamentalist missionary movements and clinical social work practices. Frank Tester (2003) has pointed out the problems with the language of oppression. According to Tester, the label "oppressed" is both demeaning and disempowering and compounds the tendency to analyze people and communities as problems. I understand Levinas to be using the term "for the other" in the sense of orientation toward, rather than helping, the Other.

2 It is not that politics, negotiation, and even regulation are not important, but these Levinas relegates to the field of morality: "This distinction between the ethical and the moral is very important here. By morality I mean a series of rules relating to social behaviour and civic duty . . . ethics cannot itself legislate for society or produce rules of conduct whereby society might be revolutionized or transformed" (1996: 29).

3 Throughout Levinas' writing, what is never knowable about another is ultimately *other than* being, *other than* the person who faces us. What Levinas means by "the Other" is not a particular person—though a person is inevitably who we actually address and are addressed by—but the

responsibility that exists prior to being summoned, prior to all knowledge and understanding (hence the name of his major work, *Otherwise Than Being*).

4 The performance I just described could be considered a testimonial. Testimony as a discursive act implies certain assumptions about its form. Ernst Van Alphen, writing about holocaust literature and art, calls testimony "a documentary realist genre" (1997: 4) that is valued (together with autobiography and the diary) because of its "presumed directness" (1997: 11). Van Alphen makes a distinction between historical and imaginative discourses within representation. He places testimony as a trope within the former and addresses the tensions produced when the realm of the imaginative intersects with what is more trusted as historical: "Documentary realism has become the mode of representation that novelists and artists must adopt if they are to persuade their audience of their moral integrity" (1997: 20). The kind of sentimentalized tragic form I am discussing feeds into this dichotomy, and maintains a preoccupation with experience—considering it authentic and untouchable—that both disregards the complexity of negotiating life in the midst of loss and presumes that approaching experience as transparent maintains an innocent listening.

5 From personal conversation.

6 See Simon and Eppert (1997) and Felman and Laub (1992).

7 See Salverson (1999) and (2001).

8 For a valuable debate about the relationship between the notion of victim and performance, see Arlene Croce's (1998) discussion of Bill T. Jones' dance piece "Still/Here."

9 I thank Rosemary Jolly for pointing out this connection to me.

10 For this idea and the many helpful conversations about clown and consolation I thank my colleague at Queen's University Department of Drama, Michelle Newman. My thinking is also continuously stimulated by work and conversations with director/devisor Steven Hill (Leaky Heaven Circus, Vancouver).

Bibliography

Boal, A. (1995) *The Rainbow of Desire: The Boal method of theatre and therapy*, trans. A. Jackson. London and New York: Routledge.

Bogdan, D. (2002) "Situated sensibilities and the need for coherence: Musical experience reconsidered," *Philosophy of Music Education Review*, 10: 2: 125–28.

Britzman, D.P. (1998) *Lost Subjects, Contested Objects: Toward a psychoanalytic inquiry of learning*. Albany, NY: SUNY Press.

Butler, J. (1997) *Excitable Speech: A politics of the performative*. New York and London: Routledge.

Caruana, J. (1998) "The catastrophic 'site and non-site' of proximity: Redeeming the disaster of being," *International Studies in Philosophy* 30: 1: 33–46.

Cornell, D. (1992) *The Philosophy of the Limit*. New York and London: Routledge.

Croce, A. (1998) "Discussing the undiscussable," in M. Berger (ed.) *Crisis of Criticism*. New York: The New Press.

Diamond, E. (1997) *Unmaking Mimesis*. New York and London: Routledge.

Felman, S. and Laub, D. (1992) *Testimony: Crises of witnessing in literature, psychoanalysis, and history*. New York and London: Routledge.

Hare, D. (1991) *Writing Left-Handed*. London and Boston, MA: Faber and Faber.

Handelman, S.A. (1991) *Fragments of Redemption: Jewish thought and literary theory in Benjamin, Scholem, and Levinas*. Bloomington and Indianapolis, ID: Indiana University Press.

Jolly, R. (2004) "Cultured violence: narrative as social form in the wake of South Africa's Truth and Reconciliation Commission," unpublished manuscript.

Kearney, R. (2002) "Levinas and the ethics of imagining," in D. Glowacka and S. Boos (eds) *Between Ethics and Aesthetics: Crossing the boundaries*. Albany, NY: SUNY Press.

Levinas, E. (1985) *Ethics and Infinity: Conversations with Phillip Nemo*. Pittsburgh, PA: Duquesne University Press.
—— (1996) *Basic Philosophical Writings*, A.T. Peperzak, S.Critchley, and R. Bernasconi (eds). Bloomington and Indianapolis, ID: Indiana University Press.
—— (1998) *Otherwise Than Being or Beyond Essence*, trans. A. Lingis. Pittsburgh, PA: Duquesne University Press.
Martin, J. (2002) "The theatre which does not exist: Neutrality to interculturalism," in F. Chamberlain and R. Yarrow (eds) *Jacques Lecoq and the British Theatre*. London and New York: Routledge.
Mooney, E.F. (1991) *Knights of Faith and Resignation: Reading Kierkegaard's* Fear and Trembling. Albany, NY: SUNY Press.
Salverson, J. (1999) "Transgressive storytelling or an aesthetic of injury: Performance, pedagogy and ethics," *Theatre Research in Canada*, 20: 1: 35–51.
—— (2001) "Change on whose terms?: Testimony and an erotics of injury," *Theater*, special edition, A. Solomon (ed.), *Theater and Social Change*, 31: 3: 118–25.
Schutzman, M. (1999) *The Real Thing: Performance, hysteria, and advertising*. Hanover, NH, and London: Wesleyan University Press.
Showalter, E. (1997) *Hystories: Hysterical epidemics and modern media*. New York: Columbia University Press.
Simon, R. and Eppert, C. (1997) "Remembering obligation: Pedagogy and the witnessing of historical trauma," *Canadian Journal of Education* 22: 2: 175–91.
Solomon, A. (2001) "Irony and deeper significance: Where are the plays?," in A. Solomon (ed.) *Theater: Theater and social change*, 31: 3: 2–12.
Tester, F. (2003) "Anti-oppressive theory and practice as the organizing theme for social work education: The case against," *Canadian Social Work Review*, 20: 1: 127–32.
Van Alphen, E. (1997) *Caught by History: Holocaust effects in contemporary art, literature, and theory*. Stanford, CA: Stanford University Press.
Young, J.E. (2000) *At Memory's Edge: After-images of the holocaust in contemporary art and architecture*. New Haven, CT, and London: Yale University Press.

Section 3

Ideologies

Reenvisioning theatre, activism, and citizenship in neocolonial contexts

Awam Amkpa

Political situations in neocolonial Africa in the 1970s instigated several artistic strategies through which people understood their new oppressions and sought cultural and political means of transcending them. Theatre for Development (TFD) emerged as one such cultural practice that helped communities produce forms of resistance by using performance traditions not only to tell stories of their oppression but also to galvanize them into social actions. As practiced in most of Africa, TFD brings together amateur and professional actors, social workers and health functionaries, in a broader movement to help communities coerced into poverty and under-development transform themselves into voluntary social organizations seeking more proactive citizenships. Its distinguishing feature is extending theatre of political consciousness into a programmatic activism whereby communities set agendas for their own social development, as well as devising means of negotiating with government and non-government organizations. Theatre for Development in Nigeria, where this vision of development became a broad-based movement, will be the focus of this chapter.

In the first section, I look at how a neocolonial historical context in Nigeria stimulated the emergence of TFD. In the second section, through a story derived from a case study in northern Nigeria, I draw attention to characteristics of TFD with inferences to training facilitators, creating performances, and organizing communities to use performances to understand and transcend neocolonial oppressions. Seen through the prism of postcolonial theory, I stress, in the third and fourth sections, how both TFD and Theatre of the Oppressed (TO), enhancing citizenship and activism in different ways, incorporate the empowering strategies of theatre practices into theatre training and scholarship.

A neocolony and the emergence of TFD

Forty-four years after independence from British rule, a large section of the Nigerian population still suffers from poverty and a structurally-induced paralysis of agency. Divided by class, gender, and ethnic rivalries, Nigeria has become what is typically understood as a neocolonial state, that is, one alienated from its civil society, despite the promise of a formidable anti-imperialist nationalism that galvanized the population into resisting colonialism. By imperialism I allude to the expansion of nations to other parts of the world through a combination of military, cultural, economic, and political incorporation. Colonialism is a systemic process absorbing other cultures and economies into the colonizer's political orbit. Such a system includes using the colonizer's language, education, forms of knowledge, and culture to define and limit the social reality of the colonized. After formal severance of colonially-defined societies from their domination, several of such countries found themselves still economically, politically, and culturally subordinated to their former masters. Neocolonialism is that dependent system now run by the formerly colonized but still dominated by the economies and politics of the imperialist nations. There are two broad kinds of nationalism: the colonial one that incorporates the colonized into the national culture of the colonizer, and the anticolonial one that seeks a nationalism in which the colonized wrest themselves from the colonizer and forge their own independence. Anticolonial nationalism is a moment within decolonization in which the colonized reform and reinvent themselves into an independent nation.

The British colonization of Nigeria was itself part of the larger story of the second wave of Western imperialism, driven by European power rivalries and the economic imperatives of the Industrial Revolution—an often violently competitive quest for markets, raw materials, and sites for the investment of surplus capital. In 1884, the German Chancellor Otto Von Bismarck convened a landmark conference of European nations at Berlin to regulate the terms of Western engagement in Africa. The Berlin meeting effectively formalized the "Scramble for Africa" by demarcating spheres of political influence and economic interest that the various European powers would subsequently consolidate by force and chicanery. What I call colonial modernity located Nigeria within a global entity by giving it a uniquely dependent identity that perpetuates Nigeria's continued subservience to imperialist economies while signifying a quasi-independent national reality within and against which citizenship was negotiated.

Yet formal independence from British colonialism did not bring freedom to Nigeria's hopeful multitudes. Colonialism left the legacy of a dysfunctional parliamentary democracy destroyed by ethnic and regional rivalries. In the post-World War II period, Nigeria's British masters designed a series of constitutions in the course of their negotiations with various nationalists and other factions in its colony, granting a disproportionate amount of influence to their client chieftains in the north. The colonial tradition of privileging one section of the country over another accentuated conflicts among the ethnic groups reorganized by the British, often arbitrarily. Thus, the departure of the British was followed by a series of political crises culminating in the overthrow of civilian rule by military coups from the late 1960s to the 1990s. The anticolonial hope of self-determination yielded to Nigeria's long nightmare of neocolonial dictatorships.

Oil lubricated the machinery of the neocolonial state. European and North American investments in Nigeria's oil firmed up support for various military dictators thereby derailing democratic processes with impunity. Conscripting their subjects into a unitary nationalism that paid no heed to the country's ethnic complexity, the dictators turned Nigerians into a people who produced things they could not consume, while developing a taste for consumer goods they could never produce. The unequal terms of Nigeria's ties to the industrialized West signify what Nkrumah called the "worst form of imperialism. For those who practice it, it means power without responsibility and for those who suffer from it, it means exploitation without redress" (1965: xi). Citizens in neocolonial states were largely citizens in name only.

Decolonization is the strategic disengagement and resistance to colonization. Led largely by educated elites, decolonizing movements challenge education, language, economies, and political institutions by developing more culturally-specific strategies of independence. In Nigeria and elsewhere, such movements led to independence and postcolonial states, some of which sought new affiliations as world politics changed through World War II and the Cold War. Decolonization, however, was erroneously applied to the work of both managers of new nations—who were, in some cases, neocolonialists—for which decolonization was automatically accomplished through independence and to the efforts of those who insisted that decolonization should be a perpetual political culture and direction that challenges local and international inequities. The undemocratic neocolonial nationalism of the state is continuously locked in combat with a resilient culture of decolonization with which individuals and groups analyze, resist, and refuse a neocolonial belonging. The practices of TFD are located within this oppositional culture of decolonization.

Theatre for Development originated in northern Nigeria's Ahmadu Bello University (ABU) in Zaria, evolving from its training program in community theatre traditions. In developing nations relegated to the margins of European modernity,[1] TFD made conscious use of the performing arts to achieve what Canadian theatre animator Ross Kidd (1982) noted as "a process of social change; changes in self-concept, attitude, awareness, skill, or behavior." Its art goes beyond metaphorical representations of underdevelopment to facilitating actions on social problems. Theatre becomes a forum for organizing communities into participatory decolonizing discourses, thereby providing a means of negotiating the cultural and political terms of their own social progress. Theatre for Development reconceptualizes the very notion of development in postcolonial Africa to mean not simply the provision of water, hospitals, and shelters for underprivileged communities but, more broadly, to encompass a complex process that uses theatre to enact, critique, and sustain strategies for the full and effective participation of marginalized communities in society.

If power entails the ability to act, thereby enabling the effective participation of people in society, oppression suggests the contrary. It means being structurally disadvantaged, lacking the social and cultural capital to enact any form of citizenship other than one that objectifies and subjects people to poverty. Being aware of oppression is an act of political consciousness whose goal is to transform such a recognizable identity into forms of political and social activism. Oppression does not only exist within the realms of material economic poverty but also encompasses cultural, psychic, mental, and social poverty, and it is the process of transforming these that politicizes and empowers the oppressed to change their culture and society.

Theatre for Development began in the 1970s in a climate of radical political activism when political ideologies such as Marxism, Pan-Africanism, and a spectrum of anticolonial nationalisms provided postcolonial universities with a framework for resisting the colonial epistemologies underpinning existing scholarship.[2] The community-based ABU Drama Program aimed at building relationships with less privileged sections of the society surrounding the University. The ABU program embraced a Freirean pedagogy combining formal learning with informal and nonformal epistemologies. Insisting that transformative education could not be achieved through formal institutions alone, informal education referred to experiences accumulated through everyday social interactions with family, friends, and peers. Non-formal education stemmed from social organizations seeking to foster critical awareness of the identities and environments of individuals and groups in a complex, pluralistic, but hierarchical society. As a primary elucidation on the role of theatre in empowering practitioners and the communities they work with, Augusto Boal's *Theatre of the Oppressed*, along with works by other Latin American, Asian, and African cultural activists, became an energizing relief for ABU's theatre makers and scholars. Inspired by such examples, the ABU Drama Program integrated nonformal cultural practices with a formal curriculum distinctly anticolonial in tenor. As the sole source of social mobility in countries like Nigeria, formal education alienated those it endowed with cultural and political capital from the vast populace excluded from its institutions. Validating informal and nonformal pedagogical modes for education and socialization, ABU drama students began to forge partnerships with base groups drawn from local communities by exploring and connecting with their local activism.[3]

By 1980, ABU had established stable outreach structures such as its now famous Samaru Street Theatre and Community Drama projects. Typically, first year students spend an initial three to four weeks in participant observation, studying a community in relation to their newly adopted one in the university. Data derived from the research are used in an open-ended performance inviting audience participation. The performance text is itself an index of the students' own development. In taking theatre outside, they expose their own fears, conceptions, and misconceptions of the community. Long hours of dialogue follow up such presentations. In the second year, students spend weeks with a base group and non-government development agencies researching social issues affecting structural underdevelopment. The students and people from the base group make performances that entertain while communicating such issues.

Ahmadu Bello University's large-scale community work drew national attention to its drama program, thereby legitimizing the practice of TFD as an academic discipline and a forum for activist theatre training. The ABU group did not rely on any fixed or institutionally derived methodology. Rather, its methods were project specific and geared toward developmental goals. Rejecting top-down models of development, the group shifted the meaning of development from a traditional social science paradigm to a cultural statement enabling marginalized people and communities to represent their histories in their own voices. They attempted to answer questions such as: What is education and how does it enable effective citizenship? What factors shape the disparate experiences of different social groups? Can one group claim to be developed when a large majority of its fellow citizens have no access to basic resources, whether material, social, or political? How can cultural practices like theatre nurture the growth of agency and social activism from below? Students were cautioned to avoid a patronizing posture toward the community members they purported to help and to appreciate the process of mutual learning that resulted from community theatre. This was initially a challenge, as a founding member of the ABU group observed:

> In wanting to help others who are clearly perceived to be less fortunate than ourselves, we find it very difficult to see how they can *materially* help us. We recognize that we may achieve humility, or selflessness, but we do not see how the very poor can improve our own material living standards. At best, all we acknowledge is that we may need to lower our own standards of living. *Determining in advance how our consciousness may be raised, we actually preclude it happening.*

> (Etherton 1988: 3)

Diligent research on performance traditions of target communities helped the students create performance texts that were forums for intergroup dialogue between townspeople and students. The parties to the dialogue then moved on to analyze the global contexts of their work by examining international case studies and studying the work of cultural theorists such as Boal (1979), Freire (1970), and Renato Constantino (1978). Refusing fixed spatial moorings, TFD in ABU happened in nonconventional places such as courtyards and back alleys, on the streets, and in market places. The open-endedness of their performances provided ideological and presentational flexibility for both performers and their audiences.

Over the course of the 1980s, ABU developed the Zaria Popular Theatre Alliance (ZAPTA), which in turn became the foundation and model for a national organization of community-based theatre artists called the Nigerian Popular Theatre Alliance (NPTA).

A story

It was about 4 p.m. one breezy Thursday in Samaru when the muezzin's call for afternoon prayers blared over loudspeakers placed atop the largest mosque in the community. Groups of men gathered in the shade of trees and under makeshift shelters all over the small community while others walked purposefully toward the mosque. Some of the men sat, crouched, and knelt in various precarious positions as they made the mandated ablutions with water in plastic and aluminum kettles and cups before taking their places on the multi-colored mats laid out for supplicants. Most of the men were workers at the nearby university campus; others were traders, students, and passersby. Meanwhile, a troupe of student actors playing drums, gongs, and flutes strolled through the neighborhood followed by a retinue of excited children. Like a carnival of sounds and spectacles, each overlapping the other, the atmosphere in the community evolved from one focused on prayers to one of impending festivity. The crowd of young onlookers suddenly grew into an animated audience that included women and men. Before long, the actors set up a stage with a tarpaulin canvas on a short street they cordoned off for their performance.

The venue of their performance was a crossroad in Samaru, a relatively new shantytown—a sort of Nigerian ghetto spawned by ABU's rise. Samaru is separated from the sanitized campus by a major highway. Populated by people of diverse ethnic origins, almost every household in Samaru has a relative or dependent working or studying at the university. It offers poorer students and semi-skilled low-income university workers the only affordable place to live. Despite the presence of middle-class enclaves, the neighborhood is, for the most part, notorious for its poor sanitary conditions, bad housing, and disorganized road plans, all of which stand out in especially sharp relief against the privileged state of the adjoining ABU.

In 1984, 23 first-year undergraduates and three MA students (one of them, myself) were assigned the task of creating and performing a street play dealing with Samaru's civic problems. The objective was to create a link between formal theatre scholarship and training at the university and informal spaces and their performance traditions. First we visited the shantytown in groups of three and four to identify the most glaring inequities in resource distribution between the town and its prosperous neighbor across the highway. A week of interaction with the Samaru community yielded the consensus that poor sanitation and the lack of drinkable water constituted some of the crises that disenfranchised its citizens. Hence, a play drawing attention to the perennial shortage of water in Samaru was crafted. Students and community members discussed a host of issues in this regard, centering primarily on the discriminatory effects of poor urban planning and the resource gap that prevailed between Samaru and the ABU community. Moreover, the play's architects undertook participant-observation cultural tours of the town to learn about its story-telling traditions and social and political issues. There followed preliminary improvisation exercises—vignettes, tableaux, and story circles—to build an ensemble that would transform their observations and interpretations into a performance text. The outcome was a play entitled *Wasan Samaru* or *The Story of Samaru* in Hausa-language and Pidgin English.

Enacted on the streets of Samaru on an improvised stage, *The Story of Samaru* unfolded through the antics of two stock characters named Dauda and Sauna. Inseparable friends yet unable to agree on almost anything, these comical ne'er-do-wells given to excessive drinking and gambling tantalized the gathering crowd of onlookers into stepping into their internecine arguments with humor and the highly physicalized gestures typical of street theatre. The debate between the short, slow, and wiry Sauna and the taller, more intellectually pretentious Dauda revolved around Samaru's water crisis. Two other actors represented the stories of two local farmers, Malam Usman and Malam Nuhu, as they made their way to their respective farms, lamenting the failure of the rains and the impossibility of trapping enough rainwater for domestic use.

Usman returned home to find that his wife Binta had not cooked dinner due to the lack of water. Upset, he bullied every member of his household to go out in search of the precious resource, threatening to evict anyone who disobeyed him. A subtext of this scene was the domestic violence endemic in Samaru that Dauda and Sauna, as narrators, underscored by stopping the play and soliciting audience responses to the subject of violence against women. The performance picked up again with a scene set in the household of the other farmer, Malam Nuhu.

A perfect foil for the Usman character, Nuhu was a calm and supportive husband who resolved to accompany his wife Maryam in her quest for water. Maryam informed him that the neighbors had already refused her entreaties and suggested the University as a likely source of water. Judging by its lush gardens, numerous storage tanks, and a dam, it was surely in a position to alleviate the needs of its drought-ridden neighbors. Nuhu demurred: had Maryam not noticed the high security on the campus, enforced by ferocious guard dogs to ward off nonresidents? The only option left was to go to a natural spring located on the farm of a wealthy but wicked man near Samaru. As Nuhu and Maryam made their way to the natural spring, they met Usman's wife and daughter, whom they persuaded to come along, hoping a larger group would appeal to the charitable instincts of the rich farmer who was once, after all, a peasant just like them.

To their pleasant surprise, they found the spring unfortified by its traditional ambushing security system. They got their water, not realizing that the owner had contaminated the source of the spring with a dangerous detergent. Usman fell ill from drinking the adulterated water and accused his wife of attempting to poison him because he had earlier indicated a desire to take a second wife. Dauda and Sauna appeared in the scene to stop Usman from physically assaulting his wife while they invited the audience to resolve the issues raised by the play. A lively debate ensued as the onlookers probed the roots of their community's sufferings. Some of them implicated the students as active participants in the structures oppressing the Samaru community, especially for reporting Samaru residents to the security department whenever they came to the University for water. The accusations climaxed with the identification of one of the students present as having physically assaulted a woman who came to the male dormitory in search of water. This outpouring of grievances was underpinned by class tensions—the Samaru townspeople felt that upon graduation, these same students would join the rank of forces responsible for their underdevelopment. During rehearsals and performance, the irony became apparent to the students as they recognized their complicity in the social crisis they had set out to study and deconstruct.

Out of these recriminations, however, flowed constructive proposals for self-help. Someone suggested the formation of a cooperative that would levy a cash contribution upon its constituent households according to their means and the proceeds invested in digging boreholes in strategic parts of the town. The play's subtext of domestic violence generated more heated debate as the community confronted this contentious issue as part of its own shortcomings. Before the end of the play, no witness to the show was left in any doubt as to its overt political purpose, which was not simply to dramatize the unsanitary living conditions of Samaru's inhabitants but also to galvanize the local community to seek redress through social and political activism. The community did eventually get its wish as the local government responded to their plea for more potable water by building more community taps.

The student group emerged from this experience awed by the overwhelming magnitude of the problems they had touched. They had learned not only the means of analyzing inequities in social structures through the theatre process, but also acquired the cultural tools—popular and interactive performance techniques—with which to develop customized performance texts geared to specific audiences and spaces.

Culture, citizenship, and activism: a postcolonial overview

Dauda and Sauna's tale is an optimistic symbol of the larger story of postcolonial aspirations for freedom and social justice. I use this tale as a call for reenvisioning the making of theatre and its implications for cultural and political forms of activism and citizenship. By postcolonial I do not mean the time after official colonialism. Rather, I mean the moments when the reality of domination become starkly coherent for the oppressed who consequently begin to imagine strategies of limiting domination as well as transforming themselves into a broader humanity within which they are subjects, not objects, of social reality. It is simultaneous with the moments of oppression, not after it. Such a process entails corrupting the cultures of domination as well as developing new modes of representation within which a proactive sense of citizenship is fantasized and imagined, using cultural practices like theatre to produce what I call "postcolonial desires." Such desires broadly include the act of imagining, living, and negotiating a social reality based on democracy, cultural pluralism, and social justice. It represents a counterpoint to Robert Young's interpretation of "colonial desire" (1995: 159–89). If colonial desire was the drive within European or neocolonial modernity to seek out and dominate its Other, postcolonial desire signifies an act of refusal to assume that passive, static, essentialist identity. Postcolonial desires begin at the very moment in which the subordinated understand their subjugation and launch strategies of defiance and change. Thus, such reformist desires can very well inaugurate, rather than simply follow, the anticolonial nationalism that leads to independence from the colonizers. As the Irish cultural critic Declan Kiberd puts it in the context of literature, "postcolonial writing does not begin only when the occupier withdraws; rather it is initiated at that very moment when a native writer formulates a text committed to cultural resistance" (1996: 6). Postcolonial consciousness embraces an expansive vision of freedom that includes not simply the formal severance of colonial relations, but also the creation of a republican society based on democratic citizenship, equity, and tolerance of diversity.

The story of *Wasan Samaru* also illustrates how ideas of citizenship are conceptualized and used in TFD. Dauda, Sauna, the two families in their stories, and the audiences in Samaru, were mostly what I call "informal citizens" in neocolonial Nigeria. Such kinds of citizenship imply a subordinate identity that lacks the cultural capital to effectively participate in civil society. Informal citizenship is the destiny of the politically destitute consigned to the margins of society by class. It is a marker of disenfranchisement. The poor sanitary conditions, the violence of urban planning on their sense of being, and the lack of social amenities to give them a sense of belonging to a developing country, underscored the nature of citizenship Samaru people were subjected to. By contrast, "formal citizenship" gives people a sense of empowerment and cultural capital to arbitrate the terms of the society they live in. Cultural capital in a neocolonial Nigeria flowed primarily from class, followed by gender, ethnicity, and religion. For formal citizens, the specter of descent into informal citizenship ensures their acquiescence in hegemonic discourses.

The drama of *Wasan Samaru* did not simply show the progression of characters from informal to formal citizenship but also alluded to what I call "nonformal citizenship." Such a notion of citizenship suggests a more fluid, hybrid sense of self that possesses the ability to seek agency in a variety of local and global contexts. It is a counterhegemonic consciousness that defies any sense of fixed identity or destiny. Its very flexibility facilitates coalition building and empowers it to engage and contest authoritarian power across a spectrum of locations. Its antifundamentalist and antifoundationalist attitudes make it a form of utopia in a historical context where neocolonial hardships plunge its informal citizens into states of despair and dystopia. This shifting conception of identity carries the greatest promise for realizing what I call postcolonial citizenship—a sense of political and cultural becoming that resists all forms of domination while developing and negotiating a social reality based on democracy, cultural pluralism, and social justice. Thus, for the characters in *Wasan Samaru*, the political destination of informal citizenship was not formal citizenship. Such a direction would not sufficiently arm the transformed against mutations of residual and emergent injustices. Rather, nonformal citizenship was what the characters dreamt of and fantasized about. This desire informed the coalition between potentially middle-class university students and the workers, traders, prostitutes, and unemployed in Samaru.[4]

Wasan Samaru achieved greater discursive significance when the audience focused on the issues rather than their performative illustration, thereby illustrating what Harry Elam Jr. notes as "the transformative power of theatrical performance . . . [that] can transform a seemingly simple act into a powerful moment of theatrical as well as social and cultural significance" (2001: 73). But nothing guarantees the efficacy of a play despite the ideal of nonformal citizenship informing its making. In other words, audiences might not interpret the politics of the performance as intended. On such occasions, the play would only be a descriptive spectacle of an oppressive situation without necessarily galvanizing the thoughts and emotions of the audiences to action. This is not uncommon in this genre of theatre. *Wasan Samaru*, in contrast, functioned as both a show and a call to action largely because it provided a reading of the audience's particular situation that needed alteration. Nonformality arms marginalized communities with a language of subjectivity that comments on oppression as well as offers strategies for democratic relations in contrast to the narrow nationalisms and ethno-religious particularisms that perpetuate neocolonial oppression in Nigeria.

Practitioners and scholars of TFD see Augusto Boal's TO as a parallel practice with the same goal of using theatre as an empowering cultural phenomenon. Like TFD, TO engages with neocolonial oppression and poverty through the making of theatre in a subcontinent that was the site of the first wave of European imperialism from the seventeenth century. Many TFD practitioners recognize TO's systematic series of exercises such as Image Theatre, Simultaneous Dramaturgy, Forum Theatre, and Legislative Theatre as significant outcomes of Boal's intimate relationship to groups of artists and communities in South America.

There are, however, differences between the objectives and directions of TO and TFD. The latter's focus on and incorporation of the historicity of poverty into its process is a case in point. Like TO, TFD projects analyze issues of marginalization, represent them, and stimulate desires for change. But TFD incorporates strategies for initiating change by relating aesthetics to actual social development initiatives such as the construction of wells, institution of inoculation programs, and distribution of urgently needed medication. This distinction implies a closer connection between the theatre facilitator and other ancillary aspects of a community's social development.

Though TO has universalized strategies derived from specific contexts of economic, psychological, and political oppressions in South America to embrace parallel issues around the world, TFD practitioners generally shy away from such tendencies as their works stress on the sanctity of specificity. TFD rejects separating the aesthetic from communal activism as well as canonizing and institutionalizing its aesthetics as a separate phenomenon from the context that created it. While aesthetic approaches in TFD are specific to each project, attention to the historical frame extends beyond the specific into analyses of neocolonialism and imperialism, and critiques of decolonization, be they overt or indirect. TO's aesthetic strategies on the other hand, are seen as possible composite parts of understanding poverty in neocolonial societies and the dreams for postcolonial democracies.

Theatre of decolonization

It is from within the framework of decolonization that I make proposals for reenvisioning theatre's contribution to activism and notions of citizenship in neocolonial contexts. Decolonization is an ideological as well as cultural attitude that stimulates political consciousness and activism refusing local and global domination. It is neither an event nor a simple destination but rather a perpetual journey of reinvention. It binds performers and spectators together in a surreal journey of empowerment that carries real potential for collective action. Examples drawn from TFD set the tone for the decolonizing theatre that I am proposing. For instance, the storytelling traditions and the performative culture that saturate everyday life in Samaru—from the drama of prayer times, to the carnivalesque atmosphere of drinking and hustling, to the theatricality of the market place—made it possible for the ABU group to effectively situate their own theatrics on the streets of Samaru. Indigenous songs, music, and dance offer culturally specific forms that constitute a meaningful signing system for Samaru residents. Thus, beyond enabling communication, the theatre of decolonization I propose facilitates socialization through a system of signification. The dramatic arts, like language, consist of a symphony of signs which make and share meaning, flesh out identities, and galvanize agency. Consciousness of decolonizing theatre as a signing system, a forum where people's sense of individual and group identities are imagined and articulated, is imperative for the performers of this genre of theatre practice. As implied by our case study, it provides Samaru's informal and formal citizens with a crucible for producing ideas of nonformality and modes of representation much needed for reforming identities. This points to another difference between Boal's prescribed exercises and TFD, namely the latter's dependence on systems of exercises that draw attention to a community's sense of the body as a signing system drawn from performance traditions embedded in their cultures.

Just as attention is paid to the organization of the theme, characters, plot, and other stylistic devices in the corporeal form of theatre, makers of decolonizing theatre must focus equally on the social and political efficacies of their practice. It is the shifts and complexities of social and political demands that make constant revisions of TFD practices and conventions necessary. The confluence of the "performance text and performance space" (Elam 2001: 71) highlights the activist moments of the play. Audiences in Samaru and most of the so-called Third World no longer assume logocentric assimilations into the drama's theme and subject. For them, the neocolonial world framing their reality make them demand forms of representations against and within which they imagine their own subjectivity. It is from such forms that the conventions of decolonizing theatre are invented.

For TFD performers and audiences, focus on stock, archetypal characters in stories essentializes their nature, thereby going against the grain of the deconstructive interpretations of identities they seek. This raises questions about the ideas of "stereotypes" and "archetypes" in theatrical presentations. While some forms of theatre focus their stories on archetypal characters, TFD focuses instead on stereotypical characters. Theatre for Development presentations deliberately play on the multiplicity of subjectivity for characters and their contexts. The term stereotype, then, assumes a different meaning within the practices of TFD and their decolonizing energies for both spectators and performers. It assumes a multiplicity in contrast to the singularity of archetypes—an important corollary to quests for a dramaturgy of political possibilities for those trapped in impossible states of poverty and economic deprivation. It is in this context that TFD practitioners and scholars understand Boal's conception of theatre as "a rehearsal for the revolution." In Boal's simultaneous dramaturgy, spect-actors transform their demands for such pluralistic possibilities beyond the story by reinscribing the story with multiple signifiers. The more acute the neocolonial oppression, the more the demand for such imaginative leaps as audiences transform themselves into spect-actors, a phenomenon similar to what I describe as decolonizing theatre. Within the context of decolonization, theatrical activity becomes a call and response whereby images and narratives are negotiated.

Commentators have often portrayed TFD as a one-way process of acculturation in which members of a politically conscious and ideologically well-formed middle class, serving as facilitators, animators, catalysts, or consciencizers, coopt the oppressed Other into their activist world as passive objects of social activism. In such renditions of popular theatre, the subalterns frequently fail to become agents of change in their own lives and bourgeois activists remain more or less unchanged by their experience. My contention is that community-building is an open-ended process characterized by the mutual evolution of the various parties involved. The process of becoming and achieving subjectivity goes beyond the assimilation of one group into the other's reality. In TFD, actors are also transformed as they watch audiences become actors and respond to their representation. Such spect-actors become activists who relate the theatrical process to political action, underscoring the idea that theatre is a cultural practice providing communities with a context within which identity, citizenship, and representation are negotiated. In the Samaru TFD project, students' interactions with local communities became points of convergence between identities originally set upon a collision course by colonial and neocolonial histories. Such is the energy with which I demand theatre, as stimulated by work such as TO, be reenvisioned to create a broader sense of citizenship that actively engages local and global conditions of inequities and social injustices. Such a demand underscores the need for context-specific awareness as well as deeper knowledge of a given locality's global ramifications, hence making decolonization a permanent theme of developing culture, citizenship, and democracy. The social and cultural realities that once made such attitudes to theatre, citizenship, and activism meaningful and stable are different in the twenty-first century than in times past. While in the nineteenth and twentieth centuries, nation states and national senses of belonging (or nonbelonging) were important indices of citizenship, today in the twenty-first century, they are not. Capitalist formations defy nation states as sites of domination while residual infrastructures of nation states in neocolonial countries intensify the localization of marginalization.

These have become the two major and conflicting narratives of globalization in the twenty-first century. One narrative gives global capitalism a broader landscape to thrive, thereby making anyone with access to the institutions of such capital more formidable global citizens. Antithetic to such a narrative is the systematic process of denying local communities a sense of the global scale of their poverty as well as space and connections that make poverty, not simply the lack of cultural capital but also the structural inability to create coalitions with people in similar oppressed situations. The conflict between both narratives manifests itself in neocolonial nations like Nigeria where global capitalism dominates the oil- rich country with impunity as dictators frustrate democratic processes, while at the same time preventing the marginalized from connecting with each other nationally and internationally. For the rulers, a globalization of capitalist gains is sharply resisted by one thematized by resistance to global poverty, such are the conflicting narratives of contemporary neocolonial societies that TFD and TO address in their dramaturgies. The twenty-first century cultivates a culture of dystopia for the marginalized. The task of TFD and TO on the other hand, is in reenergizing and retooling its cultural practices with what Paulo Freire called "new resources of hope":

> Without a minimum of hope, we cannot so much as start the struggle. But without the struggle, hope as an ontological need dissipates, loses its bearings, and turns into hopelessness. And hopelessness can become tragic despair. Hence the need for a kind of education in hope.
>
> (Freire 1998: 8)

The challenge for theatre in the twenty-first century consists of developing this education in hope. We must articulate a postcolonial politics of representation of the global crises that confront us and translate an emerging internationalist civic consciousness into constructive discourses of decolonization and democratic citizenship in every local space.

Notes

1   Most of the world was conscripted into developments within European modernity through slavery and colonialism. Colonial nation states were structurally over-determined by transformations within European modernity in whose margins the colonized belong. Even anticolonial nationalisms were constrained by such infrastructures; hence the neocolonial reality in most of the colonized societies regardless of relative independence from their colonizers. See Amkpa 2004.

2   As in other African countries, Nigerian universities in the 1970s became hotbeds for radical political activism and advocacy against neocolonial governments, particularly military dictatorships. Leftwing politics permeated scholarship, particularly the humanities' questioning of a social reality that was spectacularly inequitable. Despite intense social activities in the faculty, one mustn't assume that the kinds of theatre produced were socialist. Rather theatre provided a forum for various political attitudes among staff, students, and community members with a common focus on engendering democracy and subjectivity.

3   Base groups are grass-roots organizations engaged in their own local social and cultural developments with their own distinctive identity and agenda. The Samaru Youth Club, ABU Drama group, and Hayin Dogo community group are such base groups whose missions of self development enhance more engaged involvement with development and political projects.

4   My use of formal, informal, and nonformal citizenship is inspired by Paulo Freire's designations of formal and informal education. The former signifies education within formal institutions and the latter gives due relevance to informal modes of education that are usually demonized by formal education. My ideas allude to how education imbues individuals with social and cultural capital and that those who lack such capital are designated informal citizens. I, however, stress nonformal education and indeed nonformal political identity as one that empowers individuals and communities with the ability to develop strategies for their own development as well as choose who to affiliate with in political processes.

Bibliography

Amkpa, A. (2004) *Theatre and Postcolonial Desires*. London and New York: Routledge.

Boal, A. (1979) *Theatre of the Oppressed*, trans. C.A. and M.-O.L. McBride. New York: Urizen Books.

Constantino, R. (1978) *Neo-colonial Identity and Counter-Consciousness: Essays on cultural decolonization*. London: Merlin Press.

Elam, Jr., H.J. (2001) *Taking it to the Streets: The social protest theater of Luis Valdez and Amiri Baraka*. Ann Arbor, MI: University of Michigan Press.

Etherton, M. (1988) "Popular theatre for change: From literacy to oralcy," *Media Development*, A journal of WACC 3, vol. 35, London: World Association for Christian Communication publications.

Freire, P. (1970) *Pedagogy of the Oppressed*, trans. M.B. Ramos. London: Continuum.

—— (1998) *Pedagogy of Hope: Reliving Pedagogy of the Oppressed*, trans. R.R. Barr. New York: Continuum.

Kiberd, D. (1996) *Inventing Ireland*. Cambridge, MA: Harvard University Press.

Kidd, R. (1982) *The Popular Performing Arts, Non-formal Education and Social Change in the Third World: A bibliography and review essay*. The Hague: Centre for the Study of Education in Developing Countries.

Nkrumah, K. (1965) *Neo-Colonialism: The last stage of imperialism*. London: Thomas Nelson and Sons.

Young, R. (1995) *Colonial Desire*. London: Routledge.

Negotiating feminist identities and Theatre of the Oppressed

Ann Elizabeth Armstrong

Definitions and problems in contemporary feminism

In 1983 Alice Jaggar defined feminism saying that "all feminists address the same problem: what constitutes the oppression of women and how can that oppression be ended?" (1983: 124). In 1990 and again in 2000, bell hooks offers a slightly different definition: "Feminism is a movement to end sexism, sexist exploitation, and oppression" (2000: vii). More recently, in 2003 Chandra Mohanty explains that feminism recognizes "that sexism, racism, misogyny, and heterosexism underlie and fuel social and political institutions of rule and thus often lead to hatred of women and . . . violence against women." In identifying oppressive forces, she adds that "[t]hese ideologies, in conjunction with the regressive politics of ethnic nationalism and capitalist consumerism, are differentially constitutive of all of our lives in the early twenty-first century" (2003: 3). With each of these definitions, we see ways in which feminist perspectives have grown to be more inclusive, sustaining a more complex view of the world. These definitions trace a movement from defining "woman" as a stable entity to more of an analysis of the relationship *between* the operations of power and their effects on real women. Jaggar situates her question around oppression that only concerns women, presumably those defined by biology. Broadening the definition, hooks links the effects of sexism with the operations of all oppressions, noting that feminism is for everybody, men and women of all races and classes. Mohanty, then, asks us to consider the interdependence of economic and political forces at both a micro and macro level as sources of sexist oppression. Definitions of feminism are as varied as are women's experiences; however, such definitions share many features. They all seek to value women in their different contexts and advocate social change that empowers women without disempowering others.

Is feminism important and relevant in today's world? Some have claimed that we live in an age of "postfeminism," that feminism has achieved equality for women and/or other aspects of identity take precedence over gender. While women today have many opportunities, there are still notable discrepancies, and many, including myself, would argue that feminism is hardly over. Violence against women is a social epidemic. Women are still paid less than men in the work place and seldom do they hold positions at the highest levels. Abortion rights are seriously threatened by the religious right and conservative politicians. Poverty and homelessness are increasingly affecting women, particularly single mothers. Global economic forces have created a widening gulf between first and third world, compounding the problems of women of the third world who are without basic legal rights or economic sustenance. Corporate media and advertising continue to promote narrow definitions of femininity and body image.

With every achievement of feminism, we seem to find yet more insidious manifestations of patriarchy that permeate every aspect of our lives.

Feminist theory is a tool that allows us to take apart our world, examine invisible assumptions, and view cause/effect relationships. By identifying sources of oppression, it can point to possible ways to disrupt oppressive structures. In the early 1970s, second-wave feminists developed consciousness-raising (CR), a methodology that allowed groups of women to recount their experiences in safe, nonhierarchical, nonjudgmental environments. Through these sessions, women shattered silences, breaking down the barriers between private and public to explore resonances between their experiences. Sheila Rowbotham explains the role of CR, a process that lies at the very heart of Theatre of the Oppressed (TO):

> An oppressed group must at once shatter the self-reflecting world which encircles it and, at the same time, project its own image onto history. In order to discover its own identity as distinct from that of the oppressor, it has to become visible to itself. All revolutionary movements create their own way of seeing.
>
> (Rowbotham, cited in MacKinnon 1998: 459)

Through the act of describing and representing their experiences, women began to theorize from these observations. Many groups even took the next step of dramatizing those experiences.[1] In this way, everyday experience became the fundamental source of knowledge that constructed a theory. This theory then became a source for strategizing practical solutions and political activism.

However, because most participants of CR groups were white, middle-class, straight women, much of early 1970s feminism is critiqued as racist, elitist, and/or heterosexist. With the energy of 1970s grass-roots organizations dissipating, the new academic discipline of women's studies became one way to sustain feminist thought and activity, and, simultaneously, to broaden the base. In spite of these efforts, current feminist theory, primarily generated by academic feminists rather than activists, has lost its connection to real women's experiences. Alienated by theoretical jargon, a harsh divide exists between pragmatic activists and abstract theorists.

Feminism, however, is invested in the inextricable relationship between theory and practice. It is the split between modern and postmodern approaches to the theory/practice divide that dogs many feminist controversies. Modernist feminist theories have assumed that "woman" could be defined as the subject of feminism, that an essential truth or commonality exists for all women, and this "truth" forms the basis for advocating the rights and emancipation of female subjects. Modernist feminism relies on an epistemological framework that posits a "women's way of knowing" (Belenky et al. 1986) and this epistemology locates the boundary between oppressed and oppressor by demarcating a "woman's" point of view. While historically the valuation of women's identity is a necessary step in organizing a movement, Linda Alcoff explains the limitations: "To the extent that [essentialist] feminism merely valorizes genuinely positive attributes [of women] developed under oppression, it cannot map our future long-range course" (1997: 336). Such an approach does not address the mechanisms of oppressive powers, but instead it only creates further constraints that tie women to particular identities, limiting her ability to transform her circumstances. Ultimately, essentialism prevents feminism from incorporating heterogeneous differences between women within the movement, a key element for sustaining the life of feminism.

On the other hand, postmodern critics note that emancipation cannot be based on so-called "universal truths" (that exclude racial and gendered Others), that knowledges are constructed by power rather than by objective standards. Postmodernism focuses upon the nature of language and representation, noting that representations of reality frequently produce "reality." Deconstruction is used to reveal how representation reflects unseen biases and assumptions; "woman," for instance, is revealed to be an illusion authored by patriarchal forces. Through deconstruction, postmodern feminists disclosed how "reality" was constructed and perhaps how it could be reconstructed.

However, in suggesting that "woman" is a construction, postmodern feminists inadvertently suggest that women's oppression is likewise a construction without a basis in a real material world. This in turn makes it nearly impossible to imagine a "real" subject for the feminist movement to liberate. Critics of postmodern feminism argue that liberation requires more than merely new representations of women. Furthermore, with no objective measure of "reality," definitions of the oppressor and oppressed become only relative categories. Lack of a stable subject makes it difficult to define the problem and imagine an appropriate solution for collective action. However, it is this very fluidity between categories that has been a strength of postmodernism, leading to a more complex notion of identity and multifaceted strategies of activism. Though postmodern feminism lacks stable ground from which to base political action, it capitalizes on this instability; seeing meaning as dependent upon context and interpretation, postmodern feminists value plurality, fluidity, hybridity, and multiplicity.

Like theorists of many other identity movements, feminist theorists have and continue to struggle with essentializing tendencies of modernism and the constructivist tendencies of postmodernism. Many keep these concepts in tension in order to move forward with transformative actions that are sustained by critical reflection. Alcoff proposes viewing gender as positionality or standpoint. She explains that theorists can resist universalizing by historicizing their analysis, making women both "subjects and subjected to social construction" (1997: 347). Hence, identity becomes a point of departure for the theorist/activist, not an end result. Similarly, Gayatri Spivak employs a temporal strategy of assuming an essentialist identity within particular circumstances. Her "strategic essentialism" (1987: 205) allows a group to admit certain "truths" *circumstantially*—when strategically beneficial to do so— while staying open *ideologically* to differences and changing truths. In formulating theoretical positions that incorporate multiple categories of difference and advocate positive strategies for change, feminists of color and third-world feminists have been most successful in navigating this terrain. Authors such as bell hooks, Cherríe Moraga, Gloria Anzaldúa, Trinh Minh Ha, Patricia Hill Collins, and others have inspired significant dialogue maintaining the intersectionality of gender with other identity categories. In the next section, I will describe two recent models of feminist theory that acknowledge the importance of a stable identity while envisioning a critical reflectiveness that can produce radical change.

Feminist theory and coalition building

Rather than seeing modern and postmodern perspectives in conflict, Paula Moya and Chela Sandoval approach the problem from a "both/and" perspective. While seeing "woman" as an appropriate category around which to organize, they don't neglect other categories of identity and emphasize the importance of coalition across different identity categories. They both draw from Cherríe Moraga's "theory of the flesh" (Moraga 1983) in order to explore the relationship between lived experience and theory, and, moreover, how theory based upon the experiences of women of color is broadly applicable to activist projects beyond gender and race.

Moya's approach complicates and rehabilitates essentialist arguments. Drawing from the strength of modernist epistemologies, she critiques postmodern theories by positing a "realist" or "post-positivist" approach to the problem of identity. A "post-positivist" approach emphasizes that identities may be both real and constructed, that they can be politically and epistemically significant while also being variable and historical (2000: 12).[2] Speaking to the advantages of deploying identity categories, Moya explains, "what is being claimed is not any a priori link between social location or identity and knowledge but a link that is historically variable and mediated through the interpretation of experience" (2000: 81). So, while different people may have similar experiences, they can have different interpretations of that same experience. Similarly, the differing social locations of individuals may actually determine the experiences that they may have. From Moya's point of view, the question becomes how we navigate such contradictions in our experiences and how we make meaning from them.

While individuals participate in constructing their own experiences, the roots of these experiences are not transparent or self-evident. For example, an individual might justifiably claim that his or her experiences are related in some way to his or her gender. But these experiences are not defined by gender alone; rather, they encompass multiple discourses (race, class, and sexuality as well as gender). While identities maintain a certain amount of stability, it is through these multiple discourses that identities are interrogated, contested, and often changed. Theory becomes the mediating factor that allows individuals to formulate connections between bodies and experiences, explaining contradictions embedded within power structures. For instance, through theory, one can explain the paradoxical ways in which one can be both oppressor and oppressed simultaneously.

Moya calls upon Cherríe Moraga's "theory of the flesh" to return identity to embodied experience and to explain how a post-positivist identity can be stable but complex enough to resist being reductive. Moraga explains:

> A theory in the flesh means one where the physical realities of our lives—our skin color, the land or concrete we grew up on, our sexual longings—all fuse to create a politic born out of necessity. Here, we attempt to bridge the contradictions in our experience.
> (Moraga 1983: 23)

Moraga goes on to explain that "we do this bridging by naming our selves and by telling our stories in our own words" (Moraga 1983: 23). Moya notes how a "theory of the flesh" understands how experiences inform, rather than determine, our politics; like a post-positivist realist approach, it maintains both the reality and the active construction of identity.

Unlike Moya, Sandoval works from a postmodern position, capitalizing upon the instability and interdependence of identity to describe a utopian vision of a postcolonial world. Sandoval defines a "differential consciousness" that "permits functioning within yet beyond the demands of dominant ideology" (Sandoval 1991: 2). A "differential consciousness" joins together what is possible with what is (Sandoval 2000: 180); situated within reality, it imagines new relationships beyond the constraints of ideology. In order to move toward this differential consciousness, Sandoval constructs a "methodology of the oppressed," which explores the "transformative effects of oppressed speech upon dominant forms of perception" (2000: 7).[3] Sandoval explains that the voices of subordinated people directly led to new modes of critical reading and analysis, and she shows how these voices have directly influenced canonical philosophers and theorists. Seeing these voices in equal concert with one another, she hypothesizes coalition building across "power differential communities." The five stages of her methodology are:

1 studying semiotics, or the science of signs in culture
2 challenging signs through deconstruction
3 meta-ideologizing, or appropriating dominant ideological forms and using them in order to transform them
4 democratics, or using the previous three technologies to create egalitarian social relations, and
5 differential movement, or using all four technologies in harmony toward a utopian vision.

Sandoval's conception of a feminist democracy links unexpected realms of discourse with a humanist aim, "love in a postmodern world." She seizes both the individual and the community within her process:

> The oppressed have only one true mode of revolutionary activity, the ability to perceive and decode dominant-order sign systems . . . and one true mode of revolutionary consciousness, which is the ability of consciousness to differentially move . . . *toward* a possible and utopian world of desire, social and psychic life, *amor en Aztlán*, differential consciousness.
>
> (Sandoval 2000: 182)

For Sandoval, love drives transformation and revolution to produce a utopian vision of decolonization within current global conditions.

How is this ability to "perceive and decode dominant sign systems" different from the CR activities of second-wave feminism? Consciousness-raising groups reinforced homogeneity rather than difference, creating new systems of dominance and exclusion through their theorizing. In contrast, Sandoval imagines a movement that goes beyond feminism and into global coalitions that engage multiple differences. She describes the force of ideologies upon one another and holds up what she calls US third world feminism as an ideology that has refused any one single position and resisted exclusionary practices.[4] From their examples, she advocates a "tactical subjectivity" that can de-center and recenter different forms of power (Sandoval 2000: 58). She quotes Aida Hurtado to explain that "women of color are more like urban guerillas trained through everyday battle with the state apparatus" (Sandoval 2000: 58).

Like Moya, Sandoval evokes Moraga's "theory of the flesh," noting the way daily survival strategies acknowledge contradiction and elevate practice to the level of theory. She describes truth as a tactical necessity since "differential consciousness and social movement are . . . linked to the necessity to stake out and hold solid identity and political positions in the social world" (Sandoval 2000: 59). However, she notes that this identity must be willing and able to expand in the crossroads between races, nations, languages, genders, sexualities, and cultures to maintain the consciousness of what Gloria Anzaldúa calls a "mestiza," Patricia Hill Collins refers to as "the outsider/within," what Alice Walker describes as a "womanist," and Gayatri Spivak terms "strategic essentialism" (Sandoval 2000: 60). Moya sees this location as inhabited by "coalitions of consciousness" that include the aims of all emancipatory movements. Rather than grounding her analysis in a critique of other feminist or patriarchal theories (Moya's approach), Sandoval instead explores theories of authors of diverse historical contexts and identity backgrounds, putting them in dialogue with one another.

Resonances between TO and feminism

As a site where liberatory theory and practice intermingle, TO resonates in significant ways with feminist theory. As with feminist consciousness-raising groups of the 1970s, consciencization is a key aim in Augusto Boal's formulation of TO.[5] The process requires several stages of reflection and critical thinking: first, the ability to define, name, and identify one's self; second, the ability to discern contradictions that are bound up within one's social reality and own behavior; and finally, the analysis of these contradictions leading to political action or transformation. The work of feminism and TO relies upon the analysis of contradiction, a Marxist dialectical process in which transformation occurs through struggle and conflict. This dialectical approach assumes certain divisions, such as those between the subject and object, the self and Other. These are the very divisions that are, according to postmodernists, illusory and false, the ones they attempt to deconstruct. However, in order to take action to produce change in our social reality, modernists note the necessity for acknowledging the reality of such boundaries. Like the feminist theorists described above, Boal's TO allows us to do both.

In rendering contradictions visible and activating this dialectic, Boal insists upon certain provisional divisions—the separation of subject and object in aesthetic space, the separation of enactment and reflection, the dual functions of the spectator/actor as spect-actor, the separation between actor and character, and the categories of the oppressor and oppressed. While necessary, these divisions are also permeable and subject to revision. "It [the stage–audience relationship] is founded on the subject–object relationship. But no one can be reduced to the condition of absolute object" (Boal 1995: 42). The provisional divisions of TO allow for collective authorship so that multiple experiences can be represented. The flexibility of the rules allow for multiplicity while the divisions maintain the authenticity of the individual authoring the representation. Feminist epistemology frequently challenges the distinction between subject and object, revaluing the position of those that frequently serve as embodied objects (gendered or racialized "Others") to knowing subjects ("universal" white men). Similarly, TO values the particularity of embodied experiences, activates the sensate body, and acknowledges the mind-in-the-body (i.e., the agency of the subject to act within particular physical/social circumstances). Instead of denying the existence of cultural boundaries, TO focuses upon displacing and reconfiguring the boundaries between subject and object, mind and body. By experimenting with this division between subject and object, body and mind, feminist and TO practices construct new epistemologies and, consequently, new communities based around those epistemologies. The body is a critical site in both TO and feminism through which to explore identity politics, locating experience within the particularities of physical and social contradictions.

Though subject–object relationships become blurred through the spect-actor, Boal's techniques have frequently been criticized for the oversimplification of relationships between the oppressor and the oppressed.[6] However, this distinction is crucial (even if it must be made provisionally) in order to distinguish the particular standpoint that lends itself to the interpretation of the embodied experiences of a particular group. Moya explains how the lack of stable boundaries in postmodernism "make[s] it difficult to figure out who is 'us' and who is 'them,' who is the 'oppressed' and who is the 'oppressor'" (2000: 78). However, like the relationship between subject and object, this relation between oppressed and oppressor is still a transitive one, conveying a reality fluid enough to respond to transformation. While it may sometimes be advantageous to keep this division stable in order to strategize, at other times this might unnecessarily simplify the problem and it may, instead, be advantageous to explore the fluidity within the division of oppressor and oppressed. As Moya notes, individuals "may be simultaneously constituted as both oppressor and oppressed" (2000: 97).

Many of the rules of Boal's techniques presume a stable oppressor or oppression; however, as Boal states, this cannot be absolute.[7] As anyone jokering the techniques discovers, it is not always self-evident who the protagonist and antagonist are in a scene. An image of liberation to one person can become an image of oppression to another. Some of the value of TO for feminist politics stems from its ability to unearth these different perspectives to find an interpretation that bridges such group differences. Implicit within TO and feminism is the understanding that oppression can be transformed and that victimhood is not inevitable.

Toward challenging the boundaries of identity, TO questions distinctions between the body and the reality of our different embodied experiences. For example, in one TO workshop, a forum scene portrayed an African American female employee (the protagonist) subjected to verbal abuse by racist customers. As various spect-actors replaced the protagonist (white male and female spect-actors), I noticed that many times the antagonists within the scene responded, perhaps unconsciously, differently to these spect-actors than they had to the original protagonist. It is difficult to discern whether or not the embodied presence of the intervening spect-actor consciously or unconsciously affected the spect-actor who played the racist antagonist and who was supposed to be responding to these protagonists "as if" they were African American women.

This example raises several relevant questions to the problem of identity politics in the practices of both TO and feminism. To examine the essentialist side of the argument, should such a forum only be presented with African American women spect-actors (presuming that they are the only ones who share this same embodied experience)? Does the situation reinforce the oppression if other bodies attempt to appropriate and portray the experiences of others? Is an underlying message sent by these interventions that "if only you could behave like a white person in this situation then your problem could be solved?" Is it possible for a white spect-actor to engage with black spect-actors in the utopian urge to reenvision a non-racist world? On the other hand, to examine postmodern constructivist positions on the situation: is it important to move beyond the boundaries of the body so that we see race and gender as social constructs? Do we really know that the spect-actors who intervened were really "white" since we know that visible markers of race can be deceiving? How do we know that they haven't been subjected to similar experiences? Even if the workshop doesn't solve this particular problem, does it still manage to create significant and relevant dialogue around responses to difference? These are questions that should be addressed in determining how gender and race interact when representing and reflecting upon such experiences.

In another workshop, a woman within a mixed group of male and female spect-actors creates an image of abuse and humiliation. Boal specifically notes that images in Rainbow of Desire techniques are to be read and interpreted by the entire group, not only by the creator of the image. Noting the integrity and reality of the image as a world in and of itself, he also reiterates that one person doesn't know more than others, that there is no one "truth" to be read from an image.[8] In reading such an image, diverging perspectives emerge, generating a multiplicity of interpretations that demarcate differences of experience. Though these interpretations and misinterpretations of an image purposefully generate dialogue, do they dilute the connection that the original abusive image had to the specificity of a gendered experience? When the spect-actor who originally created the image finds that her experiences have been misinterpreted, does she become silenced when other members of the group inflect (inflict?) their readings over hers? Does the woman in this situation gain autonomy or lose it? Does she come to a more collective place of knowledge? How would the above questions be refigured if genders were reversed in this scenario? That is, how would a feminist approach inform our interpretation of a scene in which a woman is abusing a man? On another note, would the women's voices even be heard? We have to acknowledge that women's voices within many mixed communities are less likely to be heard, even though a reciprocal dialogue is imagined.

In reading and interpreting Image Theatre, Boal explains how a group perspective enriches and expands identities. He explains: "On stage, we continue to see the world as we have always seen it, but now we also see it as others see it: we see ourselves as we see ourselves, and we see ourselves as we are seen. To our own point of view we add others" (1995: 26). In this description, the group mediates the identity of the individual, providing the necessary objectivity for theorizing an interpretive framework for an individual's self-understanding. Influenced by Brecht's and Hegel's dialectical concepts of the formation of self in relation to "other," Boal (1979) advocates the dynamic construction of the self in relationship to the group.[9] Rather than seeing the self as completely autonomous, much of the individual's agency is enabled by their identity within social groups. Likewise, it can be restricted because of their identity within a particular group. In the practice of TO, how does this advance a feminist politic that values difference within the group and membership in multiple groups? Can this become a deterministic model that restricts the subject within an identity group or does it encourage growth and alliances? These are critical questions for the Joker to consider in entering into the dynamics of a community that is inevitably composed of multiple groups.

Inspired by Freire, bell hooks is another feminist theorist negotiating the boundaries of identity. Noting that "we are always more than our race, class, or sex" (1994: 241), she posits a subject-to-subject encounter predicated on what she calls a "radical openness," that includes witnessing, listening, and meeting the Other on their own terms. hooks, echoing Sandoval's "love in a postmodern world," explains how emotion, love, hope, and specifically the yearning for transformation become a ground upon which to unite:

> I wondered, "What is uniting us?" All of us across our different experiences were expressing this longing, this deep and profound yearning, to just have this domination *end* . . . So I tried to evoke the idea that if we could come together in that site of desire and longing, it might be a potential place of community-building. Rather than thinking we would come together as "women" in an identity-based bonding we might be drawn together rather by a *commonality of feeling*.

> (hooks 1994: 217)

hooks notes that a movement cannot be solely posited "against," but must somehow transform the fear, rage, and trauma into love and hope. While retaining the ability to engage conflict and difference, "love" becomes a way to combine "acknowledgement, care, responsibility, commitment, and knowledge." She adds, "we understand there can be no love without justice" (2000: 104). Love and emotional connection then become important ingredients for coalition building.

Boal has consistently critiqued the dangers of Aristotelian catharsis in immobilizing spectators; however, his techniques instead work to channel spect-actor emotion into action. A crucial feature of both hooks and Boal's configuration of a subject-to-subject encounter is the significance of this emotional connection. Common experiences and theoretical discourses are simply not enough to unite us across differences. Boal explains the difference between empathy and sympathy and how emotions can be a source of simultaneous empowerment and collective bonding.

> [T]he *active observer (spect-actor)-character* relationship changes in essence and becomes sympathy: sym, with. We are not led, we lead. I am not penetrated by the emotion of others; instead I project my own. I guide my own actions, I am the subject. Or else someone like me guides the action: we are both subjects.
>
> (Boal 1995: 42–43)

Theatre of the Oppressed is a potential apparatus for producing the kind of "commonality of feeling" to which hooks refers. It becomes a means of excavating differences, maintaining the freedom of individual interpretations of experience while constructing group perspectives. However, it can also encourage antagonism and disagreement over different interpretations of reality. Maintaining a connectedness to the group through bonds of "common feeling" averts total dissolution and chaos by instilling a sense of obligation. This obligation in TO is the obligation to transform oppressive circumstances.

As noted earlier, like hooks, Sandoval also engages love and a commonality of feeling to drive transformation. Citing Roland Barthes, Sandoval defines the "punctum" in terms of love that breaks through whatever controls it in order to find "understanding and community," "a kind of 'rupturing' in one's everyday world that permits crossing over to another" (Sandoval 2000: 139). Boal, too, theorizes a liminality that allows for a new way of thinking through a coalitional consciousness. Boal describes an example in the evolution of his practice when his simultaneous dramaturgy gave way to create the spect-actor of Forum Theatre. Simultaneous dramaturgy was one of Boal's early experiments in which audience members gave actors suggestions for solving the scene's conflict and the actors played out those suggestions for the audience. As described in *Rainbow of Desire*, Boal recounts his early work with Peruvian peasants around a marital conflict that involved an illiterate woman who was duped by her adulterous husband. When a female audience member attempts to give actors suggestions, all attempts at language fail. The woman exclaims to Boal, "Because you are a man you don't want to try something a woman is telling you to do!" To which Boal responds, "Why don't you come on stage yourself and show us what you mean . . ." (1995: 6). After the woman had explored her rage within the scene, Boal realizes:

> When the spectator herself comes on stage and carries out the action she has in mind, she does it in a manner which is personal, unique and nontransferable, as she alone can do it, and as no artist can do it in her place. On stage the actor is an interpreter who, in the act of translating, plays false.
>
> (Boal 1995: 7)

In this case, a generative failure in communication (specifically gendered communication) created a "punctum." The Peruvian woman, in a moment of emotion and strong desire for transformation, forsakes the binaries of either/or (as does Boal) to puncture discourses in order to connect previously unrelated realms. A collision occurs between several worlds: between her and Boal, between male and female interpretations of the situation, between the actors and the audience, and between urban Brazilian actors and rural Peruvian peasants. The collision occurs both within the scene, in conflicting interpretations of the scene, and in conflicting interpretations of the rules of the game. The passionate desire for change and connection, or "love" as described by hooks and Sandoval, becomes a hermeneutic that creates a new discourse.

This example encapsulates many of the feminist arguments I have described above. First, we see that a conflict situation generates a passionate desire for, and commitment to, change. This conflict also brings identities and embodied experiences into play as the woman states, "Because you are a man you don't want to try something a woman is telling you to do!" Additionally, we have the collision of a white man from the first world with an indigenous woman of the third world. We see a failure of language in this conflict which leads the woman to take on a theatrical language as she steps on stage. However, Boal's desire to understand and the woman's desire to communicate fully engage the conflict, moving it to another level of communication. The work of the woman and the actors on the stage produce a coalition of sorts as they seek to transform oppression. Most importantly, this collaboration yields a new theory, a new apparatus for creating community: the spect-actor. As a figure that ruptures "realities," the spect-actor allows different communities to speak to each other in their own terms, in their own languages, without one necessarily dominating the other. From this collectively created standpoint, the spect-actors "perceive and decode dominant sign systems" and work out new strategies for resistance.

Feminist values rest at the very heart of TO and, with an understanding of the complexity of identity politics and the value of coalition, the combination of TO with a feminist consciousness can lead us into uncharted territories that will create new strategies of activism and techniques for generating stronger communities. However, to employ a feminist consciousness in the practice of TO, one must be cognizant of the many criticisms leveled against the techniques. Any time we encounter a game-like structure with rules, it is inevitable that a strong cultural bias and power dynamic exists. As Boal has frequently noted, we must be prepared to adapt the techniques to particular circumstances and contexts. Any methodology can become coercive when it is rigidly applied without analysis or adaptation.[10] Aware of the flows of power and working against them, I see the Joker sharing much in common with feminist theorists who are creating liminal spaces in which essentialism and constructionism are negotiated to build new coalitions. Employing feminist theory in the practice of TO, empathy can be radical, and in spite of, perhaps even through, the limits of identity, a coalition of consciousness is possible.

Notes

1 In *Feminist Theaters in the USA*, Charlotte Canning notes that several feminist theatre companies were founded directly from consciousness-raising groups (1996: 59). Furthermore, many theatre companies established relationships with their audiences that resemble Boal's use of the spect-actor (1996: 183).

2　This approach is in reaction to strong postmodern concepts such as Judith Butler's discourses of performativity. See Butler (1990).

3　Though she coincidentally echoes some of Freire's ideas, her phrase and title of her book bear no relation to Freire's *Pedagogy of the Oppressed*.

4　Sandoval uses the term "US third world" to refer to a "deliberate politics organized to point out the so-called third world *in* the first world" (2000: 192). She uses the term to express a solidarity and an international consciousness between women of color.

5　Boal borrows the term "*conscientização*" or "consciencization" from Paulo Freire's *Pedagogy of the Oppressed*.

6　In Schutzman and Cohen-Cruz (1994), several authors make important points regarding the distinction between oppressor and oppressed. See Schutzman's chapters on "Brechtian Shamanism" and "Canadian Roundtable."

7　Boal (2002: 253) notes that his "rules" are merely guidelines that can and should be adapted to the particular needs of a community.

8　Boal also notes that these techniques are therapeutic but not therapy, and many of the rules and methods of his techniques are designed to keep reality rooted in the social and political processes of the group. Berenice Fisher reiterates that the techniques can be misused if directed toward individual rather than collective problems (Fisher 1987).

9　Linda Alcoff recounts the feminist legacy of identity concepts that stem from Hegel in her essay "Who's afraid of identity politics?" in Moya (2000).

10　While Augusto Boal would not consider himself to be one, he is frequently constructed by others as a guru of sorts. Feminists in theatre have long been wary of such guru status since it frequently reiterates the myth of the lone creative genius while making invisible the labor of "others."

Bibliography

Alcoff, L. (1997) "Cultural feminism versus post-structuralism: The identity crisis in feminist theory," in L. Nicholson (ed.) *The Second Wave: A reader in feminist theory*. New York: Routledge.

Belenky, M. *et al.* (1997) [1986] *Women's Ways of Knowing: The development of self, voice and mind*. New York: Basic Books.

Boal, A. (1979) *Theatre of the Oppressed*, trans. C.A. and M.-O.L. McBride. New York: Urizen Books.

—— (1995) *Rainbow of Desire: The Boal method of theatre and therapy*, trans. A. Jackson. London and New York: Routledge.

—— (2002) *Games for Actors and Non-Actors*, 2nd edition, trans. A. Jackson. London and New York: Routledge.

Butler, J. (1990) *Gender Trouble: Feminism and the subversion of identity*. New York and London: Routledge.

Canning, C. (1996) *Feminist Theaters in the USA*. New York and London: Routledge.

Fisher, B. (1987) "The heart has its reasons: Feeling, thinking, and community-building in feminist education," *Women's Studies Quarterly* 15: 3 and 4: 47–58.

hooks, b. (1994) *Outlaw Culture: Resisting representations*. New York and London: Routledge.

—— (2000) *Feminism is for Everybody: Passionate politics*. Cambridge, MA: South End Press.

Jaggar, A. (1983) *Feminist Politics and Human Nature*. Totowa, NJ: Rowman and Allanheld.

MacKinnon, C. (1998) "Toward a feminist theory of the state" in S. Ruth (ed.) *Issues in Feminism: An introduction to women's studies*, 4th edition, Mountain View, CA: Mayfield Publishing.

Mohanty, C. (2003) *Feminism Without Borders: Decolonizing theory, practicing solidarity*. Durham, NC, and London: Duke University Press.

Moraga, C. and Alzaldúa, G. (eds) (1983) *This Bridge Called My Back: Writings by radical women of color*. New York: Kitchen Table Press.

Moya, P. (2000) "Postmodernism, 'realism,' and the politics of identity: Cherríe Moraga and Chicana feminism," in P. Moya and M. Garcia (eds) *Reclaiming Identity: realist theory and the predicament of postmodernism*. Berkeley, CA: University of California Press.

Sandoval, C. (1991) "US third world feminism: The theory and method of oppositional consciousness in the postmodern world," *Genders* 10: 1–23.

—— (2000) *Methodology of the Oppressed*. Minneapolis, MN: University of Minnesota Press.

Schutzman, M. and Cohen-Cruz, J. (eds) (1994) *Playing Boal: Theatre, therapy, activism*. London and New York: Routledge.

Spivak, G. (1987) *In Other Worlds: Essays on cultural politics*. New York: Methuen.

Unperforming "race"

Strategies for reimagining identity

Daniel Banks

> [T]he theatre is a weapon. A very efficient weapon. For this reason one must fight for it. For this reason the ruling classes strive to take permanent hold of the theatre and utilize it as a tool for domination. In so doing, they change the very concept of what "theatre" is. But the theatre can also be a weapon for liberation. For that it is necessary to create appropriate theatrical forms.
>
> (Boal 1985: ix)

> Your fictions become history.
>
> (Kruger 1983)

In the early 1890s, vaudeville performers Bert Williams and George Walker billed themselves as "The Two Real Coons." As Jean and Marshall Stearns explain, "the emphasis was upon the 'Real' and not the 'Coons,' for they were consciously rebelling against minstrel stereotypes" (Stearns 1994: 121). Williams and Walker were in dialogue with Black-face minstrelsy, a system of representation which, through its appropriation of Blackness, set in motion an expectation of what Blackness "really" was, both on and off-stage. White audience expectations, in the face of such essentializing material as the 1896 song, "All Coons Look Alike to Me" (written by Black performer Ernest Hogan), dictated which representations of Blackness could succeed in the public eye (1994: 119–20). These circumscribed roles persist today, under various guises, throughout Western culture. As a theatre director, teacher, and activist, I attempt in my work to uncover, through performance—the very medium that constructed these deleterious identities and personae—how certain expectations and practices can be dismantled and erased. My central question is, if "race" (that is, an expectation of behavior and culture based on phenotype and physical appearance)—like gender—is always already performed and if stereotypes are reiterated, how, then, to destroy the machine that perpetuates these types? In other words, in the moment-to-moment performativity of live theatre, how can the practitioner disrupt or "unperform" that which has common currency? What I will attempt to do in the pages that follow is: 1) outline how certain performances of "Blackness" have attained their currency; 2) suggest strategies for the dissolution of these performed fictions; and 3) explore how Augusto Boal's work tethers with both of these performative moments.

Belief and performance

Williams and Walker's titling of their performance invokes Plato's discussion in *The Republic* about the poet. As Plato contends, and the history of minstrelsy reveals, the artist—via art and image-making—can ignite a discursive system that will "persuade people who are as ignorant as he is, and who judge merely from his words" (Plato 1987: 367). As Boal himself suggests (1985), an audience is potentially undiscerning and impressionable, unless mobilized otherwise. Art is, in essence, propaganda and art-makers put forth personal, social, and political points of view, thus shaping a national or cultural imaginary. Our beliefs about ourselves and about others/the Other are incubated and articulated through the mediated images we ingest daily through print, film, television, and live theatrical performance. In short, if we-the-viewer see it enough, we-the-consumer tend to believe what we see.

The social mechanisms by which such stereotypes are perpetuated are of vital concern, especially as different forms of media resurrect images that invoke the history of the Black-face minstrel. For example, in the summer of 2002, two television advertisements, one for Sam Adams Lite Beer and the other for Kmart's Joe Boxer underwear, contained moments that recalled images from the history of Black-face and coon shows. The Sam Adams advertisement had a close-up frame of a Black man with his mouth wide open in a coon-show pose (enjoying his beer in an orgasmic moment); the Joe Boxer advertisement featured a Black model, Vaughn Lowery, in only boxer shorts, grinning and dancing an excited, jerky dance (the "Kmart Boxer Boogie") reminiscent of images of Zip Coon. The final title of the advertisement is "Why is this guy so happy?" Lowery performed his boxer dance repeatedly on television talk-shows, including one where he was billed "The Happiest Man in America" (Lowery 2004). The connection to the Sambo, or "happy slave," character that minstrelsy institutionalized is striking.[1]

These advertisements demonstrate a general lack of awareness of what is being re-performed in terms of a constitutive history of racialized performance and its cumulative impact. Many contemporary performances have employed actual Black-face to provoke thinking about "race" and racism, the most popular being the film *Bamboozled* (2000), Spike Lee's critique of minstrelsy and popular media. In addition to these recognizable citations of Black-face, minstrelsy has also changed its "face." For example, White popular icons, such as Eminem, Justin Timberlake, and Elizabeth Regen (who was featured on the NBC situation comedy, *Whoopi*), are discussed in terms of their "Blackness."[2] These commentaries invoke and provoke references to Norman Mailer's *The White Negro* (1957), demonstrating the cyclical nature of minstrelsy in US culture.

What is missing in terms of a national dialogue is an understanding of how the repetition of these images creates acceptance. As described above, there is an inherently performative aspect to "race." Linguist J.L. Austin proposes that "the issuing of the (performative) utterance is the performing of an action" (1962: 6)—"by saying something we do something" (1962: 94). Austin also suggests that not only is speaking acting, but that acting—a physical act—can also be speaking (1979: vi, 232). Moreover, performativity functions as a reiteration of a previous act, such that agreement has been engendered about the authority of the statement or action. Identities are thus produced through the saying and the doing; and unperforming must interrupt the mechanism of performativity and its citation of previous iterations and agreed upon "laws." It is through the performativity of the initial performance—and the reiteration of subsequent performances—that rigid, immutable identities are locked in place, that belief is constructed, and that fictions become "real."

Here is where an intersection with Boal's work is useful. Adrian Jackson (cited in Boal 1995) writes: the "process Boal calls 'ascesis'[is] the movement from the phenomenon to the law which regulates the phenomena of that kind" (1962: xx). In other words, Boal, too, addresses the fact that performance, as phenomenon, creates belief (law). Performance makes images real in the minds of spectators. Jackson continues, "There are no cops in our head, they must have come from somewhere—and if they are in our head, maybe they are in other people's heads as well. Where did they come from and what are we going to do about them?" (1995: xx). If obvious untruths are perpetuated and propagated, if certain dehumanizing images are constructed for mass consumption, then clearly they must serve some purpose. As Boal explains in *Legislative Theatre*, "law is always someone's desire—it is the desire of the powerful." And his charge to the reader is, "let's democratise this desire, let's make our desire law too!" (1998: 20). How then to change the "laws" of "racial" representation?

The technology of "race"

> I must journey back in time to trace the strands of my formation.
>
> (Ntuli 1988: 209)

> We are . . . a thinking reed, and ideas motivate human history.
>
> (Pascal, cited in Gould 1994: 69)

In order to change the so-called laws of representation, the performance practitioner must understand the discursive process by which the laws attained authority and fixity and propose alternative ways of knowing. Louis Althusser discusses a process of identity formation he terms "interpellation." He writes, "all ideology hails or interpellates concrete individuals as concrete subjects" (1971: 173). In this process, the subject is, as Judith Butler elaborates, "constituted by being hailed, addressed, named" (1997: 95); and, in this way, the state apparatus polices the parameters of the subject's psyche, forming the subject's internal and external sense of self—Boal's Cop-in-the-Head. Althusser, himself, invokes this particular metaphor: he writes that ideology "'recruits' subjects" or "'transforms' . . . individuals into subjects" through the process of "hailing," which "can be imagined along the lines of the most commonplace everyday police" (1971: 174). Hailing, thus, constitutes a form of imprisonment—predetermining, naming, and delineating the self for the subject—and "race," as such, is an ideology, a system that structures and organizes (i.e., polices) our culture, setting up a false fixity in an otherwise fluid existence.

Race (and gender) theory addresses this construction of identity—how language, regulations, and an expectation of behavior "hail" or institutionalize certain roles and rituals. For much of the 20th century, critical race theorists struggled to off-set the pseudo-science of "race," explaining it as a social or political construction as well as "completely arbitrary" (Omi and Winant 1994: 55; see also Gould 1994). Paul Gilroy argues against the perpetual reiteration of racial difference and the language of raciology. He advocates "leaving 'race' behind . . . setting aside its disabling use as we move out of the time in which it could have been expected to make sense" (2000: 29). As a result of the contemporary postcolonial condition of racial mixing, unilateral racial identification becomes nearly impossible, what Gilroy calls "the crisis of raciological reasoning" (2000: 29).

Contemporary medical science also discredits the fiction of race. Sally Satel, M.D., writes that the Human Genome Project found that "99.9 percent of the human genetic complement is the same in everyone, regardless of race, as proof that race is biologically meaningless" (2002: 58); and J. Craig Venter, "the geneticist whose company played a key role in mapping the human genome, proclaimed, 'There is no basis in the genetic code for race . . . No serious scientist . . . believes that genetically pure populations exist'" (cited in

Satel 2002: 58). Similarly, Dr. Joseph L. Graves Jr., a professor of evolutionary biology and African-American studies, states, "Possibly only six genes determine the color of a person's skin out of between 30,000 and 40,000" (Graves, cited in Villarosa 2002: 5). Graves explains, "throughout history we have had too much gene flow between so-called races" for there to be any "distinct lineages," adding that there is "no biological rationale" for the rule of hypodescent (commonly known as the "one-drop rule"). Dr. Graves' position, like others, is that "races do not exist and that race is simply a social and political construct that the world would be better without" (2002: 5).

If there is, thus, no biological truth in the construct of race, what is its currency? Why does Western discourse cling to this system of classification and continue to use the word "race" as if it had concrete meaning? To answer these questions, it is necessary to understand how, through the repetition of images, "race" instills itself as truth and organizes and structures cultural life.[3]

"Race," like gender and sexuality, can be read as a "technology"—Martin Heidegger's notion of how knowledge is organized and transmitted on a societal level. Heidegger explains that technology is an "ordering" or "enframing" logic (1993: 325). Michel Foucault writes that the "different ways in our culture that humans know about themselves" constitute technologies; he explains that the "main point is not to accept this knowledge at face value but to analyze these so-called 'truth games' related to specific techniques that human beings use to understand themselves" (1988: 17–18).[4] The specific performative manifestation of the technology of "race" that has kept the ob/abjectifying interpellation of "race" intact in the Western world, especially in regard to Blackness, is Black-face minstrelsy.

What needs to be done, then, to disrupt the technology of minstrelsy and racialization is to substitute an alternative organizing mode, to demonstrate the disjunction between signifier and signified, between the minstrel and the man. In other words, the chain of representation that concretizes fictions or partial truths into fixed racial identities must be broken—Plato's "third remove" needs to be exposed. Thus, what is always already being performed in terms of supposedly authentic "racial" identities must be unperformed—not simply disavowed, but proven to be a fiction. A new system of signification must be set in order, one that does not rely on or reify the old one, that has a vocabulary specific to the ontology of the performing subjects, and that allows for multiple possibilities and what will no longer be seeming contradictions in terms of the reduction of identities to binary or essentialized locations. It is a way of seeing and describing the world that, rather than enforcing exclusive linguistic lines, creates spaces of inclusion and multiplicity.

To that end, Butler discusses strategies of "resignification," resisting, and reinterpreting—hence the "radical reoccupation" of—policed identity locations (1997: 95). She writes:

> If one misrecognizes that effort to produce the subject, the production itself falters. The one who is hailed may fail to hear, misread the call, turn the other way, answer to another name, insist on not being addressed in that way.
>
> (Butler 1997: 95)

In this way, there is a strategic refusal to ideology's "interpellation," which is what Forum Theatre stages—the resistance to the identity and role of "the oppressed." This is Boal's unique counter-technology, one that embodies a strategy for unperformance.

Unperforming "race"

The structural phenomenon of Forum Theatre allows for an interruption of a particular state or status. The so-called oppressed, who have been denied agency, find themselves in an arena where they are called to speak, to participate, to author alternative narratives. The transgressive act is that the marginalized object of the "State apparatus" attains subjectivity—actively takes it and uses it. She becomes her own capital, instead of someone else's.

Forum Theatre is thus, fundamentally, about troubling and dismantling fixed identities and creating paradigm shifts in the ontology of the acting subject. Boal describes a process whereby "the oppressed becomes artist" and through which images of oppression can be "aesthetically transubstantiated" (1995: 43). In other words, in and through performance, the so-called oppressed gains agency and uses the deconstruction of a narrative of oppression as an exercise in empowerment. Through the aesthetic appropriation of the image, oppression is transformed into freedom, at least in the confines of the performance space. But, as in Boal's ideal of transubstantiation, the intent of such work is that the freedom found in performance actually becomes real, living, flesh, and translates into action and change outside the performance space.

Boal explains that once the oppressed "creates images of her own oppressive reality, she belongs to both these worlds utterly and completely, not merely 'vicariously'" (1995: 43). This is what Boal calls "the phenomenon of *metaxis*: the state of belonging completely and simultaneously to two different, autonomous worlds: the image of reality and the reality of the image" (1995: 43). This is the ambivalence of all performance, occupying two spaces, conflating two realities, simultaneously proposing two truths (or fictions). The editors of the online Theatre of the Oppressed (TO) journal, *Metaxis*, write, "Metaxis is a Greek word. Its meaning in Plato is the passage between the world of ideas and that of experience" (*Metaxis* 2004). Although used there to describe the liminality of performance, taken another way the duality of metaxis reveals the risk an artist always runs of reproducing the same power system he intends to dismantle.

Julie Salverson writes, "When an image is created to work with, it forms a kind of container, allowing the theatre space itself to hold contradictory material without insisting on its resolution" (Salverson 1996: 187). Director Anne Bogart also uses the word "container," in this case to describe the notion of stereotype: "A stereotype is a container of memory . . . Representations of life are containers for meaning which embody the memory of all the other times they have been done" (Bogart 2000: 95–6). Bogart, here, reveals the potential for an image to be fixed through performance. The process Boal identifies that potentially frees and releases an image can also capture and contain it if misapplied (as in the case of minstrelsy being misrepresented and misread as "authentic" Blackness). As Boal, himself, states, "In order for metaxis to come about, the image must become autonomous. When this is the case, the image of the real is real as image" (1995: 44). This critical moment in representational strategizing reveals the risk of oppositional image-making. As Diana Taylor (discussing and quoting Ross Chambers' ideas) explains, "oppositionality is not and never can be revolutionary because it works '*within* a system of power even as it works against it'" (Taylor 1996: 219). Therefore, an oppositional image (such as the performative deconstruction of minstrelsy) will always reify and, to some degree, embody the ideology it seeks to disrupt. It points to the thing it attempts to deflate and says it is "not that." But it still draws attention to that that it is not.

In order to create a moment or an aesthetic of unperforming "race," the artist must understand how the technology constitutive of and produced by certain performances of "race" continues to reproduce itself today, as well as strategies for disrupting, dismantling, and disengaging that technology through performance without reproducing it. As in Forum Theatre, when a particular power relationship is destabilized or reversed, there is a moment in an unperformance of "race" in which an intervention troubles or alters an audience's perception of the authority of a previously articulated identity location. Through the deployment of a performance technique, the performer succeeds in altering her perceived identity, ultimately resulting in a reimagining of the self. In Heidegger's terms, what emerges is the "essence" (Heidegger 1993: 312), of the individual *as she understands herself to be*, over-writing—and ultimately substituting a renewed sense of self for—other previously inscribed identities or expectations.

What I address in the pages that follow is how, through specific techniques of performance, racializing knowledge is undone and the construction of the fiction of identity is revealed. There is a genealogy of work that attempts to destabilize the deleterious identities locked into the cultural imaginary by the authority of minstrelsy and to recuperate the subjects of this practice. Some of these sites, while compelling theatre, are ultimately unsuccessful in unperforming "race." The performers and performances enter into dialogue with the legacy of minstrelsy and reify it, drawing on it and reiterating its technological and epistemological authority. Such work includes the San Francisco Mime Troupe's *A Minstrel Show or Civil Rights in a Cracker Barrel* (1965), The Wooster Group's *Route 1 & 9* (1981), and the Donald Byrd's *The Minstrel Show: Acts for coons, jigaboos and jungle bunnies* (which Byrd worked on from 1981–95).[5]

These "alternative minstrel shows" present a critical ambivalence, while each performance differs in terms of style, mode of production, and efficacy in troubling the technology of race and raciology. In addition, each reproduces the format, structure, and style of a minstrel or coon show—including the technical act of "Blackening up"—to comment on and critique the history of the minstrel show and its vestiges of racism and racialization in the national imaginary. In this genealogy, the practice of reclaiming minstrelsy may have been an important step in problematizing its discursive power—as Davis (1975: 57) and Lecompte (in Savran 1986: 27, 31) have argued—and led to other resistant strategies. But, on a semiological level, this tactic does not serve to destabilize racialization or racial hierarchies in any meaningful or lasting way without, as Byrd's work provides, for example, a simultaneous metacritique of the restaging of minstrelsy. Byrd weaves this into his reframing of the minstrel show through gesture, silence, attitude, and direct address of the audience. He alternates having his "minstrels" stand inside and outside of minstrelsy while (re)performing it. Nevertheless, despite this canny critique and remixing, the performance still relies on a reiteration of the minstrel type as its source material.

Other performances, responding to historical and reperformed minstrelsy, have "flipped the script," using White-face as a strategy for "misrecognizing" the call of racial authenticity and identification. Notable examples of this technique can be found in the Negro Ensemble Company's productions of *Day of Absence* (1965) by Douglas Turner Ward and Ray McIver's *God Is a (Guess What?)* (1968), both of which rely on White-face performances by Black actors to call into question the immutability of "racial" fixed types. These White-face performances are farcical and demonstrate an inversion of power, in the line of carnival and other festivities in the African diaspora.

The problem, however, with rituals of inversion, as explained by Peter Stallybrass and Allon White (1986), is that they ultimately require the rebelling subject to return power to the dominant force, thus creating a resubjectification by reintegrating into a hierarchy and deepening the hegemonic power relationship. What seems like rebellion or resistance is, actually, part of a larger process of domination in which roles are reinforced through a repetition of the act of subjection. The White-face performances are keen social commentary, but do not actually alter the system of racialized identification and objectification—they merely reiterate them through inversion.

In another strategic intervention into the history of Black-face production, performers play characters locked in a history of representation or signification. Whereas these characters are also often uncritical reiterations of stereotypes—such as those found in many contemporary films and television shows—they can also serve to stretch and critique the original and, in so doing, perform a rehistoricization of the African diaspora. To a certain extent, Black Americans have been compelled to use this strategy since the advent of the Black-face minstrel. Satire and parody are often employed in an attempt to defy or rewrite mis/dis-information about the Black American, as disseminated through the theatre and other media. Nevertheless, the ambivalence of these forms lies in the originary location of the referent. As discussed above, a piece like *Day of Absence* attempts to invert the power relationship by employing the technical device of White-face and parodying the behavior and culture of White folk. But the device and the piece itself are always in dialogue with the racist portrayals they seek to undo. There is a similar ambivalence with all minstrelization, even without the Black-face mask. Such strategies produce a ghost image of the very thing they attempt to eliminate and erase, a palimpsest of prior bad acts.

In the 1980s and '90s, certain performances that portrayed these "maskless minstrels" did, however, come close to the ideal of unperforming. Writers began to recontextualize history, to reclaim subjectivity through a recomplication and rehistoricization, a performative embodiment of the Akan proverb, "Until lions have their own historians, tales of hunting will always glorify the hunter." Works of this nature, which still invoke the subject of minstrelsy or stereotype of Blackness but simultaneously strategically humanize him or her, include ntozake shange's *Spell #7* (1979), George C. Wolfe's *The Colored Museum* (1985), Carlyle Brown's *The Little Tommy Parker Celebrated Colored Minstrel Show* (1991), and Breena Clarke and Glenda Dickerson's *Re/membering Aunt Jemima: A Menstrual Show* (1992). In Brown's portrait of minstrel performers out of Black-face, for example, the audience learns of their history and struggles, as well as their victories and resistant strategies (in Elam and Alexander 1996). Only at the end of the play are they seen Blackening-up, literally to save their lives; yet they speak with their own voices, not with the dialect associated with Black-face minstrel performers. This disjuncture creates a performative rupture between expectation and reality, troubling the notion of authenticity and the production of the racialized Other. In this moment, with his brilliant discursive move, Brown successfully unperforms race by staging the contradiction between the "minstrel" and the man. Yet the minstrel mask is still present.

Wolfe's play, a structured series of museum exhibits, was groundbreaking for its complex staging of identity. In this museum, Black stereotypes come to life and are contextualized in such a way as to humanize their quest and struggle and to lift them from stereotypical objecthood to archetypal subjectivity. Wolfe did not attempt to glorify them, per se—only to explain their history, recomplicate their psychology, and reveal their "colored contradictions" (Wolfe 1985: 53). The acting subjects in the exhibits intervene at the crucial moment of hailing—the moment of having their identity fixed, misread, and misunderstood—and, through humor and satire, insert a critical, more complex narrative.

The exhibit "Symbiosis" is striking in its structural similarity to Forum Theatre. In the exhibit, a bourgeois Black man "in corporate dress" is seen throwing out the vestiges of various stages of his youth: his "first jar of Murray's Pomade," his "first can of Afro-sheen," his "first box of curl relaxer," and his copy of Eldridge Cleaver's *Soul on Ice*. His younger self, The Kid, watches on with horror, and protests: "Not *Soul on Ice!*" The Man replies, "It's been replaced on my bookshelf by *The Color Purple*" (Wolfe 1985: 33). Wolfe dramatizes a process of self-individuation where one set of values is replaced by another, both of which have specific class and cultural implications. According to a binary system of identification, The Man, according to Wolfe, is becoming more "White" because of his bourgeois aspirations. Eventually The Man succeeds in killing The Kid and stuffs him into the dumpster (while joking, "Man kills his own rage. Film at eleven" (1985: 36)) where his previous belongings, metonymic of his young Black self, have been discarded. He reveals to the audience his dilemma:

> I have no history. I have no past. I can't. It's too much. It's much too much. I must be able to smile on cue. And watch the news with an impersonal eye. I have no stake in the madness.
> Being black is too emotionally taxing; therefore I will be black only on weekends and holidays.

(Wolfe 1985: 36)

In a final act, he begins to throw out a *Temptations* album, at which point "a hand reaches from inside the can and grabs hold of The Man's arm. The Kid suddenly emerges from the can with a death grip on The Man's arm," and says "(smiling) What's happenin?" (Wolfe 1985: 37). By physically staging the internal struggle that The Man has with himself, Wolfe is his own spect-actor, interrupting and disrupting an essentialized history of signification that "others have compiled" for him (Fanon 1967: 120). In this way, Wolfe unperforms the authority of the urban-youth persona, as well as the seddity Black man.

However, the actual representational politics of Wolfe's play (as compared to his strategic intervention as spect-author), as with others who use this strategy of reworking history and historical characters, owe more to the theory of "disidentification"—found in the writings of Michel Pêcheux, Judith Butler, and José Esteban Muñoz—than to unperforming. These performances work to "queer" dominant notions by acting "on and against" identities rooted in ideology in a poststructuralist mode (Muñoz 1999: 11–12), rather than attempting to find a space that exists outside of ideology, in a more utopian gesture.

Unperforming an identity would, alternatively, defuse, dismantle, and, ultimately, make disappear the deleterious representation/image/icon. In psychological terms, it would create a "cognitive dissonance" among (some) viewers. Unperforming would, as suggested above, stage contradictions in the discursive system of "race" and raciology, revealing complexity, limitations of language, omission of history, un(der)represented populations, and contradictory subject locations (according to mainstream ideology). Most successful, therefore, in terms of unperformance, are techniques and strategies that return to the Platonic notion of *poiesis*, an "action which is the cause of a thing emerging from non-existence to existence" (Plato 1987: 85), "bringing forth," according to Heidegger, a new understanding, a new reality, an alternative epistemology.

Theatre of testimony

In my own work, I have used testimony—as have others such as Emily Mann, Anna Deavere Smith, and Ping Chong—to relate stories of complex identities, moments of oppression, and events of social discord. In these performances, which I have created in and for specific communities, the actor performs his own words, either in conjunction with extant texts or as a total piece intercut with movement and music. *Mixtries* (1998), which I created with a group of student actors, stages interventions into Langston Hughes' Jim Crow-era play, *Mulatto*.[6] As the Hughes text was performed, actors commented on the language and situations from a contemporary perspective—using selections from poetry and theoretical texts—and then reperformed verbatim interviews that I had conducted with them on the subject of oppression, racism, and their connection to the material.

In Hughes' play, Bert, the son of a Black housekeeper and a White plantation owner, attempts to identify as White rather than Black. At the end of the play, while attempting to escape a lynch mob, Bert kills himself. In *Mixtries*, Bert's wrestling with his identity was mirrored by the personal monologues of the diverse cast, wherein the actors reflected on and worked through such issues as patriarchy, patrimony, misogyny, gender, Whiteness, hate, home, hair, and culture. One actress described an incident when someone in authority had flippantly said to her in a class to "stop walking like her ancestors." She was later told by the same person that the problem with her acting was that she was a "subservient Asian woman." Having the opportunity to tell this story, to "talk back" in public—to question and process the event—provided a moment of liberation, an interruption in her view of herself as authored by an other. Her monologue also tethered with the Hughes text and the politics of the day, as a character in the play is described as "bowing and scraping."

This monologue was intercut with that of another female student, who is White, describing her constant questioning as to whether she was in the "right" body. She explained, "It's a lonely feeling when you wake up in the morning and you want to be in someone else's skin." Her statement and questioning of, in this case, her gender role, in dialogue with her Whiteness, served as keen commentary on Bert's struggle. There was, in fact, a recurrent reflection among some of the White actors who lamented the fact that, for them, Whiteness was "bland" or "boring," had no specific culture, and that they wished they could be "ethnic." Contrasted with stories of bigotry, marginalization, and cultural insensitivity combined with the oppressive climate of Hughes' text, these testimonies provided a type of cross-cultural dialogue—both in rehearsals and in the performance itself—that most of the actors had never engaged in, an uncommon situation in a climate of "political correctness."

Several of the actors are bi- or multi-ethnic and spoke of their various backgrounds. In performance they explored either their desire to find out more about their own Whiteness or their need to situate mixedness as a legitimate identity, not as something caught in-between two culturally predetermined positions. As one actress, of Japanese and Italian-American parentage, expressed, "I really do see this as water in the middle. And most people think you're going to drown out there. But you can float there too, and be just as stable." The title, *Mixtries*, was taken both from a line in the play and from an oral history from the Jim Crow-era south, where the word refered to "mysteries" and to the unspoken ontology of mixedness indicative of cultural and spiritual hybridity (Murphy 1899).

Another technique we used was the intercutting of monologues to stage moments of seeming contradiction. For example, a young Israeli woman, descended from 13 generations of rabbis in Iran, was seated in front of a young man, who stood over her right shoulder. He was from a Zoroastrian family, also from Iran, and told of the beatings his grandfather received for being of the "wrong" religion. Simultaneously, the young woman related her family's story, including the need to hide aspects of her identity from her father because of his strictness. The two look like fraternal twins and their stories, though separated by cultural affiliations, were deeply interconnected. Seeing them in close physical proximity, but interacting only through the thematic and geographical similarities of their stories, brought into bas-relief the incredible histories they share.

Finally, actors traded parts, so that, for example, the White actor playing the racist father, after a personal monologue about his relationship with his own father, became the "Black" son, and the Black actor playing Bert became the "White" father. As with Boal's Joker System (Boal 1985), this tactic served to destabilize the authority of the roles the actors played—the artificiality of the constructedness of each identity was foregrounded as dialogue was heard from the "wrong" subject position.

Unbeknownst to me at the time, visionary director Ping Chong was using a similar approach in his *Undesirable Elements* (UE) series. In these productions, of which there have been over 20 to date, Chong travels to a locale, interviews local residents—such as performers, artists, refugee children, immigrants, and lay people—and intercuts stories of their lives. (Chong has created UE productions in such cities as New York, Atlanta, Cleveland, Tokyo, and Rotterdam.) The project is described as "diverse voices challenging notions of history, culture, race, community—and America" (Chong 2000). The cast of the 2002 New York anniversary production included a Jewish, African-American woman raised by an adopted Mennonite family, a Persian woman with both Arab and Jewish parentage who grew up in Iran and the US, a Lebanese woman who lived in Beirut through the war, a South African who wrestles with being a White African, and Ping Chong, himself, a first-generation Chinese-American who, for the first time, performed in a UE piece.[7]

The performance is structured as a ritual. The set remains the same for each iteration—a semi-circle of white salt or gravel with chairs on it, an image of a full moon projected behind the performers. They enact non-narrative gestures and circle the stage intermittently. There are particular sections, personalized to each cast, that are repeated in each version—nicknames from the actors' cultures, favorite foods, historical dates, and their individual narratives in their own tongues. As the stories are intercut and intertwined, the cast breaks into call-and-response, each taking on the others' stories by repeating names, words, and dates, creating one narrative out of the many voices. Chong's staging of contradictory identities problematizes the imbricated notions of "race," culture, color, class, and ethnicity, and reveals how the seams of a seemingly seamless fabric constantly pull and strain to accommodate our country's obsession with over-simplification and reductive thinking. What makes this piece so successful in terms of unperforming is that Chong has dissolved any attempt to make these actors fit into predetermined identity locations. The audience member is left to resolve the conflict between expectation of a discrete, bounded identity and the "true-Real" of a more fluid representation in the actual moment of viewing.

Rac(e)ing Boal

The oppressed creates *images of his reality*. Then, he must play with *the reality of these images*. The oppressions remain the same, but they are presented in transubstantiated forms. The oppressed must forget the real world which was the origin of the image and play with the image itself, in its artistic embodiment. He must make an extrapolation from his social reality towards the reality which is called fiction (towards theatre, towards image) and, having played with the image, he must make a second extrapolation, now in its inverse direction, towards the social reality which is his world. *He practices in the second world (the aesthetic), in order to modify the first (the social).*

(Boal 1995: 44)

Boal recognizes the potential for performance to make—and unmake—social reality. In Forum Theatre, the oppressed artist steps into the network of signs and laws established by those in power. She can either participate in the perpetuation of such a system, or take on its unmaking. As discussed earlier, the risk in "transubstantiated forms" is that they are always connected to the original—the DNA of a matrix of power is locked into the performance, into relationships of power. Through performance, the network of laws that institutionalizes certain forms of oppression are potentially altered and disrupted. In other words, the "oppressed" protagonist finds freedom through performance and, through performance, discovers how to enact this freedom. Can Forum Theatre, then, be used to unperform "race"? What happens when, in the context of Forum Theatre, a spect-actor takes the role of someone with whom he does not share an identificatory position? Is the role of spect-actor "color blind"? The very nature of these questions requires further problematization.

In his 1989 interview with Boal, Richard Schechner remarks, "When a black plays a white or a white a black, a man a woman or a woman a man, not only does it liberate the performers but we see that we construct our realities including race and gender. Your theatre is an unfancy way of blowing apart these constructions" (Taussig and Schechner 1994: 27). Although this is the ideal of unperformance, it is also important to remember that the nature of the encounter wherein someone from a position of traditional societal power inhabits the subject position of someone historically marginalized and disempowered is a very different thing than when the dynamic is reversed (and these power relationships are also clearly dependent on geography and historical moment). When the oppressed subject steps back from the stage to the audience, having occupied a position of power, there is a relinquishing of power, a return to the marginalized position. This is not the same dynamic when a spect-actor from a nonmarginalized position leaves the stage.

In most cases, when a self-identified White person inhabits the role of a minoritized or oppressed individual, there is an historical privilege—a freedom to enact multiple crossings. These borders are not as heavily policed in this direction and there is no imminent threat of punishment for this crossing. However, in this country, a Black man caught "passing" in the south, or even one who was thought to be "uppity" by "acting White," was often lynched; similarly a homosexual, a cross-dresser, or a transgender subject outed in the wrong circumstance might be killed, as in the cases of Matthew Shepherd, Teena Renae Brandon (a.k.a. Brandon Teena), and Sakia Gunn.

The challenge to cross-color performances and spect-actorly interventions is to avoid implying a structural interchangeability of all subject positions. In the above examples (at least in the West), one position embodies lasting power, while the other does not. As such, this disparity must be acknowledged by all parties—especially the one enacting a "licensed" pass—if any lasting learning, understanding, or progress is to happen. In fact, it is the acknowledgment of this difference that constitutes the ultimate progress in terms of destabilizing the apparatus of racism, described by David Wellman as "a system of advantages based on race" (cited in Tatum 1999: 7–8).

In the case of interventions that happen among people from marginalized positions, there are also vectors of power and privilege, in that groups have been positioned by hegemonic interests in a hierarchy of difference, such as "model minorities" and licensed alterity. A Forum Theatre in Los Angeles where an Asian-American replaces an African-American has both a visual and sociological history that is unavoidable. As practitioners, we must consider the nature of the border crossings we are staging, as well as the politics of permitting, as it were, the "subaltern" to "speak" (Spivak 1988).

David Diamond, Founder and Artistic Director of Headlines Theatre in Vancouver, BC, related to me a moment when a middle-class White woman replaced a street youth in a Forum Theatre "Power Play" with street children.[8] Diamond suggested that learning would not take place if the woman were not allowed to replace the youth; that each had to deal with the other as "real." Diamond also suggested,

> If we're serious about breaking the cycles of oppression, how do we go about doing that in the theatre? We don't go about doing it by putting on stage an evil, violent father or an evil, racist teacher, because some of them are in the audience.
>
> (Diamond 2003)

As Diamond explained, there is a difference between an "invitation to break the oppression versus an invitation to create a community of safety."

In regard to the use of Forum Theatre to combat racism, Diamond asked, "How can we call it antiracist work? That belies a result" (2003). I am moved by his reminder that the power of the work is to "create a container" (2003) where dialogue and community healing can take place (an interesting contrast to Bogart's container of stereotype and identity). The key, I submit, is a constant awareness of the positions from which we speak, an awareness of who is "allowed" to speak—and when—a consciousness of the distance from the positions we are speaking as/for, and resisting the tendency, despite a shared humanity, of speaking as if we are all the same or have the same experiences or access to power. As such, aware of unequal vectors of power, both Forum Theatre and acting subjects who unperform difference participate in the demolition of a system of signification that oppresses in perpetuity.

Ultimately, therefore, the concept and practice of unperforming is rooted in the staging of contradictions, fluidity, and overlapping identities—rendering possible the impossible, disproving the lies, transubstantiating and transforming the history of humanity in a single moment of revelation in which the lie is exposed and its power ultimately defeated. It is deeply connected to Adrian Piper's theory of "the indexical present," the moment where viewer and performer find themselves inextricably in the same moment—the "concrete, immediate here-and-now"—where meaning is made and, potentially, unmade (Piper 1996: 247). Piper writes that her work "springs from a belief that we are transformed—and occasionally reformed—by immediate experience, independent of our abstract evaluations of it and despite our attempts to resist it" (1996: 247–48). In this moment of meeting and potential transformation, our collective future waits, the empty space yet to be filled with either another fiction—another coercive image—or with a new story, a new image, a new reality. In this unique moment, perhaps, there is neither oppressed nor oppressor, only possibility.

Notes

1   See Bogle (1989) and Riggs (1988) for discussions of these stereotypes.
2   See Boyd (2002: 127) and Bazanye (2003: 15); an article in *The New York Times* calls Regen "The whitest Black girl on TV" (Dreisinger 2003: 2).
3   Although the attempt to deconstruct the mantle of "race" as a governing concept is a move away from essentializing peoples who share physical resemblances—specifically melanin—and hierarchical assessments of what those features represent, I am certainly not suggesting doing away with cultural or diasporic identification or coalitions. What is needed, however, is a more complex conversation about the inaccuracy of the term "race" as it is currently used, what an alternative, more precise semantic choice might be, and how that would change the cultural landscape.
4   See also Teresa de Lauretis (1987) on the technology of gender.
5   This discussion is condensed from a more thorough analysis in *Unperforming the Minstrel Mask: Black-face and the Technology of Representation*, a longer work-in-progress.
6   *Mixtries* was performed at the Frederick Loewe Theatre, Tisch School of the Arts, New York University. April 21–27, 1998.
7   *UE 92/02*, by Ping Chong and Talvin Wilks, was directed by Ping Chong at La MaMa Annex Theatre, New York City, October 17–20, 2002.
8   See Diamond (1994: 52) for an explanation of the use of the term Power Play instead of Theatre of the Oppressed.

Bibliography

Althusser, L. (1971) *Lenin and Philosophy and Other Essays*, trans. B. Brewster. New York and London: Monthly Review.
Austin, J.L. (1962) *How to Do Things with Words*. Cambridge, MA: Harvard.
—— (1979) *Philosophical Papers*. New York: Oxford University Press.
Bazanye, E. (2003) "Justin is black," *Sunday Vision*, March 2: 15.
Boal, A. (1985) *Theatre of the Oppressed*, trans. C.A. and M.-O.L. McBride. New York: Theatre Communications Group.
—— (1995) *The Rainbow of Desire: The Boal method of theatre and therapy*, trans. A. Jackson. London and New York: Routledge.
—— (1998) *Legislative Theatre*, trans. A. Jackson. London and New York: Routledge.
Bogart, A. (2000) *A Director Prepares: Seven essays on art and theatre*. New York and London: Routledge.
Bogle, D. (1989) *Toms, Coons, Mulattoes, Mammies, and Bucks: An interpretive history of Blacks in American films*. New York: Continuum.
Boyd, T. (2002) *The New H.N.I.C.: The death of civil rights and the reign of Hip Hop*. New York: New York University.
Butler, J. (1993) *Bodies that Matter: On the discursive limits of sex*. New York and London: Routledge.
—— (1997) *The Psychic Life of Power: Theories in subjection*. Stanford, CA: Stanford University Press.
Chong, P. (2000) *Secret History: A documentary theatre work*. Ohio Theatre, New York City (video production by Hiromi Sakamoto), Ping Chong and Co.
Davis, R.G. (1975) *The San Francisco Mime Troupe: The first ten years*. Palo Alto: Ramparts.
De Lauretis, T. (1987) *Technologies of Gender: Essays on theory, film, and fiction*. Bloomington and Indianapolis, ID: University of Indiana.
Diamond, D. (1994) "Out of the silence: Headlines Theatre and power plays," in M. Schutzman and J. Cohen-Cruz (eds) *Playing Boal: Theatre, therapy, activism*. London and New York: Routledge.
—— (2003) Unpublished interview, Vancouver, BC, August 28, 2003.
Dreisinger, B. (2003) "The whitest Black girl on TV," *New York Times*, September 28, 2: 24.

Elam, H.J., Jr. and Alexander, R. (eds) (1996) *Colored Contradictions: An anthology of contemporary African-American plays*. New York: Plume.

Fanon, F. (1967) *Black Skin, White Masks*. New York: Grove Press.

Foucault, M. (1988) "Technologies of the self," in L.H. Martin, H. Gutman, and P.H. Hutton (eds) *Technologies of the Self: A seminar with Michel Foucault*. Amherst, MA: University of Massachusetts.

Gilroy, P. (2000) *Against Race: Imagining political culture beyond the color line*. Cambridge, MA: Belknap.

Gould, S.J. (1994) "The geometer of race," *Discover Magazine*, November, 15: 65–81.

Heidegger, M. (1993) "The question concerning technology," in D.F. Krell (ed.) *Basic Writings*. San Francisco, CA: Harper San Francisco.

Kruger, B. (1983) untitled artwork [Your Fictions Become History]. Gelatin silver print. Mary Boone Gallery, New York.

Lowery, V. (2004) *Press*. Online. Available: http://www.aboutvaughn.com/pages/506199/index.htm> (accessed July 22, 2004).

Mailer, N. (1957) *The White Negro*. San Francisco, CA: City Lights Books.

Metaxis (2004) Online. Available: <http://www.ctorio.com.br/Ingles/ingles-index.html> (accessed July 22, 2004).

Muñoz, J.E. (1999) *Disidentifications: Queers of color and the performance of politics*. Minneapolis, MN: University of Minnesota.

Murphy, J.R. (1899) "The survival of African American music in America," *Popular Science Monthly* 55: 660–72.

Ntuli, P. (1988) "Orature: A self portrait," in K. Owusu (ed.) *Storms of the Heart: An anthology of black arts and culture*. London: Camden Press.

Omi, M. and Winant, H. (1994) *Racial Formation in the United States: From the 1960s to the 1990s*. New York: Routledge.

Pêcheux, Michel (1982) *Language, Semantics, and Ideology*. New York: St Martin's Press.

Piper, A. (1996) *Out of Order, Out of Sight*, vol. 1. Cambridge, MA: MIT

Plato (1987) *The Republic*, trans. D. Lee. New York: Penguin Books.

Riggs, M. (1988) *Ethnic Notions*. San Francisco, CA: California Newsreel.

Salverson, J. (1996) "Performing emergency: Witnessing, popular theatre, and the lie of the literal," *Theatre Topics* 6: 2: 181–91.

Satel, S. (2002) "I am a racially profiling doctor," *New York Times Magazine*, May 5: 58.

Savran, D. (1986) *The Wooster Group, 1975–1985: Breaking the rules*. Ann Arbor, MI: UMI Research Press.

Spivak, G. (1988) "Can the subaltern speak?," in C. Nelson and L. Grossberg (eds) *Marxism and the Interpretation of Culture*. Urbana, IL: University of Illinois.

Stallybrass, P. and White, A. (1986) *The Politics and Poetics of Transgression*. Ithaca, NY: Cornell University.

Stearns, M. and J. (1994) *Jazz Dance: The story of American vernacular dance*. New York: Da Capo Press.

Tatum, B.D. (1999) *Why Are All the Black Kids Sitting Together in the Cafeteria? And Other Conversations About Race*. New York: Basic Books.

Taussig, M. and Schechner, R. (1994) "Boal in Brazil, France, the USA: An interview with Augusto Boal," in M. Schutzman and J. Cohen-Cruz (eds) *Playing Boal: Theatre, therapy, activism*. New York and London: Routledge.

Taylor, D. (1996) *Disappearing Acts: Spectacles of gender and nationalism in Argentina's "dirty war."* Durham, NC: Duke University.

Villarosa, L. (2002) "Beyond black and white in biology and medicine," *New York Times*, January 1, 5.

Wolfe, G.C. (1985) *The Colored Museum*. New York: Grove.

Index

Related titles from Routledge

Augusto Boal

Routledge Performance Practitioners

by Frances Babbage

The work of Augusto Boal has had a tremendous impact on contemporary theatre. This volume looks at the scope of Boal's career—from his early work as a playwright and director in São Paulo in the 1950s, to the development of his groundbreaking manifesto in the 1970s for a 'Theatre of the Oppressed'.

Augusto Boal will be fascinating reading for anyone interested in the role that theatre can play in stimulating social and personal change. This useful study combines:

- a biographical and historical overview of Boal's career as theatre practitioner and director;
- in-depth analysis of Boal's classic text on radical theatre, *The Theatre of the Oppressed*;
- exploration of training and production techniques;
- practical guidance to Boal's workshop methods.

As a first step toward critical understanding, and as an initial exploration before going on to further primary research, *Routledge Performance Practitioners* are unbeatable value for today's student.

ISBN 0–415–27325–0 (hbk)
ISBN 0–415–27326–9 (pbk)

Available at all good bookshops
For ordering and further information please visit:
www.routledge.com

Related titles from Routledge

Games for Actors and Non-actors

2nd edition

by Augusto Boal

'Boal's analysis of the art of the Actor makes *Games for Actors and Non-actors* compulsory reading.'

Plays and Players

'This is a useful handbook for those who want to explore Boal's Theatre of the Oppressed and as such is greatly to be welcomed. Boal's work deserves and demands emulation.'

Theatre Research International

Games for Actors and Non-actors is the classic and best selling book by the founder of Theatre of the Oppressed, Augusto Boal. It sets out the principles and practice of Boal's revolutionary method, showing how theatre can be used to transform and liberate everyone—actors and non-actors alike!

This thoroughly updated and substantially revised second edition includes:

- two new essays by Boal on major recent projects in Brazil;
- Boal's description of his work with the Royal Shakespeare Company;
- a revised introduction and translator's preface;
- a collection of photographs taken during Boal's workshops, commissioned for this edition;
- new reflections on Forum Theatre.

ISBN 0–415–26761–7 (hbk)
ISBN 0–415–26708–0 (pbk)

Available at all good bookshops
For ordering and further information please visit:
www.routledge.com

Related titles from Routledge

Hamlet and the Baker's Son: My life in theatre and politics

by Augusto Boal

Hamlet and the Baker's Son is the autobiography of Augusto Boal, inventor of the internationally renowned Forum Theatre system, Theatre of the Oppressed and author of *Games for Actors and Non-actors* and *Legislative Theatre*. Continuing to travel the world giving workshops and inspiration to teachers, prisoners, actors, and careworkers, Augusto Boal is a visionary as well as a product of his times—the Brazil of military dictatorship and artistic and social repression—and was once imprisoned for his subversive activities.

From his early days in Brazil's political theatre movement to his recent experiments with theatre as a democratic political process, Boal's story is a moving and memorable one. He has devised a unique way of using the stage to empower the disempowered, and taken his methods everywhere from the favelas of Rio to the rehearsal studios of the Royal Shakespeare Company.

ISBN 0–415–22988–X (hbk)
ISBN 0–415–22989–8 (pbk)

Available at all good bookshops
For ordering and further information please visit:
www.routledge.com

Related titles from Routledge

Playing Boal: Theatre, therapy and activism

edited by Mady Schutzman and Jan Cohen-Cruz

Playing Boal is the first book to examine the techniques in application of Augusto Boal, creator of Theatre of the Oppressed and internationally renowned Brazilian theatre maker and political activist.

Boal's work is becoming famous, say the editors of this volume, for its ability to effect change on both a personal and social level. But what happens to the techniques when they are used in different contexts? *Playing Boal* looks at the use of Theatre of the Oppressed exercises by a variety of practitioners and scholars working in Europe, North America and Canada. It explores the possibilities of these tools for 'active learning and personal empowerment, cooperative education and healing, participatory theatre and community action.'

A fascinating collection in itself, *Playing Boal* will illuminate and invigorate discussion about Boal's work and the transformative potential of theatre. This comprehensive and in-depth volume includes two interviews with Augusto Boal, and two pieces of his writing.

ISBN 0–415–08607–8 (hbk)
ISBN 0–415–08608–6 (pbk)
ISBN 0–203–41971–5 (eB)

Available at all good bookshops
For ordering and further information please visit:
www.routledge.com

Related titles from Routledge

Legislative Theatre: Using performance to make politics

by Augusto Boal

Augusto Boal's reputation has moved beyond the realms of theatre and drama therapy, bringing him to the attention of a wider public. *Legislative Theatre* is an attempt to use Boal's method of Forum Theatre within a political system to create a truer form of democracy. It is an extraordinary experiment in the potential of theatre to affect social change.

At the heart of his method of Forum Theatre is the dual meaning of the verb 'to act': to perform and to take action. Forum Theatre invites members of the audience to take the stage and decide the outcome, becoming an integral part of the performance. As a politician in his native Rio de Janeiro, Boal used Forum Theatre to motivate the local populace in generating relevant legislation. In *Legislative Theatre* Boal creates new, theatrical, and truly revolutionary ways of involving everyone in the democratic process.

This book includes:

- a full explanation of the genesis and principles of Legislative Theatre;
- a description of the process in operation in Rio;
- Boal's essays, speeches, and lectures on popular theatre, Paolo Freire, cultural activism, the point of playwriting, and much else besides.

ISBN 0–415–18240–9 (hbk)
ISBN 0–415–18241–7 (pbk)

Available at all good bookshops
For ordering and further information please visit:
www.routledge.com

Related titles from Routledge

The Rainbow of Desire: The Boal method of theatre and therapy

by Augusto Boal, translated by Adrian Jackson

The Rainbow of Desire is a handbook of exercises with a difference. It is Augusto Boal's bold and brilliant statement about the therapeutic ability of theatre to liberate individuals and change lives. Now translated into English and comprehensively updated from the French, *The Rainbow of Desire* sets out the techniques which help us 'see' for the first time the oppressions we have internalized.

Boal, a Brazilian theatre director, writer, and politician, has been confronting oppression in various forms for over 30 years. His belief that theatre is a means to create the future has inspired hundreds of groups all over the world to use his techniques in a multitude of settings.

This book includes such exercises as:

- the Cops-in-the-Head and their anti-bodies;
- the screen image;
- the image of the future we are afraid of;
- image and counter-image;
  and many more.

The Rainbow of Desire will make fascinating reading for those already familiar with Boal's work and is also completely accessible to anyone new to Theatre of the Oppressed techniques.

ISBN 0–415–10349–5 (pbk)

Available at all good bookshops
For ordering and further information please visit:
www.routledge.com